SEVEN TYPES OF ADVENTURE TALE

ALSO BY MARTIN GREEN

SEVEN TYPES
OF
ADVENTURE TALE

AN ETIOLOGY OF A MAJOR GENRE

Martin Green

The Pennsylvania State University Press
University Park, Pennsylvania

Library of Congress Cataloging-in-Publication Data

Green, Martin Burgess, 1927–
    Seven types of adventure tale : an etiology of a major genre /
    Martin Green.

        p.   cm.
    Includes bibliographical references and index.
    ISBN 0-271-00780-X
    1. Adventure stories—History and criticism—Theory, etc.
    2. Literary form. I. Title.
    PN3448.A3G73   1991
    809.3'87—dc20   91-8476
                                                       CIP

It is the policy of The Pennsylvania State University Press to use acid-free paper for
the first printing of all clothbound books. Publications on uncoated stock satisfy the
minimum requirements of American National Standard for Information Sciences—
Permanence of Paper for Printed Library Materials, ANSI Z39.48–1984.

DEDICATED TO

Philip Winsor,
a long-term friend
and
to the memory of several seminars at Tufts,
on one or another type of adventure tale;
and especially to the graduate students in literature
who loyally went against their instinct,
and tried to take adventure seriously.

"The modern world's dismissal of adventure as an entertaining but minor experience is unprecedented."

—Paul Zweig, *The Adventurer* (1974)

"Once a glamorous figure in Western culture, the adventurer today has tumbled into disrepute, his exploits explained away psychologically, his morals somehow suspect. Nowadays, it seems, adventure is the province of small boys and vacationers."

—Joseph Frank, Foreword to *The Adventurer* (1980)

"I am suddenly struck by the fact that no-one has mentioned these archetypal (male) quest figures lately, or any of their accompanying cortege from the portrait gallery of bourgeois individualism, such as the Adventurer."

—Fredric Jameson, "Pleasure: A Political Issue" (1983)

Contents

1

Prefaces

Adventure and Literature

Like most writers, I feel that my subject has been neglected and that I have important news to give the world. In my case the subject is certain varieties of the adventure tale, a form that has been neglected by the literary critics and scholars who constitute the world of letters, or at least perform its legislative and judicial functions. They have denied adventure the attention it deserves and so deprived us of a major way to understand ourselves. But I must begin by explaining some of these terms.

What is adventure? What does it mean to be an adventurer? The best answer takes the form of examples, and I shall begin with contemporary ones. Dangerous things happen to you, at first unexpectedly and later inexplicably; a mad dog is slavering at your door, or the police you phone for help knock you over the head, or your airplane makes a forced landing in the desert. You have to take action, make decisions, of a kind remote from your daily law-abiding life. You are called on for courage, cunning, ruthlessness, endurance, leadership, and basic survival skills, and ultimately you must get ready to kill or be killed.

That is the experience we call adventure. And when you read an adventure tale, you identify with an adventurer—the protagonist of such a story—someone who becomes a hero by the energetic way he (or she, but most probably he) meets those challenges.

Most serious readers, especially those who study or teach literature, do not want to make such an identification. It goes against their faith in civilized values. There is a morality and an ideology attached to the act of reading, no matter what is read, provided the reader is serious. (Of course, some of our reading is not serious—academics are big readers of mysteries. And some of the books we take seriously attack civilized values—part of their authority is just that self-contradiction. Such complexities should not obscure the simple line of connection between reading and being civilized.)

We expect a book to satisfy our moral standards, except when it has won an exemption by being labeled fine art, in which case anything goes. The ideology amounts to an identification with civilization, in opposition to all its enemies, and so to most people of that faith, adventures are repugnant. They probably see human beings as constituted by society, and individuals acting outside that context as fragments or fantasms—not as being the more authentic for their isolation (which is what adventure suggests) but as less so.

Moreover, their feeling about civilized values is particularly strong while they are in the act of reading. People who act quite unscrupulously in an actual adventurous situation may sincerely be quite moralistic while reading. And often—though *this* does not follow automatically and varies in strength from case to case—real-life adventure itself (even its excitements and virtues) is also repugnant to such readers.

It will be clear that I am talking a language of common sense, rather than using one of the special vocabularies of theory. I take it that even today this is an acceptable option and that I don't need to prove I know that common sense—nowadays sometimes called the folklore of a subject—has its limits and its risks, especially when one goes on, as I do now, to speak of gender issues. Far from being self-evident truth, common sense is as conventional as theory, and its conventions are heterogeneous. But it has its virtues. It eschews the privileges and the mandarin abstractions of theory and invites the reader to meet the writer as an equal.

Today, then, the traditional gap or split between serious reading and adventure reading is wider than ever because of the power of feminism in the contemporary world of letters, for adventure books are and always have been masculinist—aimed at men, and celebrating manliness. In the introduction to a 1911 American edition of the collected works of Jules Verne, the science fiction adventure writer, we are told, "It is not only 'boy's literature' that begins with Verne. One might almost say that men's literature, the story that appeals to the business man, the practical man, began then also."[1]

Around 1911 there was a masculine-protest party in the parliament of letters. It was the age of Kipling; *men* then proclaimed themselves cheated by literature and by culture in general. At all times men who define themselves as men feel that traditional literature is not written for them, like women who define themselves as women. "Literature" inevitably has something androgynous in its aspiration.

Adventure belongs to men (and vice versa) for the profoundest of reasons. Adventure is the name for experience beyond the law, or on the very frontier of civilization. At least, adventure is the high-spirited way of naming that experience and suggests the feeling of power that can go with it. By contrast, women find *their* experience, their mode of power, within the limits of law. Each gender feels weak in the presence of the other's mode of power. (I am speaking in the mythical terms that apply to gender folklore.) Men as much as women feel themselves to be victims of the sex war, and in comedies of manners they depict women as throwing their weight about in society, using loud and commanding voices while the men mumble and stutter. (There are other myths of gender. One, which I associate with D. H. Lawrence, associates women with nature rather than society, but Lawrence too depicts the behavior of the sexes in the way I have just described.)

Women are said to have psychologically easier access to the constituted forms of authority, to "the law" in all its forms (and they often agree). Men, on the other hand, are believed to have access to forms of force beyond the law. This is one reason that men batter women physically while women (so men say) batter men psychologically. Women, or rather feminists, quickly determine and demand their rights in "civilized" or "social" situations, ranging from the service in a hotel to reform politics (they are more often denied those rights

1. Jules Verne, *Five Weeks in a Balloon*, Introduction, ix.

initially). Men, even masculinists, are easily embarrassed in those situations and often prefer to do without, but they are able to enter the forbidden world of violence, which is the world of adventure.

Today it is women who have the initiative in the world of ideas. And the more antimasculinist literature becomes, the more hostile it will be to adventure writing. That split has good as well as bad features, but because it maintains itself by means of a voluntary blindness in serious readers, it must be counted an intellectual scandal that must now be addressed.

My argument here, therefore, supports the cause of feminism only indirectly. I want to overcome the mutual hostility between the adventure tale and literature as a body of standards, or at least overcome the rigidity and irrationality in that prejudice. I want to make adventure and masculinism interesting and accessible to literary readers, and while that is likely to seem antifeminist to begin with, it is not, I hope, antifeminist in the long run.

A recent interview-article about a South African adventure writer gives us an example of "the adventure problem." Written by Stephen Gray and titled "Alan Scholefield and the African Adventure Novel,"[2] the article begins by noting how hard South African men of letters find it to take seriously, even to focus on, adventure stories. Why is that? "We [South Africans] feel that adventure fiction, surely, belongs to the frontier days, and see the modern version as an escape into history, a veering away from contemporary realities . . . [something] beneath serious consideration." ("We" find contemporary reality, then, unadventurous? In South Africa? Only in the sense, surely, that we believe reality to be defined as "man in society.") And yet Scholefield is, says Gray, a "remarkable writer by anyone's standards," and nine of his novels deal with the adventurous history of South Africa.

Although I believe in the category of "the gifted writer neglected because he tells adventure tales," I am not arguing that Scholefield belongs to it. That is not a critical estimate of him; I am interested not in the particulars of his case but in the generalities.

We begin to recognize the biographical elements of the adventure-writer idea when we learn that, having grown up in South Africa,

2. Stephen Gray, "Alan Scholefield and the African Adventure Novel," *Contrast* 14 (December 1982): 38–47.

Scholefield supported himself at first as a journalist but wanted from the beginning to become a novelist. He much admired Hemingway, and like Hemingway went to Spain to live when he committed himself to writing as a career. Later his autobiographical novel, *The Young Master,* was based in its school parts on Kipling's *Stalky and Co.* Thus he sketches out a career and acknowledges forebears, which belong to the adventure tradition.

Moreover, Scholefield's career as a novelist began when he got the idea of doing for African history what John Masters (another disciple of Hemingway and Kipling) had done for India in his novels, and he researches the African history of his books meticulously (partly because the South African government is likely to be upset by his revisions of official history).[3] By contrast, the reality of modernist writers is often surreal and can be quite nonfactual. If one is writing a story of personal relations or is inspired to follow Beckett or Kafka, one might have no need for any historical research.

The adventure writer could thus plausibly claim to be—from a historian's point of view—more intellectually serious than his literary rival. But Scholefield is closer to apology than to any such boasting. When asked to define his audience, he says only that he knows it includes children.[4] Such a self-definition cannot but be self-deprecatory. He offers no cultural or literary theory to explain why he is neglected by the critics, and when asked about his development he will say only that he has moved from writing thrillers to writing adventures.

Finally, Scholefield says he himself does not read either thrillers or adventures—"I don't particularly enjoy them"—and when asked for a general comment on adventure he says, "Well, all I can say is that it mustn't present the view of life that was presented by the *Boys' Own Paper.*"[5] His values, then—his serious mind—is in some sense unadventurous. He himself reads Nadine Gordimer and Dan Jacobson, the literary writers of South Africa. He accepts in advance, one might say, a negative literary verdict.

This shows us, first of all, the split between reader and writer that is inside most gifted adventure writers: as readers they belong to the

3. Ibid., 41–42.
4. Ibid., 43.
5. Ibid., 47.

world of letters, as writers they serve a nonliterary public. This split was felt keenly by, for instance, Kipling and Hemingway, Scholefield's masters; it was felt as a hostility between themselves and literature and as a split within their own identity. Indeed, the same dichotomy is to be found in many of us, at the level of taste, and in literature itself. The books we take seriously as literature are incompatible with those we read as adventure, and whatever the rational content of that distinction (the unproblematic recognition that apples are not oranges), it also signals a nonrational incompatibility of temperament or tendency. There are two dynamic drives within our reading minds, which push away from each other. It is probably right as well as inevitable—probably vital to the health of literature—that such a split should occur. But it is also vital to find some way to bridge that gap, when necessary, to connect and communicate between the two sides. Then it will be possible for adventures to receive serious attention and for a broader sense of life to surround and modify the study of literature as an art. This book attempts to build such a bridge.

In this and the next chapter I discuss adventure as a concept, with only a broad, vague context of time and place. But the subject flourishes best under a culture-history treatment, and beginning with Chapter 3 I root my seven types in specifics and continuities as much as possible. To begin, it seems prudent to make some moves toward what we now call theory, because of the present climate of literary opinion. Readers not much interested in theory might begin with Chapter 3.

Political Criticism

This book's argument is not Marxist, nor is it tied to any other political philosophy, but it tends to converge with current lines of literary criticism and historical analysis that might be called political. I associate these especially with the recent work of Benedict Anderson, and others influenced by him, on nationalism, because the adventure tale and that political force have worked reciprocally together. Anderson's *Imagined Communities* focuses primarily on how human agglomerations are made, by the force of communal imagination, into nations, and on the ways literature, particularly the novel, has helped in that process. His own literary concerns are more with "serious" literature than with adventure tales, but it is the latter that have had the most effect in that kind of history and that reveal most about it when studied. The great adventure tales *are* those acts of imagination and narration that constitute the imagined communities called nations.

That there has been a link between the nation as a political form and the novel as a literary form is not a new idea, but Anderson calls on us to think about it in a new way, less accusing and dismissive. He tells us, for instance, that "progressive cosmopolitan intellectuals" have too long insisted on attributing to the nation a "near-pathological character, rooted in fear and hatred of the other." We need to remember that nations inspire love too, and even self-sacrificing love.[6]

The phenomena of nationalism have not yet been set in order by a thinker as good as Marx or Weber, Anderson says, but we can be clear that it is a concept of the same scope as "kinship" or "religion," and certainly not one to be thought of as simply false.[7] In fact, nation-ness is the most universally legitimate value in politics today, having outlasted the impugned and doubtful values of Marxism.[8]

Anderson's lead is followed by several of the essayists in the collection called *Nation and Narration,* edited by Homi Bhabha. Timothy Brennan, for instance, in his "National Longing for Form," says that although literary and political critics in the West now take it for granted that nationalism is a form of tyranny, that is unjust, and due partly to the disturbing challenge we feel from insurgent nationalist movements. Among newly independent peoples, like the Irish, the Albanians, and the Basques, nationalist politics and nationalist novels are progressive forces.[9]

Reading the essayists in Bhabha's collection, one cannot but think how well the different types of adventure fit their categories—how well, for instance, the Three Musketeers type fits Malinowski's definition of a political myth, a charter for a social order supplying a retrospective pattern of moral and magical values to strengthen tradition, and how well the Wanderer type (concerned with spies, renegades, reporters,

6. See Benedict Anderson, *Imagined Communities,* 129.
7. Ibid., 14–15.
8. Ibid., 11–12.
9. Homi Bhabha, ed., *Nation and Narration,* 44, 57.

smugglers) ties into Geoffrey Bennington's remarks. Bennington says we must approach the idea of a nation not at its origin (always suspect to modern thought) but via the tension between inside and outside, via its borders, its policing, its suspicions.[10]

More loosely, it is toward the critical thinking associated with Raymond Williams and Terry Eagleton, and with Fredric Jameson in this country, that this book's arguments tend. This similarity derives in part, perhaps, simply from its being a genre study. Jameson at least says that genre criticism has always had a privileged relationship to historical materialism.[11] But the likeness is also a matter of our shared concern with political themes and a narrative or diachronic criticism.

Introducing his collected essays, Jameson says that his work, as well as promoting the Marxian world-view, enlarges the conception of the literary text itself so that its political, psychological, ideological, philosophical, and social resonances might become audible.[12] By a natural extension, he calls the aesthetic idea of a work of art a fetishization and an abstraction. Our effort as critics should, at least often, be to return our art monuments to their original reality in situation, as the private languages of isolated individuals in a reified society.[13]

My own effort is even less concerned with, or for, art monuments. Some of the books I deal with would not by themselves reward (or therefore deserve) any close scrutiny—that is, they are not works of fine art. Others of them do reward that scrutiny, and some have already received it but, as grouped together in this sequence, present a different aspect from the way they look in a literature course. Thus, what Jameson calls the political, social, and ideological resonances are even more central here. Above all, I recognize a similarity when Jameson says that the story of his collection of essays (the story of his development) is "a drift from the vertical to the horizontal, from the levels of one text to the multiple interweavings of a narrative, from problems of interpretation to problems of historiography."[14]

It is now a story Jameson wants to tell, a history. In the preface to *The Political Unconscious* he writes, "Always historicize! is the one absolute and 'transhistorical' imperative of all dialectical thought."[15] He calls

---

10. Ibid., 121.
11. Fredric Jameson, *The Political Unconscious*, 105.
12. Jameson, *Ideologies of Theory*, Introduction, xxviii.
13. Ibid., 177.
14. Ibid., xxix.
15. Jameson, *The Political Unconscious*, 9.

narrative the central function or instance of the human mind, and rejoices to see historicization and narrativization everywhere recovering from the synchronic or structuralist attack. This account of the types of adventure is nothing but such a narrativization, and though I limit my survey to the modern period, those adventures have historical functions that derive, in changing forms, from long before.

Thus, in "Magical Narrative" Jameson describes our cultural tradition as beginning with epics, "the monuments of power societies," and reminds us that Goethe called the *Iliad* a glimpse into hell.[16] Jameson suggests that one day such works will seem almost incomprehensible. But Goethe's phrase is one we would do well to ponder. Whether or not Goethe saw the *Iliad* as belonging exclusively to the past, we at least should insist that Goethe's own period, the time of Napoleon's wars, had its hellish aspects.

Nor was the *Iliad* totally unlike some of the *writing* of Goethe's time. It is of course an adventure tale, among other things, and my nineteenth-century adventures (Dumas's work has an especially close connection to Napoleon's imperialism) are just as much monuments to our own power societies. We may well find them too to be glimpses into hell, however gaily tinted the lens, but we cannot afford to close our eyes to those glimpses.

The political approach to literature is also taken by Raymond Williams (for instance, in *Marxism and Literature*) and by Terry Eagleton (for instance, in *The Ideology of the Aesthetic*). Williams has been particularly helpful in his discussion of specialization. He pointed out that, as late as the eighteenth century, literature meant all printed books and was not limited to or biased toward "imaginative" works. Then came a shift from learning to taste, then another shift to *national* literatures, and then a specialization of literature to mean works of imagination. The crucial thing, Williams says, is to identify literature as in modern times a specializing social and historical category.[17]

Williams thus frees critics to take into their purview all kinds of books (including these that I now consider) otherwise allotted to popular culture or history or sociology. However, it was *not* in fact anything like adventures which Williams himself went on to consider; and as we ponder that, we realize there has been in the twentieth century another

16. Ibid., 103–4.
17. Raymond Williams, *Marxism and Literature*, 47, 48, 53.

specialization of literature, which Williams does not take account of, but was himself affected by, however unconsciously. That is the specialization to a literature of refusal and accusation, a denial of equal status to lighter and brighter books.

This was not a feature of Williams's taste only. Our major critics have been more often "tragic" than not. We should remember that Adorno called art the *negative* knowledge of reality. And a recent book by Jonathan Dollimore, *Radical Tragedy,* recommends Jacobean tragedy for having been as much a theater of scandal and refusal as our own theater, that of Genet, Artaud, and Brecht. The author quotes Sartre's recommendation of those writers as especially ours. Sartre, Adorno, Williams, these are our masters; but some of us want to escape from the bullying of this minatory and apocalyptic specialization without having to join Roland Barthes, reclining among the pleasures of the text.

We also have something to learn from Barthes. For instance, the value of bodily experience, its dialectical relationship to other values, ideal or political, is a theme that is relevant to the adventure tale, and I shall return to it. And Terry Eagleton, in the most recent major book of political criticism, combines a concern for that value with the values traditional in political criticism (just as Jameson combined structural and formal concerns with that tradition). As Eagleton says, however, the meditations on the body by the later Barthes and the later Foucault read too much like a displacement of politics.[18] The body can mean something more useful to political criticism than that.

Eagleton also reminds his readers of how much that was bourgeois in its origins deserves to be prized by Marxists (and was prized by Marx and Engels), including the achievements of liberal humanism. As we shall see, Ernst Bloch has made a good argument for including the adventure tale, and even more the study of the adventure tale, in that category.

Such is the area of the theory-map on which it seems useful to locate this study of adventure types.

French Theories of Adventure

The English-speaking countries have historically been at the leading edge of the empire-building explosion of the white race outward over the rest

18. Terence Eagleton, *The Ideology of the Aesthetic,* 7.

of the world. That race's expansion has been *the* epic story of modern history, at least as the whites themselves see it. (I shall use "white" sometimes when other authors use "Western," because it was precisely the whiteness that mattered to adventure readers and to the other peoples who faced the thrust of Europe and its colonists.) The English-speaking countries therefore saw themselves, and were seen, as crucibles of the modern adventure spirit and (as a natural consequence) of the adventure tale as well. French critics and scholars, for instance, have said that the main affinity of the English writers is for the novel of action while French writers are better at the novel of passion, that British narratives excel in narrative, French ones in analysis.

We can all think of exceptions to these generalities, but perhaps for the eighteenth and nineteenth centuries they have some validity. In the twentieth century, however, and in the realm of literature theory, there has been much writing in English that excels in analysis—in theory— and that studiously ignores the adventure tale. With few exceptions, the only serious discussions of adventure in English have not been literary in character, but sociological—treating it as a specimen of "popular culture."

This term I have seen defined as "unofficial culture, the culture of the nonelite, the 'subordinate classes,' as Gramsci called them."[19] That is also the way Walter Cohen uses the term in his *Drama of a Nation,* a study with thematic concerns like this one. This formula clearly will not do for my authors, who were linked to the ruling class and even to the official culture, though repudiated by literature.

I would like to suggest that even in contemporary art and entertainment, "popular culture" is a term we should reserve for something as unlike literature as rock music and comic strips, while the adventures of, say, John Buchan, are middlebrow or genteel culture. I don't accept the intimations of superiority that come packaged with those adjectives. We are all middlebrow in some aspects of our taste, and all the men and women of letters I know are genteel. The books I want to bring to the reader's attention reward serious discussion, but they belong neither to the people nor to the connoisseur. Just for that reason they are more vividly and vigorously related to the political ideology of their times than the literature of the other two types.

Thus, one has to make something of a fresh start, theoretically. When

19. See Peter Burke, *Popular Culture in Early Modern Europe,* xi.

one begins to think about adventure, in literature or outside, one does well to turn away from English-speaking scholars to French and German ones.

At the end of the nineteenth century, two Scots men of letters, Robert Louis Stevenson and Andrew Lang, defended adventure and romance against realistic and "great characters" fiction with some spirit, and one can also find starting points for a theory of adventure in their contemporary William Morris. One sign of their unity in taste is that all three made high claims for Scott and Dumas as novelists at a time when literature's verdict had gone decisively against both. They were *for* Scott and Dumas and *against*, for instance, Tolstoy, whom they saw as a realist. But their preferences were never developed into theories, at least not in England.

The story is different in non-English-speaking countries. In Germany there has been an outburst of interest in the subject during the last twenty years, while in France such an interest was a phenomenon of the beginning of the twentieth century. *Le roman d'aventures* by Jean-Yves Tadié sums up that controversy, which involved Marcel Schwob, André Gide, Jacques Rivière, and the *Nouvelle Revue Française*. The excitement began when essays and fiction by Stevenson caught the attention of Schwob in the 1880s. Stevenson had drawn a contrast between the novel of character and the novel of incident and protested against the literary world's automatic preference for the latter. His argument was basically aesthetic: the adventure, which absorbs the reader into a completely actualized world wholly other than the writer's self-consciousness, his self-discourse, offers the reader the chance for a much freer and fuller response. He made much less of the implications of that preference, in morals and politics.

Schwob was impressed by these essays and by Stevenson's own fiction, and he began to call on French writers to tell tales of adventure. He was joined by Camille Mauclair, who, in an article published January 1, 1898, in the *Revue du Palais,* called for a new type of novel hero, someone who would no longer be the wraith of *Symboliste* stories or the primitive of Naturalist stories, but "a conqueror from the Far East, a captain, a pirate, an anarchist dictator."[20] French literature, he said, had become overintellectualized. Unless French writers and readers found new heroes in their stories and thrilled to heroic adventures, their imaginations would be killed by the spirit of criticism.

20. Kevin O'Neill, *André Gide and the roman d'aventures*, 16.

Both Schwob and Mauclair were friends of André Gide, who was already a powerful figure on the French literary scene. By 1898 he was writing *Les caves du Vatican,* which he then thought of as an adventure tale, in a bold attempt to radically alter the contemplative and speculative character of his fiction so far. They all liked Stevenson's rebellion against a detailed realism of description, especially of the Zola variety. He and they preferred a bare, stripped narrative of action.

In 1913 Jacques Rivière cited Stevenson as a model, in a three-part essay in the May, June, and July issues of the *Nouvelle Revue Française* that amplified and clarified much that had gone before. Part one was on Symbolism, the art and art doctrine to be displaced: "an art of extreme consciousness, the art of people who are terribly aware of what they want and what they are doing," its subject always an emotion, not an object or an event and with all anecdotal origin or interest removed.[21] This had been a very French kind of art. Mallarmé, Rivière said, could have belonged to no other nation but France. But now even the French had new souls and wanted new pleasures. "The Symbolists knew only the pleasures of the tired. . . . We today know more violent and lively pleasures. All of them are contained within the pleasure of living. . . . It is again morning. Everything begins again. The pleasure of being among men! The Symbolists had lost the taste for man; they had no desire to see him anymore."[22] This has the true Renaissance lustiness, and so far it seems as if the English adventure tale, with its imperialist associations, is indeed what Rivière wants.

But in part three, "Le Roman d'Aventures," Rivière tells us that this new fiction, "tout entière en actes," will be "classical."[23] Moreover, cubism is mentioned as an equivalent in the visual arts, as is a turning away from Wagner toward Bach in music; and in philosophy, Descartes is a prime example and sponsor of this classicism. All this clearly suggests something quite different and more intellectual—in fact, another attempt by the literary world to throw off the long yoke of Romanticism. And this mood and motive became stronger as time went by, especially with the experience of the Great War, which disillusioned people with imperialism and even with "the taste for man." When, in 1919, Rivière became editor of the *Nouvelle Revue Française,* he wrote,

21. Jacques Rivière, *Nouvelles études,* 244.
22. Ibid., 244, 247.
23. Ibid., 253.

in introducing the first issue, "We will speak of everything which seems to us to foretell a classical revival." This cue was taken up in many quarters—for instance, in England and in T. S. Eliot's *Criterion,* where the classical revival signified a taste for almost anything but the traditional adventure tale.

But Rivière and his friends, whatever else they came to mean by "classical," began by identifying the term with the actual English adventure. For instance, Rivière had said Defoe was an example of the perfect actualization he wanted in fiction. A seventy-six-page article on Defoe appeared in the *Nouvelle Revue Française* in 1912, and Gide's hero in *Les caves du Vatican* reads only *Aladdin, Robinson Crusoe,* and *Moll Flanders.* Camus's later adaptation of Defoe's *Plague Year,* in *La Peste,* is perhaps an example of the classicism they wanted in fiction—and better, since it included more adventurous action, Hemingway's fiction. (Rivière seems to be giving Hemingway his cue when he reminds his readers of what Stevenson told Schwob: to stop singing and tell us what happened.[24])

What concerns us, however, is the intense attention these theories led readers to give to adventure writers. This was true even of the opposition. Albert Thibaudet replied to Rivière in 1919 with a defense of the French tradition in novel-writing: "A novel, in French, is about love."[25] When Thibaudet, as a precocious child, asked for a Jules Verne novel at his parochial school, he was allowed to borrow it, against all the rules. The reason, according to the librarian, was that Verne's books weren't novels, because they contained nothing about love; they were adventure stories and therefore morally safe.

But in France, Thibaudet admitted, the adventure was developed in a mediocre way, while in England it was a genre "lively, powerful, and rooted in full humanity." At its foundation stood one of the capital books of the Anglo-Saxon race, and of all Western literature: *Robinson Crusoe.*[26] (Within French literature, equivalent books—mutatis mutandis—would be Madame de Lafayette's *La Princesse de Clèves,* exemplifying the *roman d'analyse,* and Corneille's *Le Cid,* exemplifying the heroic classical drama.) Thibaudet compared *Robinson Crusoe* with the *Odyssey,* both of them stories "about energy, about useful intelligence,

24. Ibid., 264.
25. Albert Thibaudet, *Réflexions sur la littérature,* 73.
26. Ibid., 74.

and about action," books written "for a race, not for a public."[27] These
are suggestive distinctions that allot a high destiny to the English
adventure novel, even though Thibaudet's own allegiance still goes to
the French novel.

Finally, it is appropriate to mention Pierre Mac Orlan, himself a
writer of adventures, who brought out in 1920 a *Petit manuel du parfait
aventurier*—no doubt in response to all this critical interest in the genre.
However, his remarks, though shrewd and interesting, do not move on
the same height of theoretical interest as those of Rivière and Thibaudet,
or those of Stevenson. He dwells, for instance, on the difference between
those who like to read or write about adventure and those who enjoy it
when it happens.

For Mac Orlan, as for most of these critics, Jules Verne (one of my
authors here) was simply a bad writer. Apart from Stevenson and Defoe,
the English name these critics cite most often is Conrad; Rivière was
general editor of a large translation of Conrad into French. But, as Tadié
says, the critics were more interested in the Symbolist features of
Conrad's novels than in their adventure character. This way of inviting
the adventure tale inside the city of literature was highly intellectual and
aesthetic and made its adventure action largely symbolic. It ignored not
only the minute-by-minute excitement and plausibility of the tale, but
its cultural context as well—for instance, in Conrad's case, the dour
glamour he found in the English merchant marine service.

Read this way, the cultural and moral meaning of adventure fades
from view, and what replaces it are aesthetic ideas like "the classical"
and "the modern," *literary* ideas that really have more in common with
the despised Symbolism that they have with adventure. But still, this
moment in France was one of the rare moments in cultural history when
the adventure tale, and especially the English adventure tale, received
serious critical attention.

German Theories of Adventure

The new German theories of adventure are political and philosophical
where the French were aesthetic, and they refer much more to German

27. Ibid., 75.

and French authors than to English literature. All the German theories owe much to the work of Ernst Bloch, the philosopher and man of letters who had an important career in the world of ideas in Germany for nearly sixty years.

In a sense, Bloch's contribution to adventure theory began in 1929, when he wrote a challenging article on the importance of Karl May, the German writer of Western adventures, then an equivalent in literary reputation to, say, Louis L'Amour today. "Winnetou's Silver Bullet: On Karl May's Collected Works," appeared in the *Frankfurter Allgemeine Zeitung* on March 31, 1929, and deplored the way that, thirty years before, back in 1897, that prestigious newspaper had put May on the index of proscribed authors, for people of taste.[28] This attack, made in the name of literary standards, had occurred at Christmastime 1897, and in consequence, according to Bloch, respectable parents removed copies of May's books, just purchased and wrapped as presents for their children, from under Christmas trees all over Germany. Since then his name had been a symbol of intellectual and moral sleaziness, and adventure as a whole had been tainted.

But Bloch declared that May was one of the best of German storytellers and could have been the very best. To say this was, of course, to attribute some almost mystical value to narrative skill, on a level with intellectual power. "I know only Hegel and Karl May," Bloch said. "Everything in between is an impure mixture of both." Moreover, whatever lies May had told (part of the scandal about him was that he falsely claimed to have been, like his heroes, a frontiersman in America), every boy finds the truth in his books. "So there must be something in his lie, namely the genuine love of the far-off, which fills it."[29]

Bloch was concerned to defend not only May but all *Kolportageliteratur,* the German name for what we might call thrillers. (*Kolportage* refers to the way such books were distributed, by pedlars and notably at fairs, not through bookstores.) It is different from "literature" but not inferior. "*Kolportage* has in its twists and turns no muse of contemplation overhead, but dreams of wish-fulfillment within. . . . It has overturned the absurd image of a people with no needs or dreams, repeating the cycle of the seasons in stolid contentment."[30] Just by not being so pure as literature, therefore, it is politically energizing.

28. Ernst Bloch, *Erbschaft dieser Zeit,* 170.
29. Ibid.; Gert Ueding, *Glanzvolles Elend,* 187.
30. Bloch, *Erbschaft,* 178, 179.

The title of Bloch's collected essays so far cited, *Erbschaft dieser Zeit* (The Heritage of These Times), first published in 1935, referred to Bloch's determination to find in even the despised petit-bourgeois culture of post-1918 Germany something that would be of use to the party of the future, to the revolutionary forces that would bring the future into being. Bloch wanted to build a cultural alliance between the lower middle class and the proletariat. The adventure tale is an important part of that joint culture, a basis for that alliance.

Bloch's three-volume collection of 1959 took the title *Das Prinzip Hoffnung* (The Principle of Hope) and again set a positive cultural and political value on day-dreams and wish-dreams, including the adventure tale. The day-dream, he tells us, serves "an as-far-as-possible unrestricted journey forward, so that instead of reconstituting that which is no longer conscious, the images of that which is not yet can be phantasied into life and into the world."[31] Again the title of the book from which this comes, *A Philosophy of the Future,* is significant: Bloch is reversing the humanities' habitual backward fixation. We humanists mistake the nature of thought, he says. Its true illuminating function "is as the light that shines out ahead in this world, which is divided into the inner world still replete with thoughts, and the exterior world still not wholly reconciled with it."[32] He set himself in opposition to the cultural pessimism of the Frankfurt school (Theodor Adorno and Herbert Marcuse) and implicitly, therefore, to all the philosophers of cultural rootedness, from F. R. Leavis and T. S. Eliot to Karl Mannheim and Martin Heidegger.

One of Bloch's followers, Volker Klotz, points out that the literary novel, in the hands of Goethe, Stendhal, Keller, and so on, deals like the adventure with the conflict between the self and the world, but habitually shows that conflict as ending in defeat for the central character—in Goethe's *Werther,* in Ugo Foscolo's *Jacopo Ortis,* Flaubert's *Education sentimentale,* and many more. Honor is shown to be incompatible with ambition; love lives on the absence, not the presence, of the beloved; and heroism is out of the question.[33] The adventure novel, by contrast, breathes a spirit of optimism. It has heroes, and it sets a value on the power of the individual body and of immediate life. Every adventure, Bloch says, breaks the repressive morality of "work and pray"; the pirate ship displaces the first, and curses replace the second.[34]

31. Bloch, *A Philosophy of the Future,* 86.
32. Ibid., 20.
33. Volker Klotz, *Abenteuer-Romane,* 220–21.
34. Bloch, *Das Prinzip Hoffnung,* 1:428.

Klotz carries the war between adventure and literature further into the enemy camp. He says that the serious writers' claim to reject all literary formulas (such as adventures are admittedly built on) and to create unique books, each one unmediated in its dealings with the reader (that claim on which literature's whole superiority of status rests), is just an illusion. It is just another version of bourgeois society's illusion of individual liberty.[35] Every story is structured by formulas, just as every person is structured by society. The formulas of adventure are honorable marks of its social function, and we should ingest them as a natural part of the aesthetic experience.

The books Klotz is concerned with do not belong to any English-language literature; his main authors are Eugène Sue, Karl May, "Sir John Retcliffe," "Frédéric Armand," and "Gabriel Ferry." They wrote adventure novels, but because there is no exact equivalent for them among the English-language novelists some of his remarks are at first puzzling to English-language readers. They are, however, illuminating in the long run. The nineteenth-century adventure novel, he says, had three functions: to compensate the reader with fantasy power for his or her lack of actual power in politics and the workplace; to strengthen the reader's trust and pleasure in what he or she did have, for example, family unity; and to explain social and political conditions.

Such explanation was needed because the new forms of power in the nineteenth century were characterized by invisibility—whether physical power like electricity, or social power like capital. The stock exchange and the bank account replaced the castle, and the millionaire was a private citizen, without title or public office. This invisibility is just one of five heads under which Klotz sums up the nineteenth-century social stresses the adventure novel alleviated. The other four are (1) the harsher work conditions and more calamitous trade cycles, (2) the doubt whether people *were* freer than they had been, as they had been told, (3) the splitting up of experience, political power splitting off from economic power, and so on (so that more energy went into fantasies of wholeness), and (4) the replacement of nature by society as the locus of the threatening and inscrutable. Those adventure tales need to be read even now in the context of these historical experiences, to which they answered.

Formally, too, adventure tales had an important context. The serialization of adventure novels in nineteenth-century newspapers meant that

---

35. Klotz, *Abenteuer-Romane*, 19.

they were read along with the news of the day—the major political and economic events, the murders and sex scandals. It also meant that the readers' response became known long before the story ended, much less was published as a book, and could on occasion affect the way the author developed the themes and plot. Newspapers were themselves capitalist phenomena, with their rising and falling circulations—which could be strongly affected by the popularity of their serials. Readers also were thus involved in the writing of adventures.

Serious literature turned away from all that, demanding to be read (and written) in a private area of calm and contemplation. This literature included most strikingly poetry and essays, but to some extent also the middle-class domestic novel, the popular-respectable form of, for instance, George Eliot in Victorian England. The adventure novel instead developed from prebourgeois literary forms, like the epic and the tragedy.[36] It featured heroes who were charismatic, and in effect divine on occasion. (Klotz mentions some examples of this from *The Count of Monte Cristo*.) It offered sublime actions and emotions (fear, horror, awe, enthusiasm, inspiration), while the serious domestic novel confined itself largely to the actions and emotions of the beautiful (pathos, charm, resignation, sympathy, moral realism). And the adventure novel included three of the main elements of classical tragedy—anagnorisis, peripeteia, and the tragic fall—though the adventure hero usually rebounded from a fall.

Of Klotz's ideas, the one most in tune with contemporary English-language theory is the importance of the body. The adventure tale pays quite as much attention to the body and finds as much dignity in it (when that value comes in conflict with other values) as the love story. A brief survey of my main texts will show that.

Even in *Robinson Crusoe*, a Puritan and nonsensual novel, Robinson's experience of sickness, and his self-cure, dramatize the vulnerability of the subject's body, while the description of Friday, which is reminiscent of slave-market descriptions, translates the excitement of property into somatic terms. *The Three Musketeers'* focus is characteristically on the body's forms of movement, running, leaping, riding, dueling; even in a seated and sculptural form (as in Doré's statue of d'Artagnan) the hero seems to move. In the Frontiersman adventure, perhaps the most striking evocation of the body is the series of huge, old, fierce animals that

36. See ibid., 225.

confront the hero: Parkman's buffalo, Melville's whale, London's wolf-dog, Faulkner's bear, Hemingway's lion, Mailer's bear. These are all manifestations of body that elicit from the hero a kind of worship. In the Avenger novel an archetypal image is Dantes slashing open his sackcloth shroud as it enters the ocean and wriggling free, delivering himself from an imprisoning womb, to rise to the surface and swim heroically to freedom. In the Wanderer tale, we experience the sensations of tramping and climbing and hunger and weariness—Kim's exhaustion from supporting the dead weight of his exhausted guru. In the Sagaman story we note the loving particularity with which individual weapons and the wounds they cause are described. In the Hunted Man story—for instance, as told by Dashiell Hammett or John D. MacDonald—we note the horror generated in the reader by bodily mutilation or freakishness: the fat man, the dwarf, the cripple, the martial artist. These are all different evocations of the body, its potency, its vulnerability, its necessity.

This is part of what Bloch saw the adventure tale as offering to its readers, and thus the German philosophers of literature offer us a new starting point from which to look at the genre, and ways to avoid seeing it as simply a rejected aspirant to literary status.

Method

My own argument is an attempt to impose order on the enormous mass of adventure narratives by devising a seven-part taxonomy for them. I cover only the adventure literature of the white nations, and only books written from 1700 on. Though I have read Chinese, Indian, and African adventures, I do not attempt to describe how they differ from those of white nations. Nor do I discuss the adventures of the Renaissance, the Middle Ages, or the ancient world. I set my narratives in relation to the cultural-historical forces specific to the modern world, not to other cultures' narratives.

My method is primarily logical. I identify each of my seven story types by the character of its protagonist and hope thereby to "explain" the differences between any two or more adventures. The alternative methods would be more descriptive. They would include the geographical (grouping together adventures of the Caribbean, those of the South Seas, those of mountain lands) or the national (adventures by French versus German versus English writers) or the historical (seventeenth-, eighteenth-, or nineteenth-century adventures) or the elemental (adventures of land, sea, air), and there is something to be said for each of these descriptive taxonomies, but the grouping according to protagonist seems best for analytical purposes.

The protagonist's character may be said to "generate" or at least characterize his adventures, which form the stuff of his book. Very different things happen in *Robinson Crusoe* from those that happen in *The Three Musketeers,* because a middle-class Protestant trader has desires and fears unlike those of a fiery Gascon cavalier. Crusoe's adventures have to do with storms at sea, being cast away, building a boat, planting a crop, and hiding from cannibals. D'Artagnan's adventures have to do with the King's Guard, the Cardinal's plots, a wicked seductress, swordplay, jewels, and night-rides across France. The reader is offered different kinds of heroes, and so different kinds of excitement and different views of life, under the same names of adventure and adventurer.

However, though this scheme is logical rather than chronological, because each type has a life in time (not so much a beginning and an end as periods of blossoming and fading), there is also a historical significance to the order in which I deal with them. *Robinson Crusoe* is the first specifically modern adventure, while my seventh type belongs mostly to the twentieth century. In fact, I see each subgenre in relation to certain features of political history, as the energizing myth or legend of certain political forces.

This is therefore a value-laden taxonomy, and it is in some sense nonobjective. I have named the kinds of adventure that interest *me*— which means the kinds that are relevant to the politics of manliness/ nationalism/empire. Other kinds get short shrift. And I do not include even massive phenomena that could be called relevant—for instance, I say nothing about Tarzan or Dr. Fu Manchu. My excuse is that, insofar as such stories bear upon my themes, they offer only extra and inferior examples of ideas I have named out of other books. (Tarzan is just another example of the white race atavism that inspired many adventure books at the end of the nineteenth century, and Dr. Fu Manchu is yet another example of the white race paranoia of the same period.) Where there is a choice of examples, I, like other people, choose those with more literary dignity or interest. In fact, I discuss only "respectable" adventures, a term I shall define.

Thus, I do not claim that this taxonomy allows me to place every adventure satisfactorily. For one thing, it has a bias toward Anglo-American books. I started from my own, nonsystematic reading, though I have extended my purview in thinking about the topic. If I had begun from a different point my "system" would have been somewhat different. But there is much to be said for a "spontaneous" scheme of ideas that springs from and reflects a personal taste. Taste is, in literary studies, as nature is in paintings: always a potential source of vitality/authority/pleasure. So I have wounded logic in the name of taste.

Thus my scheme is not all-inclusive or all-explaining. These are seven types of adventure tale, not *the* seven. But I hope that my method produces some order and enlightenment.

Beginning with the protagonist leads me naturally to name famous examples in each case. This is an obvious way to think of the types and to remember them, so we can call this an effect of light. As for order, this method also lets me subdivide each of the seven logically, according to certain variables. First of all, the protagonist is sometimes not an individual but a group—a couple, a family, a band of comrades, or a boatload of strangers. And these variants combine with variants in literary genre, so that the Robinson story can be told as *The Blue Lagoon,* or *The Swiss Family Robinson,* or *Lord of the Flies,* or *The Coral Island.* Then the protagonist is sometimes an adult, sometimes a child, sometimes a man, sometimes a woman (though this last rarely), sometimes white, sometimes nonwhite (though this last very rarely).

Many of the variables are quite unrelated to the protagonist, but all of them are potentially interesting. I will invoke this one or that in the course of the discussion according to the interest of the results it leads to. There is the choice of first- or third-person narrator, of epic or anecdotal style, and so on. One variable that is always important is the tone of the telling itself; the story is sometimes told straight, sometimes told satirically or negatively, especially when the writer has literary ambitions. However, I am interested only in cases where the satire acts "within" the genre and empowers adventure. A satire that is totally unsympathetic and that trivializes adventure values will not be an adventure at all.

These alternatives are not all equally available at all times. There are cultural pressures on writers, varying with history, which give a preferential weighting to one or another—for instance, there is pressure today to create women adventurers. One place where this drive has succeeded is in the detective thriller, especially in America, with the women detectives of Sue Grafton, Marcia Muller, and Sara Paretsky. Thus, if logic provides the writers with a number of options, history makes a selection from them attractive.

Finally, the story is offered sometimes as fact and sometimes as fiction. Perhaps the individual writer does not often (though he or she does sometimes) hesitate between those two options with a subject ready-formed. But if one looks at the culture as a whole, the way adventure fiction and adventure fact reflect and feed each other is obvious. It is also important for my argument, because that connection gives weight to the fictional adventure and offers insight into the factual kind—into real-life adventurers, their motives and their psychic styles. Adventure tales are an important part of any culture, and a very important part of modern white culture. They contain the experience (and even more the dreams) of the white culture's adventurers and heroes—its engineers, explorers, soldiers, governors. What we study (or should study) in adventure fiction is that experience reflected, refined, rehearsed, and reordered.

By and large, men of letters have ignored or denied the connection between adventure fiction and fact. And certainly most adventure writers fail to establish any claim to be read seriously of that kind, the claim the connection to history potentially allows them. But then critics can establish connections *for* writers; that is one of the main functions of literary studies. In the case of Jane Austen, for instance, critics have taught us to see the connection between her stories and forces in her age that she herself, as novelist, did not describe. And then one must make the more accusing point that literary readers unreasonably and irresponsibly deny the factual connections of adventure. They do so for ideological or temperamental reasons, because they don't *like* to think about factual adventure—about fighting and killing, about situations beyond the control of civilized reason. For all these considerations, in several chapters I say something about relevant nonfictional narratives and the experiences they contain—the factual adventures that form the hinterland to that type of adventure tale—and about the large historical forces mythically mirrored in the rippling surface of the narratives.

When put in the proper context, adventures of the respectable kind reveal themselves to be political documents. They reflect, and are reflected in, all the white nations' feelings about their status as nation-

states and about the imperial venture they were jointly engaged in—
about their national and international destinies. Those enthusiasms were
also reflected in some literary novels, of course, where they were com-
mented on much more critically, usually from a Little England point of
view. But if a reader wants to see the dream being dreamed, to feel the
attraction it exerted, he must turn to the adventure and set it in its
proper context. Robinson, d'Artagnan, Natty Bumppo, the Saga-hero—
each is a manifestation of a national destiny, as those destinies were
fondly imagined by the people who shaped and enforced actual policy.

But to persuade readers to study adventure in the right way, in the
right context, I must first propose a slightly unorthodox point of view
on literature as a whole. And because it is the guardians of literature,
the critics and scholars, who can allow or refuse to allow readers to
follow up this suggestion, I must try to persuade some of them, in the
next chapter.

2

Adventure, Literature, History

The arts of the Western nations—including literature, music, painting, and so culture in one sense of the word—celebrate various forms of freedom, force, and growth. They celebrate other things too, but those are characteristic themes—indeed, dominant ones—for our period, the whole sequence of modern history beginning with the Renaissance. But you can find a good deal of art with opposite themes and values in the Middle Ages (for instance, the story of Patient Griselda, and other images of sanctified suffering), and those themes show precisely the aspect of the Middle Ages against which the modern world has reacted: the resigned, ascetic, and antiadventurous aspect. One can also make a similar contrast between Western culture and, say, Hinduism. Because it has served an expanding civilization, Western culture has been characterized by motifs of expansion and self-assertion. (This has often been clearer to observers from nonwhite cultures.)

But the fine arts are a subset within the arts, a literally elite subset that often has a radically different and, these days, a deliberately antithetical ideology. Plays like *Waiting for Godot* and novels like

Lord of the Flies attack our complacent expansiveness (though when gift-wrapped with the glamour of literary prizes and fashionableness such books carry a double message). So when we approach the arts via the fine arts, as we do in the academy, we get a biased view of them. We tend to see popular poems and novels as inferior imitations of, or substitutions for, "great poetry" or "great novels," when in fact they have aims and values of their own that are significantly and sometimes proudly different. These latter, whether popular or gen-teel, serve their culture more directly and less antagonistically. So we must learn to distrust the fine arts approach. But if we approach the arts via the social sciences, diagnosing novels (for instance) according to the conceptual schemes of "popular culture," we then too miss what concerns us here: a self-respecting *art*.

This perspective is still too dizzyingly broad to help us see adventure clearly, but it can begin to be narrowed for our purposes by limiting our concern to literature, and within literature to fiction. We might call fiction a literary mode, which like poetry, drama, and so on, includes many genres, and the adventure tale is an important example of a genre. It is a form of art, though not fine art.

Within literature—and something similar is true of music, painting, etc.—the different modes of art aspire to the status of fine art in varying degrees. Poetry (at least twentieth-century poetry in English) is largely a fine art, while film (Hollywood film) is simply art. Fiction presents a more complicated case. There are and always have been large numbers of respectable novels, written with talent and conviction, that are not fine art. Some of these, with the help of intelligent commentary, make vivid and subtle statements even though they have not received intense attention as to form and style, quite apart from their lacking the implicit ideology of fine art. Such statements have a great deal to tell us, if we scrutinize them with an appropriate kind of literary sensibility. This is the case with some adventures.

The two main story types that our fiction tells over and over are the marriage tale (focusing sometimes on courtship, sometimes on marriage and adultery, sometimes on siblings growing up) and the adventure tale. Both these stories celebrate freedom, force, and growth, even though the field of action in the first place is the family, and love relationships, and personality (think what a force-field Tolstoy makes out of the family life he depicts in *War and Peace* and

Anna Karenina). But of the two types the first has much more often been the subject of a fine-arts treatment (as by the great erotic writers, such as D. H. Lawrence) or a treatment of mixed or consensual character (as by the great Victorian humanists, such as George Eliot).

The adventure tale has usually been labeled the opposite of fine art and has therefore largely been disparaged, referred to instead in such terms as "blood and thunder," "penny dreadfuls," or "dime novels," labels that refer to content or cost. I'm not denying that they deserved disparagement—most of them did—but I am suggesting that their poor quality was result as much as cause. Writers were told that quality was inappropriate for books in that genre.

Other countries have comparable labels. The Germans, as we saw, speak of *Kolportageliteratur* (something like "pedlars' stories") and of *Rettungsromanen* (something like "cliff-hangers"). This is market labeling, telling the reader what he or she is buying and implicitly denying that the book has any other value. It is taken up into general discourse only because establishment literature refused these books *its* labels, its stamps of approval, its prestige-conferring nomenclature, such as "sonnet," "satire," or "prose poem," names which—like a pass—give books access to a privileged zone of transcendent being where a protocol of respectful reading obtains. Such demarcation lines and barriers of control occur in most periods. Modernism's conflict with the middlebrow repeats that early eighteenth-century conflict between the Augustans and Grub Street, which also set up impassable barriers between true art and false (or as I put it, fine art and art, serious novels and adventure tales). But however traditional it may be, literature's way of describing such conflicts expresses its institutional interests and is prejudiced and obscurantist from the more liberal point of view I want to establish.

To escape those prejudices, let us turn away from writers and criticism, toward readers and response. The interesting source of the difference between some readers' readiness to enjoy adventure, and others' resistance, lies between two kinds of reading, but not between the responsible and the irresponsible, for both kinds of reader are intelligent and serious and culturally responsible. The one kind we might call the Pharisees, people concerned above all to see the outward-reaching energies of their society maintained: highly moral people, who disapprove, for instance, of modes of heightened sensibility and sensual freedom that threaten morality, but who associate

morality with (to take a typical instance) manliness. The other kind I
call (to make a pair with Pharisees) the Galileans, people who are
preoccupied with the inadequacy of all social morality and see the
chauvinism of manliness and its outward-reaching energies. (This
sort of terminology, if not traditional, has been used before: Swin-
burne talks of Jesus as the Galilean, and Stevenson discusses the two
kinds of morality in a way that is relevant to our concerns in his *Lay
Morals.*)

In the history of fiction, especially English fiction, the first group
of readers has read adventures and has been mostly men; the second
group has read love stories and has been mostly women. That
specification at least applies fairly well to the eighteenth and nineteenth centuries. Before the eighteenth century, love stories did not
have quite this spiritual prestige, and after the advent of modernism
the difference lay no more between the genders than between artistic
simplicity and conventionality in the first group, versus artistic com-
plexity, obscurity, and experiment in the second. Thus the Pharisees
of modern times are opposed not only by women-and-humanists but
also by artists-and-Bohemians. (In this last phase the fine-arts opposition party was inundated with highbrow men, and women have
sometimes felt a new chauvinism arising there.)

These two groups of Galileans are unlike each other and should
perhaps be given different names, but the split between them and the
other kind of reader and reading is continuous as well as manifold.
And it is not—as men and women of letters tend to assume—a
difference between intelligence-and-integrity and their opposites. The
adventure tale, when well told, appeals to just as responsible and
morally formative a reading from the Pharisee reader as the love tale
(whether in its nineteenth- or twentieth-century form) invites from
the Galilean. The adventure is about killing, conquering, dominating
other people and countries or about building up hierarchies and
empires of power. The killing and conquering is done by the reader's
cousins and leaders, and the tale most often presents those activities
from the perspective of the killers and conquerors. But that does not
make it morally insensitive; that merely names the project, and the
question of sensitiveness depends on how the project is carried out.
As for killing and conquering being repugnant to the imagination,
those surely are the experiences that *need* to be responsibly imagined,
above all others. We must know the violence that protects us in our

peaceful pursuits. Those who have found a way to abolish such activities, or a way to build a society that does not rest on them, may feel free not to think about them. The rest of us have no such excuse.

Respectability

Serious attention can be given to anything, even the most trivial matter, even the crudest adventure tale. But I am not arguing for that. I am arguing only that we should attend to the more serious or respectable examples of literary adventure. Many of these are already guaranteed by "respectable" names like Defoe and Scott. But the respectability guaranteed by those two names is surely academic in a limiting sense. Although they are large figures in literary history, occasionally taught and researched, it has been a long time since they were the foci of a living taste, since they seemed relevant to contemporary concerns. Scott and Defoe are not congenial authors to modernist or postmodernist readers—for one thing, because they wrote adventure tales. We need to rehabilitate the concept "respectability" as applied to adventure writers, and to do that we need to discuss how to apply it to adventure characters.

If we consider adventurers outside fiction, we can see three social classes of them, all of whom are by definition outlaws but differ in how much of their life they spend outside the law—in the *persistence* of their adventures and their *commitment* to illegality. (Let us ignore, for the moment, adventurers who challenge nature exclusively, who break only nature's laws—mountaineers, test pilots, deep sea divers.) Some are permanent and, as it were, absolute outlaws; romantic literary examples would be smugglers, gypsies, pirates, and highwaymen, and modern, realistic examples would be pimps, drug-dealers, and protection-racketeers. Others, such as C.I.A. or F.B.I. agents, private investigators, or Green Berets, are commissioned by society to control outlaws, and in so doing themselves pass beyond the law periodically, trespassing in the liminal areas of violence forbidden to citizens. Still others, the easiest for the readers to identify with, are citizens who get involved with people of the first two classes accidentally and temporarily. The reader as reader (even if he is a pimp or a C.I.A. agent in his working life) must find it easier to invest his serious moral feelings in a story about adventurers of the third kind, because that kind of story is designed to explore the relations between adventure and morality. (Let me point out how rarely a writer or a critic considers the reactions of a reader who is by trade a pimp or a C.I.A. agent. This brings to light briefly the hidden structure of "literature" as a social activity, its unspoken exclusions and biases.)

All three classes have adventures written about them, but the more respectable stories are written about the more respectable classes—primarily about the third one, to a lesser degree the second, and to the least degree the first. This is true of the past as well as the present. Robinson Crusoe and Edward Waverley, Natty Bumppo and Huckleberry Finn and Richard Hannay, and so on, belong to the third class—those accidentally involved in adventure. Athos, Porthos, and Aramis, Philip Marlowe and the Kim of the Secret Service, belong to the second. And a great mass of adventure tales that offer the reader the excitements of rape, slaughter, and sinfulness belong to the first class of adventurer. We have to assume that the writers of the latter feel, or ought to feel, some loss of self-respect at providing the mental fodder they do.

I am ignoring the way writers bridle at the word "respectable." Writers like to think of themselves as naughty, but they also resent moral reproach, because like other people they believe some things are worth doing and others are not. I think we can dismiss their protest and call this knot of complication a matter of wording only.

Respectability here refers to the self-respect of both the writer and the reader. These are two different feelings, but they are parallel and mutually dependent. Both writer and reader of respectable adventure, we deduce from the text, believe in what they are doing, believe in adventure tales as a mythology of moral culture. At the same time, they don't believe in themselves as great artists. This is surely true of Sir Walter Scott and John Buchan, of Kipling and Jules Verne, of Defoe and Dumas.

Adventures and adventurers show their respectability in more than one way. A historical novel will be respectable if the author shows a serious interest in history, but it will also be respectable with only a minimum of historical knowledge if the writer is seriously investigating a moral problem or dramatizing the experience of, say, battle. To fail in one of these respects is not a final failure.

The writers' names I have invoked are all out of the past, and that is significant. The respectable adventure genre as a whole has had a career, which now seems to be in decline. That career is comparable and related to the career of white empire; more exactly, that career corresponds to the self-respect and self-image of empire. In terms of power, and of secret pride in that power, the white empire has never been so great as today. (And we should always be skeptical also about the decline of adventure fiction when it is men of letters who give us that news.) But empire's self-consciousness is uneasy today—in part accepting censure, in part resenting it, and as a whole preferring not to invite attention. This corresponds to an uneasiness in the adventure tale, which nowadays shows itself in a crude, self-disfiguring violence, or in an attempt at self-satire, or in would-be blends of adventure with comedy. All this can be seen in the James Bond stories, which could not be less like Defoe or Scott and their readers, with their happy and "innocent" zest for life.

The greater part of this argument will therefore refer to eighteenth- and nineteenth-century examples of the adventure genre. But that does not mean that the argument has no relevance to the twentieth century. Men of conscience still read adventures, even if they don't write them. A genre's power over readers is often quite out of phase with its power over writers—at least if we mean self-respecting writers who are always, if resentfully, controlled by "literature," that is, current critical opinion. People went on reading *Robinson Crusoe* and *The Three Musketeers* long after the critics washed their hands of them. And among those readers, men of action and men of power were always prominent.

John Buchan, perhaps the last of the respectable adventure writers in this century, is an example, at least with his kind of respectability. Long before his death, Buchan was for serious critics a figure of fun, or else a proto-Fascist. But his tales were loved not only by successive English prime ministers (Balfour, Baldwin, Attlee) but also by later and non-English leaders—for example, the Kennedys. John F. Kennedy's widow has said that Buchan's autobiography was a favorite book of her husband, who especially loved Buchan's commemoration of his Oxford friends who died in the Great War. One can see that the Kennedys' sense of themselves would make them find Buchan's romantic cult of his friends congenial. And it was around those friends—men like Raymond Asquith and Bron Herbert, favorite sons of a great nation and destined from earliest youth to share in ruling—that Buchan constructed his adventure fantasies.

Then Rose Kennedy, in her *Times to Remember* (1974), quotes one of Buchan's poems to express her feelings about her dead sons. The poem, addressed to Buchan's dead brother, relates, "On ballad ways, and martial joys, / We fed our fancies, you and I," while "little, wandering boys." Its main message is: "While young men in their pride make haste, / The wrong to right, the bond to free, / And plant a garden in the waste, / Still rides our Scottish chivalry."[1] That image of boys playing at war and at becoming knights warms Buchan's heart, and it warms the Kennedy mother's heart too. It is the sort of public elegy for a public man that our fine-arts poets rarely write nowadays. Buchan's sensibility, the same in his adventure tales as in his verse and autobiography, expresses feelings about young men of great promise that still persist among those who admire such young men.

To return to the general case, you can find the respectable adventure in publishers' lists of young-adult reading and in what publishers call, or used to call, classics. There were, indeed there are, lists of "classic thrillers" and "classic sea tales," but even more striking are those lists that mix the genres, and so claim to base their choice entirely on quality. There you find Scott and Dumas side by side with Austen and Eliot. But when young people begin to study literature at the university level, they are likely to be taught to draw a sharp distinction between the two pairs, between literature and entertainment.

The respectability of the writers named distinguishes them from merely pastime writers and readers, but it also cuts them off from the opposite class, those devoted to fine art, to art. There is a kind of seriousness that Scott and his ilk do not actively ascribe to themselves and that they know other writers and readers actively deny them. This kind of seriousness is sufficiently suggested by the words "literature" and "art," which are awarded as an accolade by men and women of letters. It is literary scholars and critics who decide which writers are "serious"—which ones belong in the canon, which ones deserve to be taught and studied, and so on. Roughly speaking—there are exceptions, for these categories are not logically perfect or immutable and these judgments are assumed rather than argued—adventure stories are not considered to be art, not to be taken seriously, even when written by men of extraordinary talent and dedication, like Kipling and Stevenson.

That is why the idea of "respectability" (closely linked to that other social idea, the "bourgeoisie," the hegemonic class, and therefore scorned by the intellectual and literary class) is so appropriate here, but also so ambiguous. What is respectable in the world of letters is different from—in some ways the opposite of—what is respectable in society. We

1. John Buchan, "Fratri Dilectissimo," *Montrose*, v.

do not ordinarily think of the bourgeois mind as adventurous, but in fact the body of respectable adventure was and is produced for and consumed by a bourgeois readership, while the intelligentsia, though temperamentally committed to rebellion and marginality, has usually read books of an opposite character, works of theoretical analysis and abstraction, or fantasy explorations of the unconscious. Adventure was not something to be read seriously. Why not? No doubt just because it was written for those others, the respectable classes. It seems to be a special trait of Western or white culture to tell so many tales of respectable adventure, because they have fueled the imperial enterprise, but the Western *mind,* Western *literature,* is possessed by an animus of corresponding passion *against* adventure.

Scott is a good example of the powerful self-respect of some adventure writers, a self-respect deeply involved with his respect for his country and its rulers. By his writing and by his life outside writing, he played an important part in the history of Scotland, a past of which he was proud. But he also exemplifies the limits of that self-respect in his inability to claim, for literature in general and especially for his own books, any final dignity as a life work. As Buchan says, Scott believed "the simplest soldier who carried a gun for his country [was] a sounder fellow than he was."[2]

He saw writers not as prophets or law-givers, but as entertainers, men of more or less taste or talent. ("Art" is a category invented to save writers from this self-shame.) Moreover, he explicitly *preferred* adventurers to respectable citizens, and preferred the more irresponsible over the less so. He called his first novel's (respectable) hero Waverley, "a sneaking piece of imbecility," preferring the Jacobite rebels among whom that hero moved. In his second novel, *Guy Mannering,* Scott turned from the comparative respectability of *Waverley's* political rebels to smugglers and gypsies (adventurers of the first and least respectable class). He said he preferred "the dubious characters of Borderers, buccaneers, Highland robbers, and all others of a Robin Hood description."[3] Thus Scott is a paradigm of all these writers of respectable adventure who disavow art and moral intensity and lay claim only to worldly wisdom and wit.

A hostility runs between such writers and the scholars and critics who

2. Buchan, *Homilies and Recreations,* 25.
3. See Buchan, *Sir Walter Scott,* 133.

today represent literature. In tendency at least, the latter speak for the spirit with a severe purity, unspotted by the world, and so the adventure tale, however respectable, is cast out as unclean. (Scott was cast out on these grounds, notably by Carlyle.) But I want to bring the two parties together so that respectable adventures may be given literary scrutiny, because they are a primary part of our literature. If by English literature we mean (among other things) the literature of that political entity called "England," then nothing is more central to the concept than the respectable adventure.

I am not suggesting we should enlarge or change "the canon," a concept that seems unwieldy or impalpable except when anchored to a field as limited as "the English major at X College." But adventure tales constitute a body of books, sorted out into interconnecting groups and connected also to the developing history of major Western countries, that richly rewards serious reading.

The Conflict with Literature

The adventure tale genre of literature claims to be dealing, in its own way, with truth and morals. I, for instance, in this argument, am interested only in adventures that satisfy my mind by throwing light on history or empire or courage or power. Of course, the light adventure throws on such topics is vivid and enhancing—though not only that— and, so treated, those themes constitute values that are uncongenial to the literary reader today. We don't want to see "empire" or power enhanced in a book, and even courage of an ordinary kind makes some of us uneasy.

Thus, one book about adventure tales is Irving Leonard's *Books of the Brave*. It discusses the Spanish romances of the fifteenth century and their close relation to the Spanish knights' defeat of the Moors and the subsequent conquest of Mexico and Peru. If we turn to the texts literature departments teach today, and if we take as examples those Lionel Trilling discusses in "The Teaching of Modern Literature," we shall see that they might be called "Books of the Unbrave." They are built around figures like Stephen Dedalus in Joyce's *Portrait of the Artist as a Young Man,* or Flaubert's Frédéric Moreau in *Education sentimentale,* or Dostoevsky's Underground Man, or Proust's or Kafka's heroes.

The powerful influence such books exert on their readers is toward qualities other than bravery.

Trilling, of course, belongs to the past, and he was speaking of modernism, which also (we are told) belongs to the past, but I don't see a great change in literature between his day and ours. I want to avoid the complex debate over defining postmodernism, but surely by any definition it does not differ from its predecessor by any impulse to celebrate the simple virtues or the attributes of manliness. Both cultural moods are, for good and for ill, alienated from everything simple or ordinary.

What I am claiming to find in the study of adventure, however, is not moral regeneration but an intellectual illumination of history, empire, and so on. And this criterion, "illuminating the mind," is on other themes exactly what one brings to literary study: we study serious literature to bring out and reinforce such illumination. Why then should the study of adventure seem so different? The answer lies in the way that criterion translates into literary sensibility in the two cases. Only one of the two, the traditional kind, do we usually call literary sensibility; the other we are likely to think of as insensibility.

It is not easy to describe the differences, because literature and adventure are both enormous categories and include many exceptions to every generalization. But perhaps, with goodwill on the reader's part, we can pull further toward the light some things we already know at the back of our minds.

Please think of examples, not exceptions, for the following hypotheses about our different expectations from literature and from adventure in form, language, and subject-matter. Even if one does not always get it, one expects (1) from literature a sense of aesthetic form shaping the material of experience, and from adventure a submersion in the experience; (2) from literature a sense of language that crystallizes critical thought into a play with words, and from adventure a language of action that is often remote from critical thinking or verbal play; (3) from literature a sense of critical judgment being made on society's harshness, and from adventure an exploration of the weakness of social laws and guarantees; (4) from literature an exploration of real and possible relationships, love, and consciousness, and from adventure an exploration of forbidden violence, and above all the experience of inflicting it. (I need not say that some books fall partly in both camps.) These propositions, I hope, leave adventure distinct from literature in the institutional sense and yet susceptible to literary scrutiny in a more liberal sense of that term, for in this book my argument is largely a literary one.

My argument is partly extraliterary too. It will not make sense to those who don't believe in the values of adventure—in the adventurous forms of courage, cunning, leadership, endurance—or who don't believe that people can learn something of those values by reading and via the imagination. I do believe in both propositions, and although, following Gandhi, I see the consequences of Western adventurism as a blight on world history, I don't, any more than he did, turn away from or refuse to recognize adventure values. (Gandhi tried to transform them, to serve nonviolent ends.) Those historical consequences are precisely why I am interested in the literature that embodies those values.

I also believe in that idea of culture which some feminists now repudiate indignantly as a masculinist myth—the idea that all human societies have a center where their laws are promulgated and revered, and a frontier where they are partially ignored, but where the law-making power fights life-or-death battles. This dichotomy is often imaged as a campfire around which people cluster and a fringe of darkness where dangers lurk. In terms of individual countries, this translates into capital cities versus national frontiers. But it also translates into the city's daytime and official activities versus its criminal nightlife. In all such cases, the frontier requires things of men (and of women, but especially of men) that are different from what the center requires; it demands skills and qualities that are not those of the law-abiding citizen. The frontier is always the locus of adventure, and men read adventures to prepare themselves imaginatively for those encounters, so I believe. Such beliefs and perceptions are scarcely demonstrable, and they stand outside the structure of my argument, but my argument is built on them.

I am concerned, therefore, with values that are in some ways opposed to literary values (of the traditional kind) and certainly distinct from them, the values of action and violence. Literature as an institution has traditionally turned away from adventure, or severely criticized it, with rare periods of exception, such as 1880–1914 in England and 1945–70 in America. (In those decades of Anglo-American triumphalism, adventure imposed itself on writers and readers as the natural mate of literature, with Kipling and Stevenson, and later Hemingway and Faulkner, as exemplary authors.) But that opposition can be named and interpreted in various ways. Men and women of letters call it a conflict between literary quality and lack of quality; students of popular culture sometimes call it a conflict between elite and popular values. My own interpretation differs from both.

I cannot, for instance, beg the reader's interest for formulaic fiction as opposed to literature, as John Cawelti does in his book on adventure. From my point of view, Jane Austen and George Eliot are also formula writers; that I don't *respond* to their novels formulaically is another matter. I respond to their stories as true and important experiences, and so I give them access to my deepest responses, my strongest sentiments, because I judge them to be significant works of art. But part of that response is *treating* them as significant works of art—cause and consequence are mixed up together—and so I do the same for some adventure tales (only some, of course). The adventures that interest me engage my mind as much as Jane Austen's novels, once I have built up around them an interpretive context. When you approach adventures from the right point of view, their formulas become the conventions of truth.

The anxieties of awaking to hear someone try the door of your room, and the subsequent straining of eyes and ears, the glimpse of a knife raised above you, the twist of your body just in time to escape the thrust—such a sequence may fairly represent the clichés or conventions of adventure. But there are comparable sequences in the stories we take seriously—the anxiety of finding no letter from your beloved, and reading in a friend's letter that he has paid attentions to a rich merchant's daughter, and then seeing him at the ball, having returned to town but neglected to call on you. In both cases the pattern of events is familiar, and it arouses a familiar pattern of feelings. And in both situations the pattern *can* cease to be cliché; in certain contexts it *does* carry a strong emotional charge, and even a strong intellectual interest, because we connect it to moral, social, and political ideas.

Adventure's Social Function

There has always been a great deal of adventure writing and reading. It is one of the most important arts of the white world. But because of police action by men and women of letters, the adventure tale has usually had to be smuggled into high culture, into "serious people's reading." That is done in three ways. First, much of adventure writing is nonfiction and labeled biography, sailing/climbing/diving narrative, explorer books, or descriptions of revolutions, battles, and guerrilla warfare. When contemporary, and far off in space, this is journalism; when far off in time, even if nearby, it is history. This is adventure reading without being called adventure, and it forms a large part of the intellectual diet of men of power and action.

Second, a large section of adventure writing is labeled as fiction—and so art—but specifically as historical novels, where their adventure elements are disguised as history, things that happened so distantly they can be imagined without guilt. (They are in effect bracketed off, and the reader thinks he is studying the history, not participating in the adventure.) This historical fiction had its greatest prestige in the nineteenth century, but it still attracts many serious writers and readers. One subject current in England is the troubles in Ireland, and another is the empire in India. Two contemporary such writers are J. G. Farrell and James Carroll. Again the adventure elements, though obvious, are in some sense conceptually masked.

Third, and perhaps the most important, is the section of adventure writing called boys' reading, and therefore deemed not suitable for serious consideration by adults. But what is meant by "boys' reading"? Many of the most famous historical examples (*Robinson Crusoe, The Pilgrim's Progress,* and *Gulliver's Travels*) were written for adults, read by them, and handed over to children later, and such handing over became part of the career of historical novels, for instance Scott's. Books written for adults are often later judged good for children, however serious their themes or their writers. If Swift, Bunyan, and Defoe are children's authors, who is too good for such a fate? While among the books that *were* written for children, some are highly wrought fine art: Stevenson's *Treasure Island,* Barrie's *Peter Pan,* Kipling's *Puck of Pook's Hill.* Writing for boys can be done, has been done, with a refinement of taste and technique that quite equals anything done for men.

Moreover, the books parents give their sons to read surely contain the myths they want to shape their imaginations and orient their drives. They are more, not less, important than their adult reading in activating certain forces in their mind and repressing others. Boys' reading, then, and adventure in its other disguises, forms an important but disguised or secret force in our literary culture. These adventure tales are assigned a space that appears to be limited and subordinate—we don't talk about them in our departments of literature—but in propaganda terms this is strategically advantageous. This is a phenomenon we can recognize more easily by looking at a culture other than our own.

Hindu culture, for instance, has a picture of the whole range of human values that divides them up and assigns them to different slices of society and different phases of life, so that each has its own space within the culture and all are endorsed in turn, however they may contradict each other. Brahmin virtues are unlike Kshatriya virtues; the moral duty of the householder is incompatible with that of the old man preparing for death. Hinduism endorses such incompatibilities, making a virtue out of inconsistency.

Our own culture regards inconsistency as a vice of thought, but it too endorses irreconcilably different values, as when it gives boys reading matter with values that contradict those of men's reading and of religious reading. But the two cultural schemes are profoundly different in their effects. In India, the period of childhood and adolescence (called the time of the *antevasin* in the Hindu scheme) is the time for young people to devote themselves to the highest, purest human values, just as in general the Brahmin caste, which has the highest prestige, is the purest. The idea is that the highest or most sublimated ideas and feelings should establish themselves first, in people of all castes, before the young person begins to sample the intoxications of passions.

The West has followed a similar idea as far as the sexual passions go—or so it has done until recently—but as for the passions of adventure, combat, dominance, and force, we have tried to establish them early. (Different agents of the culture have operated differently and on different schedules. As far as literature goes, a notable development began when *boys'* books began to be written, in the mid-nineteenth century, and the fiercer virtues replaced the meekness and prudence hitherto recommended to children.) And then we have overlaid those passions, covered them up, with a different set of values communicated in a different set of books. (Fairy tales, read *before* boys' books, had yet another set of values.) But we have disguised what we are doing by talking lightly of "blood and thunder" or "derring-do." That is the more shameful side of our honorable aversion of attention from adventure.

This began to happen in post-Renaissance Europe, in step with the beginnings of white empire, and it established itself in the nineteenth century. Hegel said that young people first recognize the valuable in what is far off; only later do they see what they should cherish close at hand. This tendency was surely intensified by the popularity of adventure and by the giving of such stories to the young to read. (Hegel makes his remark apropos *Robinson Crusoe*.) But if the sense of the valuable is aroused by adventure images, rather than by the direct exhortations to meekness and obedience found in earlier children's literature, has not the sense of the valuable—even in adults—been affected by, shaped, and changed by its history? Isn't our sense of values made permanently, if invisibly, adventurous?

According to the pattern assumed by pedagogues and corroborated in many autobiographies, at least in the nineteenth century boys read adventures up to adolescence, then turned to serious literature (domestic novels) and theories of society (at first Mill and Spencer, later Marx and Engels). They then, at least if they were intellectuals, forgot about adventure. But what happened to that original stimulus? Did it go for nothing?

Surely we must expect what in fact we find described in Nikos Kazantzakis's autobiography, *Report to Greco:* The transubstantiation of traditional moral schemes by the zest for adventure. Kazantzakis relates: "Time passed; I grew bigger. . . . The saints' legends [which he was told as a child] were too confining; they stifled me. It was not that I had ceased to believe. I believed, but the saints struck me now as much too submissive. . . . I had a presentiment that the true man is he who resists, struggles, and is not afraid, in time of greatest need, to say no, even to God" (pp. 78–79). When given money as a boy, he "ran the next day to Mr. Louka's tiny bookstore and bought pamphlets about distant lands and great explorers. The seed of Robinson Crusoe had obviously fallen into me. Now it had begun to bear fruit. . . . Savages with red feathers stepped inside me, danced, lighted fires, roasted human beings, and the islands surrounding them smiled like new-born infants. These new saints did not beg for alms. Whatever they desired, they took by the sword. . . . Hero together with saint; that was the perfect man. . . . The earth now seemed like a tropical jungle with colorful birds and beasts . . . [the saints] now merged with the great explorers, and the ships of Columbus which departed from a tiny Spanish port were the same . . . as the ships which up to that point had departed within me for the desert, loaded with saints" (p. 79). Such testimony can be corroborated from a thousand sources, and it surely means that it would be foolish to dismiss adventure reading as premoral or amoral. That reading transforms the sense of values and leaves a profound imprint. However different the ideas that came next in Kazantzakis's development, they had to be upper stories built on that adventurous foundation and drawing on that power system, the system of heroic manliness, of adventure.

As everyone *knows,* adventure was and is the *rite de passage* from white boyhood into white manhood, and the ritual of that religion of manliness which in mainstream books of the nineteenth century quite displaced Christian values. (In the twentieth century, manliness has had other opponents and is in retreat in the world of ideas, but I doubt it is any weaker outside that arena.) Manhood was the affirmed or superior term in dozens of value-bearing polarities of thought. Any male had to strive always to be a man and not a boy, in Kipling adventures; a man and not a slave, in slavery narratives; and, similarly, a man and not a coward, a man and not a mouse, a man and not a woman. At the same time, manhood—*being* such a sacred value—spread out to mean humanity, spread beyond these antitheses to include the inferior or rejected term in each case; manhood/humanity included boys and women and slaves and cowards. But the supreme human relationship was that between a man and other men, all engaged in adventure—the relations of comradeship or of enmity—and the great test and field of display for manhood was the supreme adventure, war.

Adventure exists in many forms, and the most powerful, or at least the most permanent in all phases of social development, may well be nonliterary. Most cultures, in most historical phases, have adventurous *rites de passage* for their male adolescents. (In Western society, however, most women and some classes of men can avoid that ordeal, never go through that *rite de passage.* And it may be that in the world of letters such men and women together constitute the dominant party, which if true would be an important clue to the relations between literature and adventure.) But the literary form studied here is especially interesting because it signals the adoption of adventure by the writers of a society, its cultural priesthood, and long after the tribal stage of that society was passed. The same thing can be seen in the revival of hunting among the empire-builders of Britain.

It is presumably because boys' adventures have this important function that they have often been read by ambitious or rebellious girls, as the biographies and autobiographies of notable women often declare, whereas boys much more rarely read, or admit to reading, girls' books. (It is an advantage to a girl to be a tomboy, but no advantage to a boy to be a sissy.) Indeed, the girls who read boys' books often boast of refusing to read girls' books. Adventure has not traditionally performed the same important function for girls, though it has for some. Most girls have found a comparable function in "romances," which prepared them for the life of women.

Literature's Censorship

Such, then, is this book's subject: a cultural phenomenon so pregnant with significance that it is usually covered up. For it is difficult to find for the purposes of study. If you look up "adventure" in the annual bibliography of the Modern Language Association or the Bibliographic Index, you will find a brief and fragmented entry with bizarre subheadings like "Shipwreck" and "The Mayhem Novel." (For an entry that makes sense, turn to "fantasy," a genre with which the literary mind is at ease.) If you look in the Bibliography volume of the *Literary History of the United States,* or in the index of that history, you will find nothing under "Adventure," even though the United States is the one country whose literature is *based* on adventure; one is less surprised to find that the same is true of the *Cambridge History of English Literature.* But, just to show that this is not a law of nature, the first entry in the *Reallexikon der deutschen Literaturgeschichte* is a long article on the "Abenteuer-Roman," which refers the reader to several other articles and discusses adventure as a genre for adult readers.

Even in the English-language literatures, everyone knows that there *are* adventure novels. The 1970 edition of Marryatt's *Masterman Ready,* for instance, advertises on its back flap "Some Great Adventure Stories in Everyman's Library," and the authors listed are Defoe, Blackmore, Dumas, Hudson, Hugo, Kingsley, Scott, and Stevenson. Juvenile and young adult series always advertise such authors. For publishers and booksellers adventure is a major category. Only when we rise to the level of *study*, literary study, does the adventure disappear from view.

This is no accident, but a semiconscious, semideliberate occlusion of the vision, a semipurposeful ignorance. Humanism, perhaps especially Anglo-American humanism, is powerfully oriented toward the past and toward "home"—away, that is, from the future and the empire, away from expansion and adventure. The golden age for humanists is that of the "organic society," a *natural* social growth with internal conflicts contained by a *natural* form, the opposite of empire and something forever in the past. (The term "organic society" belongs to a British tradition of culture criticism, but I use it here to represent a whole class of similar ideas.) And blended with this implicit idealism about the past is moral anxiety and moral "realism" about the present, feelings that *stress* contemporary conflicts and that are harshly skeptical about official values and heroes or exhortations.

This is a typical literary philosophy, because literature is usually allied to the critical and resistant forces of culture, which can root themselves in various social groups and make various cultural alliances; one alliance we have suggested is with women against men, another is with the Galileans against the Pharisees. Thus the men and women of letters are partly ignorant of adventure and partly hostile to it, and the two parts are intertwined inextricably.

But it is essential that these men and women turn their serious attention to this subject, for the sake of their own breadth of mind, for the sake of other readers' depth of response, and above all for the sake of literature as a field, as an idea, as a discipline. Easy as that proposition may be to argue logically, it is difficult to mobilize support for it. Because it is difficult to interest men and women of letters in this subject, their assent or dissent is lukewarm. That is because very few of them ever made any emotional investment in adventure; they turned away from it too early, in order to become men and women of letters.

This creates a problem, because their assent is crucial. The only response to adventure worth arousing must be critical and sophisticated as well as generous. It is the relation of adventure to the subject-field of literature that must be changed. The correct response must be in some loose sense deconstructive and involve critics in dissenting from the adventure writer quite as much as they assent. Because of the popularity of deconstruction today, and the unpopularity of adventure, such a reading might seem easy to arrange. But the deconstructionists work with, tease, an emotional affect in their readers that is missing as far as adventures go. Men and women of letters have made an emotional investment in literature, which makes them both resistant and responsive to deconstructing it. The same phenomenon can be seen outside literature, and Jane Gallop, in *Reading Lacan*, gives a vivid account of her rebellious but fascinated response to Lacan's deconstruction of psychoanalysis. She made a transference of her strong feelings about analysis to Lacan even as she struggled against his desecration of those feelings.

Gallop is talking about one particular writing personality; for men and women of letters, there are a number of deconstructionist critics to choose from. But their feelings about reading are much like her feelings about analysis. And the abstraction—reading—signifies certain authors, varying with the individual, those to whom one has affiliated oneself. We are appalled, but also fascinated, to see such fathers-in-the-spirit deconstructed before our eyes.

That feeling, which is the strength of deconstruction, is something to which no study of adventure can aspire. Men and women of letters have had those feelings about D. H. Lawrence and T. S. Eliot, Milton and Wordsworth, not about Scott and Buchan, Kipling and Verne. But as students of adventure, we have one corresponding and countering advantage, which lies in our turning away from such deeply personal history, opening our minds to new experiences as well as to new categories. Deconstruction is likely to enchain readers in yet another self-referring, self-narrowing relationship—in becoming strong readers who struggle against strong writers. The study of adventure turns our minds to something new and unexplored, the kind of experience we shrugged off too early and too completely as the concern of others.

Moreover, the relation of the adventure to literature is an intricate dialectic that teaches us the hidden structure of the field, the forces that included some books and excluded others from literature. Today we are all familiar with "women's books" and "proletarian books" as examples of such exclusion, but the same is true of "men's books," at least as far as criticism is concerned. And as we discover those books critically, we also see the operation of the cultural politics that relegated them to an unvisited periphery of the canon.

Gustav Klaus has a study of proletarian novels in nineteenth-century England in which he discusses the way workingmen's novels were "forgotten" and literature was so defined as to exclude them. He says we get to the heart of the literary culture of any period by "exploring the nature of this complex, interpenetrating and yet, 'in the last instance,' dominant relational process"[4]—the process of excluding working-class fiction from literature. That dominant relational process is always a literary one, though it has its roots outside literature. And in the case of adventure the process of relegation and domination is further complicated by the fact that the subordinated literary form belonged to a dominant group in society.

4. Gustav Klaus, *The Literature of Labour*, xii.

Adventure served and serves the interests of an alliance of imperialists, chauvinists, entrepreneurs, and some of the clerisy (like some of the public school headmasters in late nineteenth-century England). Such an alliance usually disposes of more literal power in society than literary criticism or the world of letters does—even cultural-aesthetic power, of a low prestige level. But within the world of letters all this power is held in check, subordinate to literary values. The hierarchy of power is in some ways reversed, so that, for instance, the more gifted writers usually refuse to write adventures, and serious readers never study it. Adventure was and is culturally repressed, as far as the most intelligent and sensitive people go.

To understand how this happens brings out literature's strange combination of strength and weakness with a clarity we rarely see. But that is only a by-product of our enterprise, the main aim of which is to know this important and valuable body of writing in and for itself—to *know* adventure in the form of these seven types.

3

The Robinson Crusoe Story
The First Type

The seven types together give us the self-imagined history of the white race from 1700 on, as it expanded over the other four continents and its domination over the other races. And though many sections of the white race—a whole country, such as Hungary; a whole gender, such as women—took little active part in that expansion, they were all profoundly affected by it in their consciousness of themselves when they came in contact with other races.

This first adventure type is unlike the others because it is so identified with one particular example, one narrative, that is highly specific as to time and place, action and motivation, ways and means, weather and wording. To say "Robinson Crusoe" is to name one particular (highly particular) book, but it is also to name a type of book, a subgenre. The importance, and in some ways the import, of Defoe's story persisted through all the later retellings in different languages and different centuries, though certain features of the significance changed profoundly. We must use Defoe's title. Even though it was not the first treatment of a castaway surviving on a desert island, this one subsumed all earlier versions, just as it has overshadowed all subsequent ones.

The story has had this power because of a series of alliances it made with major forces in Western culture. It has been the supreme symbolic expression of Enlightenment ideology, the supreme expression of Protestant capitalist enterprise, and the supreme expression of "the English temperament" as displayed to the world in the making of the British Empire.

Yet we can define this adventure type, much more than the others, in terms of one narration, one plot. It is the story of a man cast away on an island (by a number of possible mechanisms; a man with a number of possible histories) who at first is in danger of dying but gradually learns how to survive, and later how to accumulate goods and crops and comforts, until he is monarch of all he surveys. (In anti-Robinsons, satirical versions of the story, only the first part of the plot follows the model; the ending is likely to be quite different.) Robinson accomplishes all that by hard, physical work and by the exercise of technical and moral shrewdness. In the first part of the story, the reader's attention is called to Robinson's skills and tools, his practical successes and failures, and above all his persistence and ability to learn. In the second half of the story, he meets other people, some of his own color and some of darker skins, and they present different problems. He has to defend his self-made property from them, and to that end must resort to violence. But, in nonsatirical versions of the story, Robinson resolves these difficulties and his life grows the richer and grander for all the other people it involves.

Not all stories of the Robinson species, however, follow that plot closely. Some motifs vary a good deal. *The Swiss Family Robinson,* for instance, is about a family, not a single man; *The Coral Island* is about three young comrades; *Lord of the Flies* is about a large number of schoolboys. Consequently, solitude in the individual sense cannot be the theme in any of those three. Other motifs, like the island, are more or less invariable. The geographical setting and historical period of the story differ from case to case, but the southern hemisphere is much more frequent than the northern, and contemporary times are usual, except when the author wants to play his version off against Defoe's by setting it back in the eighteenth century. The meaning or ideology also differs from case to case, even though much thematic material is implicit in the plot and so is constant.

Because the Robinson story has been so entwined with key ideas of modern politics, economics, exploration, science, and so on, it can be retold again and again, and each time with a different point.

Robinson Crusoe was very popular from the day of its publication (1719). It has, of course, a "mythical" or legendary basis. The Philoctetes episode in *The Odyssey,* and the Sinbad story in the *Arabian Nights,* show how evocative the idea of a man alone on an island has always been. And Defoe did not neglect that kind of direct appeal to the imagination. When Robinson opens his eyes on the morning after the storm that wrecked his ship, he sees a new world around him and begins a new life, reborn. When he fires his musket, it is the first time a gunshot has ever been heard on that island, and all the birds rise up into the air, complaining, to mark the arrival of history.

But it is not that potential in the material which Defoe primarily develops. The legendary and symbolic aspects of the story are subdued to what we might call the anecdotal—which practical problems are faced and how they are solved, in detail. Defoe reminds his audience of the many anecdotes they have read and heard about shipwrecked sailors and desert islands. One that had drawn general attention just before Defoe began to write was the story of Alexander Selkirk, but there had been large compilations of sea narratives a century earlier, such as Richard Hakluyt's *Voyages* and Samuel Purchas's *Pilgrims.* These resulted from and memorialized English explorations and trading expeditions (other countries had their equivalents) and were designed to inspire more of the same. For that reason, the East India Company had put copies of Hakluyt's book into their captains' cabins.

Such stories were part of the motor power of the great historical adventure by means of which the white nations were taking the rest of the world in fee. Although Defoe's novel was not even a semi-official document of policy, like Hakluyt's and Purchas's, but a fiction offered mostly to pass the time, it was so authentic in detail and so close in spirit to Hakluyt (one might call it a crystallization of all his various short narratives into one that is long and self-consistent) that it could have a similarly inspiring effect on its readers, and there is much evidence that it did.

The novel was popular not only in England but also in Holland, France, and Germany. It was translated immediately, and before long each language had several translations. It was also adapted, to naturalize the story abroad. There were German and French and Dutch Robinsons, and within Germany there were Prussian and Saxon and Westphalian Robinsons, and a baker, a butcher, and a barber Robinson. Perhaps the most striking testimony to the story's popularity in Germany is that earlier books were *re*published with "Robinson Crusoe" in the title, on the calculation that they would now sell, with that endorsement.

However, neither the book nor its author was taken seriously. In England, for instance, literary law-givers and taste-makers like Swift and Pope stigmatized Defoe as a fake man of letters, a figure from the inferior world of journalism and not from the world of literature. *Gulliver's Travels* was written as a satire on the voyage literature *Robinson Crusoe* imitated. Even the French *philosophes* who so admired England and valued the type of practical intelligence Crusoe exemplified did not ask to meet Defoe when they came to London. Part of the book's character was that it was *not* literature.

In 1762, however, *Robinson Crusoe* did begin to be taken seriously, in Jean-Jacques Rousseau's *Emile,* with which this adventure type reached the second stage in its career. In his book Rousseau described an ideal scheme of education, which avoided books in favor of "learning by doing," and when the time came for his ideal pupil, Emile, to read, the only book he was allowed for a long time was *Robinson Crusoe.* This was to constitute his education, as far as literature went, up to the age of fifteen; that book contained everything he needed, and in the best possible form.

Robinson Crusoe thus became the Enlightenment's major text-book, for Rousseau's treatise was quite influential for half a century at least, and it set a pattern whereby teachers and preachers recommended *Robinson Crusoe,* and other adventures of this type, in a way hitherto reserved for religious or classical texts. The story thus acquired powerful allies. Wherever these new ideas about education were put forward, *Robinson Crusoe* was recommended or discussed.

Rousseau, moreover, edited Defoe's text and cut away much of it. He ignored volumes two and three and within volume one explicitly rejected everything that took place before Robinson arrived on the island and after he left. That meant the novel ceased to be a picaresque fiction—with one episode, the island episode, dispropor-tionately long and vivid—which was what it had appeared to be, perhaps to Defoe himself. In fact, *Robinson Crusoe* became in some ways the reverse of picaresque: a quite static story of survival by means of work, with a hero who was no rogue but an exemplar of the civic virtues. Further, by what he did *not* say, Rousseau secularized and modernized the story, ignoring its passages of Protestant piety. And in the same way, he rejected its Romantic potential by ignoring Friday, the noble savage, and the island as a landscape background to reverie. It was essentially an Enlightenment story, with a *philosophe* hero, that Rousseau recommended to the educationists of his time.

His recommendation was enthusiastically taken up in France and Germany, and in 1779 two German writers—in conscious rivalry—both produced remarkable revisions of the Robinson story. One of these, J. H. Campe's *Robinson der Juengere*, was widely translated and went through many reprintings, especially in Germany. Campe was an influential figure in the history of education. Thanks to him, some version of *Robinson Crusoe* was often the integrating text in year-long curriculums of "modern studies"—geography, natural science, mathematics, technology, modern history.

Then in 1812 came the first part of the version known so widely as *The Swiss Family Robinson*. This was inspired by Campe's success, but it is in some ways almost opposite in its political tendency. Johann David Wyss told his story of a shipwrecked family in a way that reinforced patriarchal authority and justified by implication the patriarchal state. Whereas Campe was a liberal, and loved the story because it showed how much a free man, a man not trapped at the bottom of a feudal hierarchy, could accomplish, Wyss was a reactionary in the sense that Burke and Scott were. The French Revolution had occurred between 1779 and 1812, and Wyss like other people had been appalled by the bloodshed of the Paris Terror. The story was thus recommended to a large new public.

In 1841 Captain Frederick Marryat published *Masterman Ready*, the first interesting English version of the story since Defoe's. This was clearly designed as a boys' story and was Victorian and Evangelical in tone. It seems that the Robinson story was revived in England in response to the Evangelical movement; it was the type of adventure most compatible with Christian feeling, and the Evangelicals were propagandists for nineteenth-century nationalism, sponsoring magazines that published adventure for boys. This is a paradox, and *Masterman Ready* is a rather paradoxical adventure, because Evangelical religion was so full of moral anxiety and therefore antiadventurousness. But Marryat was a gifted writer, and *Masterman Ready* (and his other Robinson, *The Little Savage*) are interesting, in part because of their inner conflicts but also because Marryat was knowledgeable about islands and castaways. They make sense as adventures, despite their moral self-contradictions.

Quite soon after this, in 1847, came the most interesting and convincing of the American versions, James Fenimore Cooper's *The Crater*. This is striking for its combining of the author's enthusiasm for anecdotes of development and economic growth with his antidemocratic politics. Cooper was an eccentric, but he was not alone among American intellectuals in loving technical progress and economic expansion and yet distrusting democracy and liberalism. By the end of the nineteenth century, the Robinson story was likely to be a favorite with conservatives as much as with liberals.

In Britain, in the second half of the nineteenth century, the story began to show the effects of so much repetition. In R. M. Ballantyne's *Coral Island* (1858), for instance, it was clear that the author was in some sense not taking the story seriously. He presented the whole experience of being shipwrecked as fun. His three boy protagonists are delighted to be cast away and *expect* an island to be furnished to them. Of the three, moreover, it is the most impractical and least adventurer-like, Peterkin Gay, who most endears himself to the writer and the reader. In other words, the story has become decadent, even though Ballantyne himself was one of the most pious of all the Robinson writers.

Peterkin Gay is in fact a precursor for Peter Pan, as of course the names suggest. And far from reducing the story's appeal, these changes installed it more firmly than before in the realm of pleasure and fun. But this decadence did not prevail everywhere. In France, for instance, the last quarter of the nineteenth century was the period of Jules Verne's immense and immensely popular productivity. Verne wrote several *Robinsonaden,* of which *The Mysterious Island* (1874) was the most notable, and the greater part of his large oeuvre can be said to teach the values of Defoe's story in its nineteenth-century form—the enthusiasms for work and technical skill, and the faith in progress and reason. Verne was one of the founders of science fiction, but he so expanded the story's scale in *The Mysterious Island* (employing six protagonists instead of one) and speeded up the action (their technical triumphs take no time at all) that the reader becomes uneasy—at least the man of letters, the potential writer, does, for, after Jules Verne, French writers told the Robinson story satirically.

In Britain, and notably in Scotland (Ballantyne also was a Scot), we find two striking literary uses of the story: in Robert Louis Stevenson's *Treasure Island* (1883) and James Barrie's *Peter Pan* (1904). Neither are retellings of *Robinson Crusoe;* in both that story has blended into other kinds of adventure, and the writer treats his material nostalgically and playfully, though this effect is subtly implicit in Stevenson and is fully developed only in Barrie. Together, however, they mark an important stage in the story's career, when the title was in a sense on everyone's lips but always accompanied by an indulgent smile. At the same time, earlier versions of the story were quite widely read (which was why it was difficult to retell), and in schools and with official sponsorship. It remained a readers' favorite even when writers turned away or approached it obliquely.

In the twentieth century, we can say that the story fell into the hands of its enemies, in that the most notable versions have been satiric. This does not mean that the writers were flatly unresponsive to the story—satire inevitably pays some tribute to its object—but clearly the alteration in their response marks an important new stage in the story's career. After the Great War, World War I—and in reaction against its horrors—there was a revulsion of feeling against many ideals of patriotic manliness and imperialism and economic enterprise, which were seen as having contributed to the war. The traditional adventure genre became suspect, and it was not surprising that in the early 1920s there were two French revisions of the Robinson story that set out to subvert its myth, with a frivolous tone but an underlying seriousness.

The same thing happened in England after World War II. William Golding's *Lord of the Flies* and Muriel Spark's *Robinson* appeared in 1954 and 1958. They differed from their French equivalents most strikingly in their use of a religious ideology, attacking the Robinson story as a Protestant and post-Protestant myth, from the point of view of the Catholic writer. The anti-Robinsons (as was true also of versions of the story more faithful to Defoe) use a great variety of conceptual languages to make their points about the story.

Finally, in 1967 Michel Tournier published his *Vendredi ou les limbes du Pacifique,* which used the conceptual language of the avant-garde of the 1960s and won a literary prize. It retold the familiar story and kept faith with the original plot quite strikingly for the first half of the book, but it revised the values from the perspective of contemporary Paris. Tournier focused his attack on the idea of manliness, first by his depiction of "otherness"—the process of mutuality that constitutes some men as men and so condemns them to the fate of being, for instance, white imperialists—and then by his suggestion of a nongenital sexuality, which could let us escape that fate. Friday, who is not an other to Robinson and whose sexuality is purely playful, is the hero of the story. He has everything to teach us, and Robinson nothing, and the author wants to dedicate his story to the Fridays of contemporary France, her Third World migrant workers.

This brief summary of the ways the Robinson story has been retold during the 250 years between 1719 and 1967 has focused on writers rather than readers, and on the literary status of the story rather than its broader cultural significance. Our next step must be to consider the cultural forces (political, economic, scientific, imperialist, or whatever) that seem to have been in some collusion with the story, that relate to it in constant mutual reference and reinforcement.

But preliminarily we might consider the Robinson story simply as one of the adventure types, and therefore in collusion with the idea of adventure itself—teaching the adventure virtues, such as courage, cunning, leadership, fortitude, perseverance, and so on. These concepts are moral truisms, in that no one speaks against them, but in the forms they take in the adventure tale, even in the Robinson story, they are not what all moralists at all times put at the head of their prescriptions.

This is so primarily because those virtues, within the adventure tale, are shaped by the expectation of, by the movement toward, violence. There is less of this in the Robinson story than in other types of adventure (which is why it has been the one most recommended by the clerisy), and Crusoe engages in some moral debate before he kills. But finally he does shoot the native who chases Friday, and the cannibals who are ready to sacrifice the Spaniards. His triumph, his very survival, would be more in doubt, and at best much smaller in scale, if he did not engage in violence.

For all Defoe's praise of wheelbarrows and grindstones and other such objects as embodying the true values of English civilization, it is the gun that is Robinson's crucial tool, on which his superiority to the savage—his simple power to survive—is based. The fundamental fact about adventure, for its enemies but also (though more implicitly) for its admirers, is that it is about violence. More than that, one can say that adventure tales prepare their readers, via their identification with the protagonist, to inflict violence, to kill. They take readers across the frontiers of civilization and into the forbidden zones of the illegal or alegal, where one makes one's own laws. (There are, of course, adventure tales that do not involve the reader in the committing of violence, but as long as we are situated inside the circle of white culture and are discussing the idea of adventure as it is defined there, they must be called incomplete adventures. Conceptually and experientially, they are subsumed within the violent kind.)

And besides the adventure tale itself, there are other social forces that value violence. Some of them value violence in and for itself, or for the power and excitement it brings, and we associate that trait with crime. But the love of violence is not confined to criminals, nor is it unmixed, even in them. In sports like boxing, wrestling, and the martial arts, but also in American football and ice hockey, violence is clearly part of the attraction, but mixed with moral ideals in a variety of ways. The moral ideals of the masculine personality, as most societies define it, have to involve violence, although that involvement may include a strong disapproval of violence. In the armed services, and in the professions of jailer, policeman, and secret agent, some people some of the time see violence as the least desirable option, but they are trained to employ it, physically and mentally. Apart from the question of liking or disliking, approving or disapproving, such people know about and care about violence, and know they are associated with it in other people's minds. They feel the disapproval of refined and liberal moralists. For them, the adventure tale at least alludes to that great fact—so important in their lives—which the rest of literature and culture keeps quiet, as a dirty secret. They are part of the audience for adventure, one of its allies.

Before we get to the point of killing, however, which must constitute a moral climax and transition, a fatal self-commitment, the Robinson Crusoe story takes us into a frontier land of freedom and creativity, where the only laws binding on Crusoe come from nature or from his own conscience. Each day when he gets up, he does what he has decided should be done, and for the reader this constitutes a promise of exhilarating freedom. (The upward gaze of his subjects on him, his cat and dog beside him as he eats, objectifies the excitement he feels at his own power.) And this is not just a matter of "How shall I pass the time today?" It is also a matter of "Which trade shall I practice? Shall I be a baker or bricklayer or carpenter or fort-builder?" Moreover, the modern reader needs to reinforce this excitement by reminding himself of the system of guilds and apprenticeships in Defoe's England, which imposed so many restrictions on a young man's choice of and practice of a trade. An important step toward social mobility, toward the modern world, is implicit in this excitement. It is an excitement about work.

The Robinson story has often been called antiadventurous. After all, Crusoe's courage and cunning are characterized by their reference to work quite as much as by their reference to violence. He is brave and persistent and strong-willed and clever in projects like building a boat and trying to bake bread and getting a load of iron off a raft and onto a steeply rising shore. These are homely and practical forms of courage and cunning. One could contrast them with the forms those virtues took in the Spanish romances (such as *Amadis de Gaule*), which were popular just before Defoe invented the modern adventure and were lavishly fanciful stories in which men never lifted a brick or used a spade, and were extravagantly and unreally brave. But, however homely, Defoe's moral scheme is quite original, compared with other moral schemes in books. This is a moral imagination that is thoroughly rooted in praxis and material things, in tools and techniques. It is not what most philosophers and theologians had meant by courage and fortitude. To use the terms of the history of ideas, it is a *philosophe,* an Enlightenment, imagination and morality. To use contemporary terms, it is the do-it-yourself enthusiasm we see reflected in the Robinson story.

Cultural Alliances

But if we are to think of this and other adventure types in terms of the cultural forces to which they were allied, perhaps the most important cultural force is masculinism—meaning a stress on the masculine specific to the modern world. Western, or white, civilization has, like most other civilizations, always been patriarchal. But in the phase of history with which we are concerned here, there has been a new emphasis on the priority of men. That emphasis is new in that it is felt and conceptualized in new terms—which, paradoxically, are terms of a proud liberalism—using slogans like liberty, equality, and fraternity. The liberation of men to which the Enlightenment summoned humanity turned out to entail, almost unquestioningly and yet quite explicitly, the imposition of limited roles on women. And this can be seen happening in the career of the Robinson story, and indeed in the careers of other adventure types.

It is most convenient to begin with *Emile*. Rousseau's theory of education was devised for boys and young men exclusively. When his attention was called to that fact, and he added a section on the education of a girl and woman, her training was all directed to producing a bride fit for Emile, fit primarily because of her readiness to subdue herself and support him. "He for God only, she for God in him"—the Miltonic formula fits Rousseau's prescriptions perfectly, despite everything that separated the two men ideologically. Rousseau had rejected most of the biblical theology that might appear to have inspired Milton's patriarchal authoritarianism. But his gender doctrine is just as severe, and that is all the more surprising because of Rousseau's coterie of women disciples and his authorship of *La nouvelle Héloise*, a novel famous for being about and for women.

But then we remember that the one book Emile is to read is *Robinson Crusoe*, a book in which no woman appears and no need for a woman is felt during the more than twenty years Robinson spent on his island. Robinson's feelings for other people are focused first on Friday, a man of another race, and later on the Spaniards. After leaving the island and returning to England, Robinson marries, but his choice of a wife and his experience of marriage are covered in only a few lines, as if they were of no interest. We cannot say that this constitutes an attack on women, but it is an attack, implicitly, on the mutuality of the genders, on the importance of personal relations—on love. But love is the topic to which the great novelists have given greatest reverence, and many men and women of letters, novelists and lovers of novels, have felt Defoe's slighting of love and resented it.

Yet Defoe was also the author of novels, two of which, *Moll Flanders* and *Roxana*, suggest an unusual interest in women's experience and a readiness to give women a voice. Like Rousseau, Defoe seems to have been a man of sufficiently mixed gender to have some female traits and some sense of female experience, but while in the world of the adventure tale (in this case the Robinson story), he felt no need for women. Rousseau too, while he was seeing all intellectual and moral development in terms of that story, felt no need of or interest in women, and though we cannot lump together all the Enlightenment philosophers in this regard, Defoe and Rousseau were not the only ones to subordinate women in this way.

Subsequent tellings of the Robinson story exhibit the same phenomenon. *The Swiss Family Robinson* includes a wife-and-mother, but her action is limited to being social cement. She helps hold the family together by staying at the fireside to welcome the men and boys home from their expeditions. For herself she does nothing. She is referred to and even addressed as the Little Mother. And that is a pattern often repeated. Most versions of the story include no woman, and those that do exclude her from the adventures and reduce her to admiring the men's successes and consoling them for their failures. (The other adventure types do not so strikingly exclude women, but we shall find that, in a variety of ways, they all limit them to minor roles.)

This enserfment of women apparently came about as a "natural" consequence of the ennobling of men. The ideology of the Enlightenment called on men to assert their manhood against feudal tyrants, class privilege, religious superstition, soulless bureaucracy—all the enemies of freedom. It constituted men as a kind of gender yeomanry of the human race—men rather than women, or children, or unmanly homosexuals, or the sick, aged, and infirm, or any other division of humanity.

The reward promised to men resembled that promised to yeomen in legends like that of the Norman yoke said to oppress Saxon England; each freeman was morally entitled to have an independent "kingdom" of his own, with a deferential consort, dependent youngsters and oldsters as subjects, and animals and crops as inalienable property. In that mock kingdom the supreme authority was vested in the (normally masculine) head of the family. This is what *Robinson Crusoe* and *The Swiss Family Robinson* and all the other versions promise the ardent reader, in their various fictional ways. It is what all the types of adventure promise. Though the others do so less directly, all of them show us men winning their freedom, becoming men, outside the law and against authority. And whether or not the men settle down at the end into such a "kingdom," the women are usually minor and centrifugal. They form the disturbance, the distraction, the reward, the decoration, the horizon point, for the heroes of this male enterprise. Thus, while the adventure tale is part of the ideology of masculinism, it is inseparably linked with consecrated political ideas like liberty, equality, and fraternity. The three things act on each other and reinforce each other—adventure, masculinism, and Enlightenment ideology.

Masculinism is a pervasive presence within many ideas, a continuum that links them to each other. Something else in the same sequence is the modern idea of science. Feminist scholars, such as Evelyn Fox Keller and Sandra Harding, have shown the way that Bacon's and the Royal Society's idea of science—with which and from which modern science began its extraordinary career of cultural dominance—characterized itself by masculine concepts and metaphors. It saw earlier and alternative forms of science, like scholasticism and alchemy, as soft or vague or mystifying, as involved in nature mysticism and the cult of the Great Mother (or involved in the arid and impractical abstraction of scholasticism). The new science was to be clear and firm and practical above all, measurable and experimental, predictive and verifiable, free from feelings and appearances, free from everything but reality. It set man in opposition to Nature, first to interrogate her, then to bend her to his will.

The new investigator meets Nature face-to-face, without preconceptions, without assumptions deriving from philosophy or theology, from tradition or from books. He acts on Nature, interfering with her processes, forcing her to yield her secrets. And he does so with his hands, like a skilled worker, not with prayers or incantations, like a monk or a magician. And where better than in *Robinson Crusoe* do we find this empirical and pragmatic experimentation depicted in art? The work of the Royal Society was a systematization and refinement of the work of Crusoe on his island. (The London Huguenot circle, which made propaganda for the Society, and some of whose members were fellows thereof, included the first translators of *Robinson Crusoe* into French.)

From the beginning, the Robinson story belonged to the Huguenots in France and to the Protestants in Holland and Germany. There are pre-Defoe adventures of this kind that figure Huguenot protagonists, but none that I know of with Catholics. And this link persists throughout the career of the story. Even in Jules Verne's *robinsonnades,* much later, propaganda is made for Protestantism.

There is also a link to the *philosophe* movement, the Enlightenment, as we saw when discussing Rousseau. And in England the rise of Evangelical Christianity led to a revival of the Robinson story, with Protestant missionary martyrs appearing in it. Thus we have three quite different "religious" ideas, all making alliance at different times and

places with Robinson. But different as they are, all three are linked by
their hostility to Catholicism.

The Robinson story was also linked to ideas of work and value and
property, to the "science" of economics in general—or political economy, as it was first called. The doctrines called mercantilism in England,
and associated with Adam Smith there and with the Physiocrats in
France, were held to derive at least their inspiration from the *Robinsonade.* That story was thought to demonstrate the way an entrepreneur
created value—out of inert raw materials and the mindless labor he
employed. Consequently, the opponents of mercantilism or physiocracy,
like Marx, also referred to the Robinson story in attacking them.

In a less specifically capitalist sense, the Robinson story made each
reader feel the excitement and nobility of work, the primal thrill of
making something or making something work or putting something to
use, especially something that had hitherto had no use. In Defoe's version
the protagonist starts with two things of no use—a wrecked ship and a
desert island—but by seeing the leftovers and fragments of the former as
embodying the secrets of white civilization and putting them to use on
the latter, he created a valuable property of infinite potential.

In versions like *The Swiss Family Robinson,* more striking is the
function of *knowledge* as the encapsulation of earlier work, knowing
which animal and vegetable species are tamable and edible. In Jules
Verne's version, the work done is the reenacting on a miniature scale of
the industrial history of Europe—the making of mines, kilns, factories,
explosives. And all along the way there are the small but essential
problems of survival that must be solved: how to make fire without
matches, how to make bread without yeast, how to make ink.

One feature of the story that still attracts nonliterary readers and
offends literary readers, such as graduate students in English, is its
factuality. Facts, those nuggets or building units of truth that offer
themselves to be snapped into place to construct whatever, are rarely
found in poetry or imaginative prose and are repellent to many lovers of
the latter. Just for that reason, of course, they have special value for us.
As Terence Eagleton says about literary theory, "The patrician disdain
which the literary mind has always evinced for such prosaic phenomena
as the facts" is recognizable in many a sophisticated textual theory.[1]

Besides these exercises in ingenuity, there are the more moral aspects

1. Terence Eagleton, *The Ideology of the Aesthetic,* 380.

of work, like patience, perseverance, endurance of fatigue and disappointment, continuity in purpose, correction of mistakes, and record-keeping. Such experience finds more expression in this type of adventure than in most others (or most domestic fiction), and probably it has never been done as well as Defoe did it. This is the do-it-yourself aspect of the story.

These emphases become starkly predominant in one's image of *Robinson Crusoe* only after one has edited the text the way Rousseau edited it. Without that editing, Defoe's story is a picaresque tale about a wanderer; with the editing, it is an essentially static story. Crusoe stays where he is, improving the place in which he finds himself. These two facts, plus Crusoe's ambivalent devotion to prudence, his self-reproach for his wandering, have made some critics deny him the title of adventurer. But that is a mistake, for all Crusoe's life on the island takes place beyond the limits and safeguards of civilization, beyond the social frontier, and so is *necessarily* adventurous. To call adventurous only people who love to take risks, either out of some self-destructiveness or as an element in a stylish self-image, is to exclude half of those who have been true heroes of adventure, and so to empty the concept of half its serious meaning. In any case, Crusoe's devotion to prudence is ambivalent, for it is matched by a persistent boldness and inventiveness (as in his maneuvers against the mutineers). In such a complex of qualities, prudence is as much the adventurer's virtue as the others. (This is a prominent trait of many fictional as well as nonfictional adventurers—for instance, Allan Quatermaine in Rider Haggard's tales.)

Then this story is more associated with education than are the other types of adventure. This is especially true because Rousseau built the Defoe version into his scheme of an ideal education in the eighteenth century. But Rousseau only recognized a potential that was there before and that is there even later, in anti-Rousseauist versions; *Lord of the Flies*, for instance, has been used in schools on a very large scale. Many of the versions of the Robinson story I have listed have been taught in schools all over Europe and became the integrating element in curriculums, especially where the goal is to make education an adventure. It has also been widely read outside Europe, in mission schools and wherever Western civilization has presented itself to people of another culture. (It seems that nonwhite readers identify with Crusoe just as easily as whites do, if they read the book when they are young and innocent. They begin to identify with Friday instead only when their political consciousness has been aroused.)

Robinson Crusoe is very suitable for these uses because it is a brilliant anthropological romance—not for what it tells us about the other races Robinson meets but because of the way it deals with the pride and anxiety, the glee and guilt, that Englishmen and other white nationals felt when they measured themselves against those others in survival situations. Can the white man survive in those circumstances? Ought he to survive and enslave the others by making use of his tools and guns? How does he feel about his extraordinary cultural advantages? Such questions permit a wide variety of answers. The story can perhaps be told, and read, in simple complacency, as demonstrating Robinson's deserved superiority. But more often, even as the story is told by Defoe, other moods must arise in the reader's mind, and do not seem to go against Defoe's intention.

Then, as well as being an anthropological romance in this sense, the story is a geographical romance. Campe's *New Robinson* and *The Swiss Family Robinson,* for example, make much of the flora and fauna, the climate and geology and marine life, of the southern hemisphere, but it is a geographical romance also in the sense that the element of the dangerous derives from the events being so remote in *space.* (In the Three Musketeers type of adventure, the dangerous and challenging elements derive from our going back in *time,* meeting forms of life unlike our own because they belong to the past.)

In the eighteenth and nineteenth centuries, geography was actually taught in conjunction with the Robinson story, and in a good many places sight of a map or chart evoked thoughts of islands and castaways. *Treasure Island* began as a story in Stevenson's mind after he drew a map of an imaginary island to amuse his stepson. And many biographies and autobiographies, over two hundred years, relate how reading *Robinson Crusoe* or *Treasure Island* started a lifelong love of maps.

There was indeed a wide subculture of adventure, designated for boys in particular. It involved almost anything to do with the sea and the navy, Royal and Merchant—evidenced by, for instance, the fashion of sailor suits for toddlers and the singing of sea chanties in schools. By the same token, it involved almost anything to do with swimming, boating, hiking, camping, and of course endurance tests, scouting, and singing around the campfire. At a somewhat higher intellectual level, but still promoted by schools, were the institutions of exploration and immigration, such as the Royal Geographical Society and the National Geographic magazine, and, promoted by the churches, missionary adventures.

Finally, there is the idea of empire. Defoe's story was not overtly about imperialism, but at the end the island is going to become part of the British Empire. That is an end to several stories of this kind—for instance, *The Swiss Family Robinson* and *The Mysterious Island* (in the latter the United States, not Britain, is the residuary legatee, but the continuity between the two Anglo-Saxon empires is notable). The Robinson story is the idyll of white imperialism, which represents in fanciful form the preimperial phase of imperial history. Castaways or other adventurers find such an island; their story tells of how they subdued its dangers and settled its best areas, and the climax is the handing of the island over to the official authorities. These brave young men unwittingly did the will of their masters (an idea richly developed in another adventure type, the Three Musketeers story), and as long as the empire was a living idea, whether calling itself an empire or not, the Robinson story was a living myth.

For perhaps a quarter of a century, that myth has been failing decisively, and Defoe's book has fallen into the hands of the men and women of letters. Of course, they had their hands on it before, but now they have it to themselves and can destroy its mythic potency with the formic acid of exact scholarship. In accordance with the cult of texts, they go behind Rousseau to the three-volume work begun in 1719, to treat that as a literary whole or even a religious allegory. When one gives as much attention to the rest as to the island part, the myth expires on the page. But if we reconstitute its late eighteenth- and nineteenth-century context, its place in cultural history, the story again becomes vivid as an imperialist or nationalist myth. Its energizing function was always clear to readers who looked at England and empire from a little distance.

In Ireland, for instance, in the early twentieth century, both George Moore and James Joyce gave *Robinson Crusoe* a historical reading of great enthusiasm and remarked on the fullness with which Robinson represented England. (Moore, in *Avowals,* "edited" the book, offering an interesting revision of the plot that would, he thought, win it literary prestige.) Joyce, in one of the best general essays on Defoe, a lecture delivered in 1912, called him the first author to present specifically English characters in specifically English stories. (He said he had read every line of Defoe, and the only other English author of whom that was true was Ben Jonson.) Clearly, Joyce was using "English" to mean the modern England he knew. He praised Defoe's typically English men and women—Moll Flanders, Roxana, Mother Ross—for the "realism" of their depiction, and he added that realism was not the right word, insofar as it suggested a reaction against some earlier idealism. Defoe, Joyce said, was prophesying, not reacting; he attributed to Defoe a prevision of what England was to become in the years between 1719 and 1912. His women have the indecency and continence of beasts; his men are strong and silent as trees. English feminism and English imperialism already lurk in those souls, which are just emerging from the animal kingdom. The African proconsul descends in a direct line from Captain Singleton. *Robinson Crusoe,* more than any other single book, reveals the wary and heroic instinct of the rational animal and the prophecy of the empire. The true symbol of the British conquest is Robinson Crusoe, as Friday is the symbol of the subject races. The whole Anglo-Saxon spirit is in Crusoe: the manly independence, the unconscious cruelty, the persistence, the slow yet efficient intelligence, the sexual apathy, the practical and well-balanced religiousness, the calculating taciturnity.[2]

That the Robinson of Defoe's book was taciturn and apathetic could be denied with some plausibility, on the evidence of the dreams and terrors and passions of weeping that Defoe attributes to him. But the majority of readers have, like Joyce, dismissed those passages of emotional melodrama as literary conventions, no doubt because of the greater and incompatible intensity that Defoe generates around Robinson's practical skills.

However we imagine Robinson "the man," it is recognizably the same figure who recurs in the long series of Robinson stories. And he can be seen as a national emblem, and so as an alternative to John Bull, and a much better emblem of the progressive/aggressive energies that other countries saw in England. John Bull was a country squire (cousin to Squire Booby, Sir Roger de Coverley, Sir Stentor Stile, Squire Allworthy), an embodiment of eighteenth-century conservatism, political, moral, and intellectual, of that part of England which hung back and resisted the technical and imaginative innovations of each new age and spoke for a semifeudal countryside. John Bull was the keel of the ship of state, or possibly the ballast; Crusoe was the prow of the boat and the sail. We

2. James Joyce, *Daniel Defoe.*

find him reborn in men like Captain Dampier and Captain Cook, England's explorers and empire-builders.

We also see Robinson's progeny in later heroes of white empire, such as Natty Bumppo and Jules Verne's Englishmen and Kipling's Scots engineers and Conrad's sea captains—all famous for their dour inexpressiveness. What these men feel can be deduced only from their characters, since the action is designed to bring out their strong silences—their strengths of decency and reliability, of the limited imagination, as Conrad says. They are emblems of masculinism. It is in situations of storm, shipwreck, mutiny, savagery, and danger that their virtues will find play, not in the situations of social life or the comedy of manners or heart-sympathy, or erotic passions. Such situations belong much more to the domestic novel, to women rather than to men. The Robinson hero, as Joyce and other Irishmen perceived him, belongs in the adventure novel and among men.

In France, a little later, Paul Dottin stressed the book's energizing function for Englishmen in the most literal sense of energizing. He said *Robinson Crusoe* was a patriotic book that "induces maritime vocations, . . . helps to maintain the cohesion of the great British Empire, . . . contributes to increasing the Anglo-Saxon hegemony in the world."[3] And the Anglo-Saxons themselves said the same things. In an American book entitled *Robinson Crusoe: Social Engineer,* Henry Jackson recommended that all those driven to despair by the problems of postwar America read Defoe's book: "Crusoe is typically Anglo-Saxon in his patient acceptance of fate, and his effort to make the best of it. Crusoe's gospel is the same as that of Kipling. It is the gospel of work and the gospel of courage" (p. 47). Jackson quoted the Victorian intellectual Frederick Harrison, saying, "*Robinson Crusoe* contains, not for boys but for men, more religion, more philosophy, more political economy, more anthropology, than are found in many elaborate treatises on these special subjects" (p. 47).

In 1851 George Borrow described the fascination the book had for him from earliest boyhood and called it "a book which exerted over the minds of Englishmen an influence certainly greater than any other of modern times, which has been in most people's hands . . . a book, moreover, to which, from the hardy deeds which it narrates, and the spirit of strange and romantic enterprise which it tends to awaken,

---

3. Paul Dottin, *Daniel Defoe et ses romans;* quotation from p. 374.

England owes many of her astonishing discoveries by sea and land, and
no inconsiderable part of her naval glory."[4] These things are true of
other versions of the Robinson story and of other white nations, but the
story has belonged in a special sense to England.

There are distinctions to be made between the various tellings. The
family stories put the stress on the organic social cell, the self-integrating
group that is the core or heart of life, while the boy-comrade stories put
the stress on freedom and exhilaration, except when the story is told
sardonically. And among group-protagonists we must distinguish between groups that contain a Robinson figure (as Verne's *Mysterious
Island* does) and those that do not (as *The Swiss Family Robinson* and
The Coral Island do not). The former are purer specimens of the
Robinson species. There is, in each of the latter groups, a natural leader
who is full of practical skills and information: the father in the first, Jack
in the second. They therefore remain *Robinsonaden,* but the father and
Jack are not of the taciturn engineer type, and the special character of
their adventures (so patriarchal in *The Swiss Family Robinson,* so boyish
in *The Coral Island*) derive from the somewhat deviant character of their
Robinsons.

The character of the protagonist crystallized out in his physique over
the course of the story's career. Defoe does not describe his hero, who
therefore has no physical identity, but later writers of *Robinsonaden*
evolve a physique for him—dry-skinned, narrow-faced, lanky, and often
red-haired. Most clear in French versions, this physical description is
associated with French ideas of the English national type. The process
by which a character evolves as he or she passes from one author's hands
to another is natural to myth. It allows for, indeed invites, multiple and
contradictory evolutions. We can perfectly well imagine—we might
like—a fat and jolly Robinson, but the piquancy of the idea derives from
its going against the grain.

There were some women Robinsons, and several girl companions to
boy Robinsons, but in the cases I know they seem to have been ingenious
and in some sense paradoxical extensions of the Robinson idea. One
exception, in eighteenth-century Germany, produced several female *Robinsonaden,* in some of which the castaway experience turns women
into figures of strength and protectors of other women. Unless they have
been misrepresented, they had and deserved no *literary* fame, but their

4. George Borrow, *Lavengro,* 55.

recent emergence on the scholarly field is striking enough to suggest that there may be other such phenomena undiscovered.

I have come across no nonwhite Robinsons, though there is one in which a white boy follows his black friend when the latter is marooned on an island.[5] On the whole the story has been overwhelmingly white and male. One exception is Scott O'Dell's *Island of the Blue Dolphin,* in which an Indian girl is left alone on an island off the coast of California during the nineteenth century. The story is based on historical fact but was written in the second half of the twentieth century and is obviously a response to a liberal desire to have nonwhite, nonmale adventurers. It has a lyric or idyllic character, rather than the quasi-epic force of the best *Robinsonaden,* but that difference does not seem to express the writer's intention, or the way the story is written, so much as its relationship to energizing social myths. It is a would-be counter-myth.

As for the hero's age, there have been Robinsons of every stage of life, but there is a tendency of pattern within the variations. That tendency is suggested by the title of the first significant retelling on our list, Campe's *Robinson der Juengere.* Defoe's hero was half through his three-score years and ten when he arrived on the island, but later writers have wanted to make him younger. The story requires, or at least requests, a long future perspective, and so it has a vested interest in youth and adaptability. Campe made Robinson eighteen years old, and the tendency remained steady through much of the series. *Vendredi* made Robinson in his early twenties, for instance, and in the freer variants, such as *Treasure Island* and *Peter Pan,* the protagonist became a boy and then a child. (Perhaps in the postnuclear *Robinsonaden,* which one can predict will be written, there will be old Robinsons, partial repositories of the huge and broken science of the past.)

With these formal variations, the Robinson story was rewritten and in a sense reenacted throughout white culture for hundreds of years. It was therefore also reenacted in the other cultures on which whites made such an impact. A recent literary expression of that impact is Derek Walcott's play *Pantomime,* where a white man and a black man in the contemporary Caribbean work out their relationship by playing at being Robinson and Friday to each other. The play is based on the Robinson story, the author says, because everyone in the Caribbean is in a Robinson situation—that is, they have suffered a "historical shipwreck" and have to

5. Anne Bowman, *The Boy Voyagers* (1859).

put together a life out of "bits and pieces" derived from that shipwreck.[6]

Thus the story represented much that was powerful in Western culture. It derived its own power over our imaginations from all that it represented, but it also gave imaginative power to those other forces, through its narrative and character patterns and its emotional and evaluative dynamism. The same is true of the other adventure types, but because the forces represented differ from case to case, the patterns of meaning do too.

6. *Boston Globe,* June 8, 1986, B33.

4

The Three Musketeers Story
The Second Type

The Three Musketeers type of adventure tale differs from the Robinson story formally in almost every way, and thematically in being associated with France as opposed to England, with state nationalism as opposed to economic individualism, with the nineteenth century as opposed to the eighteenth century, and with historical glamour or military glory as opposed to commercial and technological rationality. The books I refer to as the Three Musketeers type are often grouped under the heading "historical novels." The difference between that concept and the one I have employed is clear enough: a novel can be historical without being adventurous. One can easily imagine, and indeed point to, stories of quiet domestic life in the past, replete with authentic detail and local color. However, a great many historical novels, and notably some by the founders of the genre—Scott and Dumas—do have adventure plots. Those are the ones I refer to as Three Musketeers stories, and they seem to exert a certain hegemony over the other kinds of historical fiction (which is an example of the hegemony of violent adventures over the nonviolent kinds).

It is appropriate here to discuss the relations between all seven adventure types and the more usual classifications to which they roughly correspond. What I call the Robinson stories are to be found in a group sometimes called "island stories"; the Frontiersman story is a part of a group called "Westerns"; the Wanderer story is sometimes called picaresque; the Avenger story is one of a group of nineteenth-century "Gothic" stories; modern Sagaman stories were sometimes called "Viking romances"; and the Hunted Man story is a kind of thriller.

So why invent a new set of names? Well, there are a number of differences between my seven and their alternatives. Some of those differences vary from case to case, but one large feature is common to all, which is the more systematic character of my seven. The system is not very rigorous, but it to some extent aligns the seven and allows some comparisons to be drawn. And the most important consequence is this idea of a formal hegemony exerted by the type over the other stories in the larger, looser category. The function of this idea is like that of "hegemony" in social and political theory. It points to the power—an implicit, shifting power of precedence and influence—which some individuals in a species have over the others who are ostensibly their equals. Robinson is *primus inter pares* among island stories, as they used to say of the prime minister in England. The Three Musketeers story *matters* more than other forms of historical fiction, in various ways, as the Robinson story matters more than other forms of island story, and so on.

In the Three Musketeers type of adventure, as in most of the others, we do not find, as we did in the first type, a single plot that is recognizable in each case despite variations. We can generalize only about the type's themes and motifs. This sort of adventure usually features young men beginning adult life; their warm loyalty to other young men in their group; their keen rivalry with other such groups; their gallant love affairs; their tutelary subordination to older men who wield power; a political situation involving rival statesmen; a picturesque pageant of figures from some national past. We also find a mass of colorful detail out of history: period clothes, local dialects, forgotten foodstuffs, buildings *we* know only as ruins, quarters that survive only as names, the Paris of the Middle Ages, Elizabethan London, the Edinburgh of the '45. What we get is a panorama of society that looks all-inclusive, though often with an emphasis on the court or the army, the church or secret diplomacy. The human qualities most warmly recommended are courage, gaiety, warmth, and virility. The authors in this category we think of first are Scott and Dumas, then Marryat and Tolstoy.

Although I aim to describe a type as a whole, I must begin with individual books and individual authors—in fact, with Scott's *Waverly* of 1814 and Dumas's *Les trois Mousquetaires* of 1844. I will give Dumas the priority here, despite Scott's deserving it chronologically and on some other grounds, because Dumas developed the group protagonist. The focus of this adventure type can of course be on a single figure, but the story gains when it is on a group. In Dumas's prototypical case, there are three—or rather four, when d'Artagnan adds himself. The image of a band of comrades strongly bonded together strengthens the appeal of this story in particular. Every type of adventure can accommodate the group protagonist and profit by the cult of male comradeship, because every adventure is masculinist, but some (for instance, the *Robinsonade*) also have a strong affinity for the solitary hero. The historical romance of the Three Musketeers type seems especially linked to the band of brothers.

Alexandre Dumas

Alexandre Dumas's story of *The Three Musketeers* is set in early seventeenth-century France, where Cardinal Richelieu is the minister all-powerful with the king, Louis XIII. The action begins with d'Artagnan's arrival in Paris from Gascony, as a very poor and very young man, with a letter of recommendation to the Captain of the king's Musketeers, the regiment he wants to join. He wins the friendship of the three Musketeers called Athos, Porthos, and Aramis, and he joins them in their sporadic brawling with rivals, the Cardinal's Guard. D'Artagnan lodges with Monsieur Bonacieu, whose pretty young wife is a devoted servant of the Queen. Attracted to Madame Bonacieu, d'Artagnan becomes involved in the love affair between the Queen and France's national enemy, the English Duke of Buckingham. The Cardinal tries to ruin the Queen by exposing this affair, and his beautiful spy, Milady, matches herself against d'Artagnan in various contests of intrigue. The Musketeers take part in many historically important events, such as the siege of the Protestant stronghold of La Rochelle. At the end, Milady is executed and the Cardinal is reconciled to d'Artagnan, who gets his commission into his regiment. Issues of "moral" right and wrong, in love and war, are lightly treated. What is most affirmed is the charm of the young men's mutual loyalty and the overwhelming importance of France—her national unity and international greatness.

Women play a much more important part in Dumas's novel, and in most adventures of this type, than in the Robinson story. There are at least three good "parts" for women: the Queen, Madame Bonacieu, and above all Milady, the wicked seductress. There is even a certain bonding of woman to woman in the devotion of Madame Bonacieu to the Queen. But it is feeble next to the male bonding of the four Musketeers to each other, which is moreover shadowed in the bonding of the four heroes' valets. The women are there more as motives for the actions of the men than as actors in themselves. They give occasion for the latter's reckless deeds. Even Milady is less a person than an incarnation of evil and sexuality. As the Cardinal's instrument, she manifests his character of being beyond good and evil, and as an exaggeration of his amorality she deflects our disapproval of him onto herself. The Cardinal has to be excused because he is an embodiment of France, and the manipulation of Milady's character to that end is typical of the way the women are manipulated within this story. All the characters are drawn according to a highly colored and simplified scheme—like a child's book of historical costumes—but the women are more loosely imagined than the men, and less invigorating to identify with.

The Three Musketeers adventure type offers striking examples of what Eve Kosofsky Sedgwick calls male homosocial desire. It shows men promoting the happiness of other men in transactions—even involving heterosexual love-relationships—that pass through and make use of women. Some larger cases of this will be cited later in discussing Tolstoy and Marryat, but the idea is relevant to Dumas, and indeed to many other writers of this story type. Sedgwick cites a definition of patriarchy as relations between men, with a material base, that establish the interdependence and solidarity between men that helps them dominate women.[1]

Works by Dorothy Dinnerstein and René Girard are Sedgwick's

1. Eve Kosofsky Sedgwick, *Between Men*, 3.

starting points. The latter analyzes triangular love-relationships in fiction, tending to show that in any erotic rivalry the bond that links two rivals is as intense and potent as the bond that links either to the beloved. In many cases the very choice of the latter was predetermined by her relation to the other. Sedgwick goes on to show us more subtle and complex patterns of desire, but none are more so than those found in *The Three Musketeers*. The hostility between d'Artagnan and Milady leads d'Artagnan to impersonate the man she loves in her bed; this fantasy dramatizes a very complex set of desires, including the feelings of Milady's maid for d'Artagnan. But all d'Artagnan's dealings with Milady are a part of or in the service of his dealings with the Cardinal.

Milady is an adventuress and not an adventurer, and that is a morally inferior destiny. This can be illustrated (if the reader will follow a lateral leap) from the script of the film *Palm Beach Story*, in which Claudette Colbert declares she is going to become an adventuress. When Joel McCrea says skeptically that he can't see her setting off for China in a twenty-seven-foot boat, she replies something like this: "That's an adventurer. An adventuress never sails in anything under three hundred feet and with a large crew." In a screwball comedy the adventuress has the last word, but not in a respectable adventure.

Thus, if we compare this second adventure type with the first from the point of view of sexism, we see immediately that this one does include women (and the idea of sexuality, and the idea of intimate relations). But on the other hand, these themes and values are all presented in the second type in ways that give a priority to men and to the idea of adventure, a priority of many kinds. Women are assigned a place in men's lives and are made secondary to what passes between a man and other men. In comparable ways, if we turn from gender to class, we see that Scott's and Dumas's people are always being assigned to their rightful places in an elaborate social hierarchy, and we are asked to enjoy both kinds of hierarchical differentiation.

Robert Louis Stevenson describes Dumas's moral teaching in an essay on Dumas's *Le Vicomte de Bragelonne*, a sequel to *The Three Musketeers*. (Stevenson's essay is entitled "A Gossip on a Novel of Dumas's" and was published in his *Memories and Portraits* [1887].) He says that *Vicomte* is among the few books that have influenced him morally and that he feels he is at all times under the scrutiny of the older d'Artagnan, the hero of the story, "a man so witty, rough, kind and upright, that he takes the heart by storm."[2]

2. Robert Louis Stevenson, *Memories and Portraits*, 144.

In the opening scenes of the *Vicomte de Bragelonne,* the old d'Artagnan teaches the young King Louis XIV how to be a man, and it is clear
that what attracts Stevenson is the masculinism of d'Artagnan's and
Dumas's morality—the *natural* (as opposed to pious) morality of *men,*
as opposed to other human groups. He says: "There is nothing of the
copy-book about his virtues, nothing of the drawing room in his fine,
natural civility; he will sail near the wind; he is no district visitor—no
Wesley or Robespierre; his conscience is void of all refinement whether
for good or evil; but the whole man rings true like a good sovereign. . . .
if I am to choose virtues for myself or my friends, let me choose the
virtues of d'Artagnan."[3] Andrew Lang, following Stevenson, says the
young should learn frankness, kindness, and generosity from Dumas.[4]

Moreover, the band of protagonists in Dumas's novel constitutes not
only a static morality or myth, but also a ritual of the cult of young
manhood, because of the interactions of the four men. Athos, Porthos,
and Aramis, are clearly differentiated from each other: Athos the distinguished, severe, reserved; Porthos, the loud, boastful, exuberant; Aramis
the discreet, sentimental, seductive. And the interaction between them is
a mutual appreciation for the zest with which each performs his own
particular style of young manhood. D'Artagnan is welcomed into their
inner circle for the ardor with which he concentrates on the essentials of
the cult. In his aspiration to the young manly qualities, he is more direct
than any of them. His single-mindedness exposes him to ridicule by
other people, but the Musketeers, and all those who know—right up to
the Cardinal—see his value. Thus, instead of a fourth member compli-
cating the image of the protagonist, he simplifies it. He reinforces the
central image of young manhood.

This cult is fused with that of France, of patriotic French feeling, and
that fusion brings the Musketeers to serve the Cardinal, and he to favor
them, despite their being on opposite "political" sides. The ultimate
reconciliation of these antagonists gives the story its satisfactory ending.
But simply in themselves the young men *represent* France, coming as
they do from different parts and embodying different French tempera-
ments, but loving each other. (In adventures of this type, the individuals
often represent different geographical areas. In British stories with three
boys, for instance, the one will be English, the second Scots, the third
Irish.)

3. Ibid.
4. Andrew Lang, *Essays in Little,* 1.

This was clearly perceived and appreciated by Dumas's immediate audience. Said Hippolyte Parigot: "A very lively sense of nationality . . . in that lies the secret charm of the four heroes . . . epitomes of that gracious, courageous, light-hearted France which we still like to recover through the imagination. . . . If Danton and Napoleon were exemplars of Gallic energy, Dumas, in *The Three Musketeers,* is the national novelist who put it into words."[5] When Dumas's remains were buried at Villers-Cotterêts in 1872, Victor Hugo sent a letter to be read at the ceremony, saying, among other things, that Dumas had been an embodiment of "the French idea" and so a seminal mind for all humanity: "Alexandre Dumas is one of those men one can call sowers of civilization: he sanitizes and improves minds by who knows what strong, gay clarity; he fecundates souls, brains, intelligences; he creates a thirst for reading; he opens up the human genius and fertilizes it. What he sows is the French idea. The French idea contains such a quantity of humanity that wherever it penetrates, it produces progress. . . . [He] charms, fascinates, interests, amuses, teaches. From all Dumas's works, so many, so varied, so living, so charming, emanates the sort of light proper to France."[6]

André Maurois also connects Dumas's work with the history of nineteenth-century France, but with the Napoleonic empire in particular: "Corneille and Racine bored him [Dumas as a boy] to tears. General Dumas's son, like all the young men of his generation, had heard too many thrilling stories to be content with the analysis of human emotions. What he wanted was action, no matter how mad. . . . He had been nourished on tales of adventure marked by both splendour and the shedding of blood. . . . [He loved] the more than life-size figures of the Empire, who had conquered hearts as they had conquered provinces."[7]

These comments followed up clues that Dumas gave about his own sense of himself. He made a profession of exuberance in more than one sense of profession, inviting others to see him as a force of nature. Jules Michelet, the historian of France, wrote him: "I admire and love you because you are one of the forces of nature." Dumas fused together personal, literary, and nationalist exuberance, especially from the moment he first saw English actors playing Shakespeare: "I recognized that

5. Hippolyte Parigot, *Alexandre Dumas Père,* 140–41.
6. See Claude Schoop, *Alexandre Dumas,* 526–27.
7. André Maurois, *The Titans,* 47.

next to the Creator himself, Shakespeare had created more than any other being. From that moment my career was decided. I felt that I had received that special call which comes to every man. I felt a confidence in my own powers that until then I had lacked."[8]

In those days Shakespeare seemed to be the poetic voice of nationalism, and a suitable sponsor for adventure writers. He stood behind Scott and (in a play like *Henry V*) was the originator of all the adventure types, connecting adventure with the Renaissance and the beginning of modern empire. In historical date and in literary form, he was out of line with these authors of mine, but he was their beloved father—their Homer, perhaps, or what the poets of Rome made of Homer.

Dumas's own creativity came into full play, however, only when he began to write historical novels. Before then, before 1840, he tells us, he had not been conscious of "the marvellous quality of mirth which was latent in me. At that time, the only permissible mirth was Satanic."[9] He means the laughter of Byron's Manfred and Goethe's Mephistopheles, the two great sneerers of the period, as he calls them. "In common with others I had put a mask on my face, which is evidenced by the portraits of me of that period."[10] Deveria's 1831 portrait of him, said Dumas, could have been a portrait of "Antony" (the hero of Dumas's bourgeois tragedy by that name, a contemporary Manfred, who broods over his illegitimate birth and murders the woman he loves). Indeed, Dumas's early melodramas (in the genre later perfected by Ibsen and Strindberg) read more like "realistic" fiction than like the novels he went on to write, as F.W.J. Hemmings has remarked.[11] A big change had to come over him before he could begin *Les trois Mousquetaires*.

When he read some of Augustin Thierry's histories, Dumas tells us, he saw that there was more for him in the past than in the present. Turning to the historical novel, he discovered *continuity*. He saw all of France's past as a brilliant tapestry or standard that floated from the battlements of the nation-state to exhilarate all its citizens: "The studies of the French monarchy I was compelled to undergo, from Caesar's invasion of the Gauls [*sic*] to the invasion of the French Republic in Europe, unfolded before me that magnificent continuity of eighteen centuries,

8. Alexandre Dumas, *My Memoirs*, 119.
9. Ibid., 226.
10. Ibid.
11. F.W.J. Hemmings, *The King of Romance*, 103.

wrongly styled the history of France, under Charlemagne, Philippe-Auguste, François I, Louis XIV, Napoleon, which has become the history of the world . . . wonderful material . . . [celebrating] all who had worn a crown, whether of laurels, of flowers, or of gold."[12]

This nationalism had an imperialist dimension in a quite literal sense, but it did not mean that Dumas was politically conservative. When Algiers fell to the French, in July 1830, Dumas immediately planned a tour of inspection, but he canceled his plan when he realized that a revolution in Paris was imminent. He took part in the fighting, hoping to see the Bourbon regime replaced by a republic, not by the constitutional monarchy that in fact came to power then. He risked his life, going to Soissons to seize arms for the insurgents in Paris. In 1846 he again planned a tour of French North Africa, this time financed by the government, to make propaganda for the colony and encourage French emigration; the government promised him a warship in which to sail. In 1860 he played a prominent part in the rebellion Garibaldi led in Sicily and Naples that brought about the unification of Italy.

This connection between Dumas's adventure type and a cult of France (national and imperial) will remind us of how the Robinson story represented England. D'Artagnan was to France as Crusoe was to England, and that is neither a trivial coincidence nor a unique one. In this matter, as in others, Dumas follows Scott, and is like Scott's other followers, as a nationalist novelist. Tolstoy, for instance, made Pierre, in *War and Peace,* an embodiment of Russia.

Scott's novels—both the sentimental-humorous kind, which focused on his historical characters and anecdotes, and the heroic-revolt kind, which made people thrill to his pictures of rebellions, like that of 1745 in Scotland—were a major stimulus to Scottish, and English, nationalism. Scott's imitators across Europe, moreover, raised national consciousness among people who did not yet have their independence.

Modern nationalism was contemporary in its growth with the modern adventure tale. The two sprouted from the same cultural tendency, and adventures, especially those of the Three Musketeers kind, supplied various national movements with their icons and liturgies. If England was linked to the Robinson story, as we have seen, our third adventure type supplied the United States with its image of American heroism; the Sagas supplied imperial Germany with its heroic style and myth; and so

12. Dumas, *My Memoirs,* 249, 252.

on. These adventure-born images showed how each nation "thought" of itself, especially in international contexts. In Jules Verne's novel about space travel, *From the Earth to the Moon,* the Frenchman (called Ardan, meaning ardent) is not at all like the serious Anglo-Saxons with their technical expertise, because he is primarily dashing.

These national affiliations were recognizable across international borders, for all the white world was playing the adventure game. In *Discoveries in England* (1930), Emile Cammaerts, a Frenchman resident in England, says he had long been struck by the number of Englishmen who had big parts in Jules Verne's stories, and suddenly realized that Phineas Fogg (in *Around the World in Eighty Days*) was Robinson redivivus. Cammaerts had loved Crusoe since his childhood and found him the ideal type of adventurer—courageous, patient, as well as wise and just in his relations with the savages.[13] Cammaerts was an ardent English patriot who wrote texts for some of Elgar's war music. He knew early in life that he personally could not emulate d'Artagnan's bravado, or the military dash of French adventure heroes in general. That was why he preferred to live in England, to be an Englishman. (Just so, some Englishmen saw themselves as being frontiersmen by temperament and therefore emigrated to America.) Crusoe was a *settler,* not a Musketeer. He carried in a kind of frog, instead of a sword and dagger, a little saw and hatchet, one on one side, one on the other.[14] The English adventure novel, Cammaerts says, is geographical, while the French is historical. The English dream is in a sense outside history, at least the history of domination and militarism. And this national contrast was noted by several commentators foreign to both countries—for instance, the Russian radical Alexander Herzen, in his memoirs, and "Sir John Retcliffe," the German adventure-writer, in his novel *Puebla.*

Then there are formal differences between the types of adventure, which correspond to the ideological differences. Defoe's *Robinson Crusoe,* for instance, is told in the first person, and that precedent is often followed in retellings, as in *Treasure Island.* Third-person narrators are usually transparently similar to the protagonist, as in *The Swiss Family Robinson,* and the language in which the protagonist's thoughts and actions are reported is, in a literary sense, naive and colorless. When we turn to Scott and Dumas, we find something quite different. The author's

13. Emile Cammaerts, *Discoveries in England.*
14. Ibid.

persona stands midway between the protagonist and the reader and treats with both as interpreter and commentator, in an elaborate style, with humor, nostalgia, and irony, a blend of historian and master of ceremonies.

Comparing themes and values, we see that the Musketeers story has no sense of the dignity of work, indeed, takes no interest in practical techniques, to compare with the Robinson story. What it does have is a keen sense of social and gender power, prestige, and hierarchy. We might follow Cammaerts and call this essentially historical romance, while the *Robinsonade* is geographical, but we should stress the word "romance." Dumas's sense of history focused on the personalities of kings and ministers, on intrigues and love affairs, on costume and manners and titles and forms of address. This is history identified with its colorfulness, history as seen from the top, from the king's point of view. To approach the point another way, this is a mode of conceiving history that is indelibly marked by the conventions of theater (conventions that play no part in the Robinson story).

Dumas actually wrote plays before he wrote novels, but Scott, who did not, has the same theatricality, to use the word literally as well as metaphorically. Scott, in fact, borrowed some characters' traits from famous actors' interpretations of Shakespearean roles. It appears that, early in the nineteenth century, all Europe was excited by a conjunction of Shakespearean theater with a new sense of history (as a fictive world corresponding to bourgeois nationalism) and with the world triumph of England. Dumas was inspired by some English actors of Shakespeare when they came to Paris in 1827. He saw passion and genius in Kean, Kemble, and Smithson, as did other young writers, such as Victor Hugo, and this experience led to a new Romantic theater in France. As for the sense of history as a drama, that had been awakened by the enormous events of the Revolution and the Empire. Maurois says, "A people which had *made* history, and witnessed vast changes, was longing to be taken behind the scenes" to see the equivalent in earlier ages.[15] And Scott had shaped that interest into a new and extraordinarily popular form of fiction by writing (as Shakespeare had before him) the foundation epic of England. But Scott himself, like Dumas after him, was also responding to twin political phenomena of the greatest kind: the extraordinary successes of Napoleon and the solid invincibility of Britain.

15. Maurois, *The Titans*, 172.

We should not, therefore, dismiss too quickly the historical claims of these authors' work, however romantic it seems to us. Dumas came to novel-writing through history-writing. Beginning in 1831, he wrote "scènes historiques," semidramatized reconstructions of the past, for the *Revue des Deux Mondes,* and these were later published in book form as "historical compilations." It was not until 1844 that he published *The Three Musketeers,* and for the preceding seven years he had served his apprenticeship to history writing.

In the nineteenth century, Scott was regarded as a notable historian, and he inspired many scholars. Thierry said, "I regard him as the greatest master that has ever been seen of the *instinctive* understanding of history."[16] It is a mark of the seriousness of his and Dumas's genre of fiction that the latter set out to cover all French history, from 1572 up to the Revolution. Indeed, Dumas once boasted of having covered five and a half centuries, from *La Comtesse de Salisbury* to *Le Comte de Monte Cristo.* Scott did the same for English history, starting much further back, and Cooper did the same for white American history, beginning with Columbus. Each was giving his countrymen their national history in the form of a foundation epic, explaining how their nation-state came to be and how its parts fitted together. The historical novel justified the nation-as-empire while at the same time sympathizing with nationalist revolts against foreign empires. Scott managed to do both in writing about Scotland's relations with England.

It remains true, however, that Dumas's understanding of history was theatrical and romantic, or baroque—in the sense that it featured flowing costumes and lavish curves, in gestures and in action. Gustave Doré's 1883 sculpture of d'Artagnan presents him in feathered hat and curling moustache and flowing cape, and in a posture equivalent to his costume—arms akimbo, legs astride as he sits, every limb at a jaunty angle to the rest. He is about to move. The fun is about to start, for life was fun in historical times.

This stress on fun and entertainment and mirth militated against Dumas's literary reputation. Literary values were associated with a more solemn or intense sense of truth. (In a less blatant way, the same thing happened to Scott.) Even Dumas's defenders, such as Stevenson and Lang, associated him with Porthos rather than with, say, Athos. Stevenson also referred to him as a frivolous giant and as "the ventripotent

16. Ibid., 127.

mulatto." This tone expresses a gradual acceptance of inferior status by the champions of adventure, an acceptance of their exclusion from literature.

We could explain this exclusion as a gradual recognition by Dumas's readers of the philistine and complacent character of his "mirth," its reinforcement of the nineteenth-century French reader's pride in being French, in being bourgeois. But from our point of view this gaiety deserves to be looked at as a formal phenomenon too. From the start, there was an emphasis on fun in the Musketeers adventure—a mood in some ways the opposite of the Robinson mood. It is easy to translate that difference into ideological terms. All true Robinsons are middle-class and serious-minded in a Protestant way, and the culture they serve and represent is a congeries of commercial and technical practices. The heroes of this second adventure type are nobly born but impoverished or disinherited. They have to make their way in life, but their destiny cannot be anything but aristocratic. Within their respective nations, d'Artagnan comes from Gascony, and Scott's heroes often are from Scotland—in both cases the home of proud but impoverished gentry, far from the affluent bourgeoisie of Paris and London. They are lighthearted and even lightminded—readers are encouraged to think themselves more serious than they—the writer presents them as essentially *young* men. And the culture they represent is a colorful panorama of nobles, priests, peasants, and merchants (a society of castes), within which the heroes will, once they settle down, bear arms, dispense justice, and manifest authority and splendor.

The complementary part of "history," the part from which young men are excluded, is the bureaucratic and organizational and essentially duplicitous or secret policies of the Cardinal. This is the domain of the old men—not necessarily old in years, but men shriveled in soul and alienated from youth and nature, from ardor and gaiety, charm and warmth. This conception is just as exciting to Dumas and Scott (and to Kipling, who writes the same story, in *Puck of Pook's Hill*) as the romance the Musketeers represent. Adventures of this type put the two things together, to make "history." This idea of history omits nearly everything that, for instance, Karl Marx meant by the term (and of course the sociologists and the *Annalistes*). But we should not too easily give Marx the advantage. In his dealings with contemporary events, Marx was himself ready to believe conspiracy rumors as romantic as any Dumas plot.

Dumas's idea of Richelieu may sound to us very nineteenth-century romantic, but it is expressed in the portraits of him in his own time—the painting by Philippe de Champaigne, for example, and verbal portraits by writers in various memoirs. This latter genre began to appear in the seventeenth century, the work of or the report on contemporary men of action looking back over their lives. Much was written about Richelieu (and about such comparable figures as Cardinal Retz) in memoirs by La Rochefoucauld, Saint-Simon, the Duchesse de Nemours, and so on, as well as by the pseudo-memoirist Gatien de Courtilz, on whom Dumas in fact drew. Though a writer of fiction, Courtilz has been compared with La Rochefoucauld for his historical insights.[17] It has long been suggested that such memoirs (which replaced the "roman précieux" in popularity after 1650) engendered or led on to the modern novel. Like Defoe, Courtilz was very popular and received much blame for deceiving his public, for making them think it was real history he wrote. (The same was to be true of Karl May; adventure writers often write on the edge of literary respectability.)

In any case, Dumas's portrait of Richelieu is confirmed by, among others, Defoe, and not only in his fiction but also in his journalism and letters. Writing to Lord Oxford, his statesman-protector within the British government, Defoe recommends to him Richelieu's practice of having three successive rooms as offices, each one more private than the last and the third so private that no one was ever admitted to it except in the dark.[18] And in the second issue of his *Review* he wrote of "the most exquisite master of politics, Cardinal Richelieu, whose life and management may hereafter take up a considerable part of these papers, . . . the most refined statesman in the world."[19] Words like "refined" and "exquisite" express exactly the excitement, and thus the idea of politics, that Dumas expresses in his depiction of Richelieu. It isn't an idea to limit to the Romantic period.

That Defoe's name turns up in this second context should arouse only mild surprise. He himself wrote one of the first historical romances in English, *The Memoirs of a Cavalier*. Indeed, Defoe shaped into being nearly all the modern fictional forms—the adventures but also some kinds of domestic or erotic novel. What *is* a striking coincidence is that

17. See Luciana Bianca Alocco, *I memoirs de M. d'Artagnan*, 22.
18. G. H. Healey, ed., *The Letters of Daniel Defoe*, 39.
19. A. V. Secord, ed., *Defoe's Review*, 12.

he took his inspiration for his historical novel from none other than Gatien de Courtilz and his *Mémoires de le Comte de Rochefort,* published in Cologne in 1700—and that this was also Dumas's major source. Indeed, Richelieu plays a part in Defoe's story, which contains also Scots adventurers like those Scott was to write about.

This must be partly mere coincidence, but it can remind us of something causally substantial: the network of adventures of this type, passing from author to author and already in existence in the early eighteenth century, though not to receive international fame for another one hundred years. That network can be seen also in the manifold connections between Defoe and Scott.

Sir Walter Scott

Significantly, both Scott and Defoe were excited by their sense of Scotland, and the two ideas were similar. Of course, Scotland was only a minor concern of Defoe's, but it meant a great deal to Scott. Both, however, saw it as exemplary of the paradoxes of modern empire, as a country situated on the borders of England and so of the modern world but belonging, above all in its Highlands, to an earlier phase of cultural development. This contrast excited them and all readers who shared their strong and ambivalent sense of how much was gained or lost or changed by "progress." Defoe, for instance, was fascinated by the idea of Highland soldiers as uncivilized, uncouth, and almost grotesque but yet—indeed, *for that reason*—formidable: "The most formidable little body of men in their rude circumstances in these parts of the world."[20]

This is the way other frontier peoples were seen. The glamour of the Cossacks in Russia, the subject of many adventure tales, had the same source. In India the English saw the Gurkhas and the Pathans in the same light. In Flora Annie Steel's novel about the Indian mutiny, the real-life General Nicholson says, "By and by, unless I'm wrong, men of their stock will be our best war weapons; for mind you, war is a primitive art and needs a primitive people."[21] Primitivism is both bad and good.

In 1706 Defoe wrote a poem, *Caledonia,* as part of the English

20. Ibid., 10.
21. Flora Annie Steel, *Breath upon the Waters,* 357.

propaganda for the Act of Union between England and Scotland (1707), which was a major step in the development of Britain-as-empire. In his preface Defoe said the act should be passed in the name of "improvements," what we would call modernization. He responded to two things in Scotland: the retarded state of the economy, which must be changed, and the rude virtue of the fighting men, which must be preserved. A similar tension, between a rationalist desire for Scotland to follow England and a romantic appreciation of her anachronism, inspired the best of Scott. The suppression of the rebellion of 1745, the subject of *Waverley*, also led to "improvements." It is a theme of many writers of historical romance, though not of Dumas, and this lack shows the weaker side of Dumas's sense of history. And it is to be found in Defoe a full century before the historical romance is usually held to begin.

This is not to challenge Scott's claim to have invented a new form. Scott's was a triumph of synthesis. He combined what Defoe and others had done, with the taste of his contemporaries for the exotic and his own formidable learning in old books and manuscripts, traditional ballads and folktales, and collections of armor and weapons and costumes of various kinds. He put together a lot of "action"—quarreling, dueling, galloping, lovemaking—with the scholarly apparatus of the three-volume novel, with epigraphs to the chapters and footnoted introductions. Above all, he put together a strong sense of the advantages of modern, secular, rationalized England with an equally strong feeling for other sides of life: the noble simplicities of traditional culture, the passionate loyalties of clan life, the romantic aspiration to unconditioned values.

This complex vision of history becomes a recommendation of, as well as a parallel to, the complex unity of contemporary Britain—England and Scotland united, Britain-as-empire. It is all to be found in the original Waverley novel of 1814, in which Edward Waverley, though born to all the advantages of modern prosperous England, needs to go adventuring in the savage Highlands of Scotland in search of challenging experience before he can settle down to enjoy his prosaic and comfortable privileges.

Scott's story begins just before the 1745 rebellion of Scottish Jacobites (adherents of the Stuarts) against the rule of the Hanoverian George II. Edward Waverley is a young Englishman who lives on a country estate with his uncle, a romantic Jacobite, although his father is a Whig who stands well with the government in London. The Waverley family has prudently kept friends in both the opposed camps. But the young man, inexperienced and romantic by temperament, goes to Scotland with the English army, visits friends of his uncle, and falls under the spell of Fergus and Flora MacIvor, who are committed to the rebel cause. When the revolt breaks out, Waverley marches with Prince Charles Edward Stuart's army, which is defeated at Culloden, and so he has to go into hiding as a traitor. Reprieved by the intervention of friends, and reconciled to the march of history and to political realism, he returns to his English estates, matured by the experience.

Scott's best work is essentially a reconciliation of the mutually opposing values that belong to differing social groups or castes. (Dumas does the same thing, but with less intellectual distinction. He said he differed from Scott in his willingness to amuse the reader from the first page.[22]) One of those sets of values, however, has an "emotional" preeminence in Scott's mind—the romantic values associated with the aristo-military caste. In lesser novels like *Ivanhoe,* Scott simply made propaganda for that caste among the middle-class reading public. It was a regular pattern of social mobility in eighteenth- and nineteenth-century England for a successful middle class to spend new money becoming noble and pretending to antiquity; acquiring a title; sending the sons to Eton; buying or building oneself a fake castle; and so on. England's accession to world power, and the spread of her empire, created a need for governors and generals and ambassadors, and so a demand for stories like Scott's, which provided a fanciful energizing myth for an aristo-military class. This accounts for the least palatable aspect of Scott's work, and his repudiation by men and women of taste in the latter half of the century. He provided a fake armor for aristocratic joustings, a style of fanciful "historical" ornament to dress up the facts of power and wealth. But another side of his work, his strong feeling for Scotland as a conquered nation, made him a model for writers inspired by their country's aspirations to liberty and unity, the writers of Poland, Hungary, Germany, Italy, Greece. And the Musketeers story could serve both purposes.

Scott's historical romances were phenomenally popular, both in the Anglo-Saxon countries and, in translation, throughout Europe and beyond. If one added together all the editions of his works, and those of the writers who professed to have copied him, one would have a genre

22. See Jean-Yves Tadié, *Le roman d'aventures,* 58.

much larger than the *Robinsonade*. One problem of that genre, however, he failed to solve: that of the hero. Scott himself always spoke scornfully of the central male figures in his stories, who are indeed pallid by comparison with the other characters. The reason for that failure is perhaps also the reason for the stories' best qualities—Scott's complex balance of mind. In the long run, in the final accounting, he always endorses common sense and rejects the more brilliant alternatives. The plots image well enough the debate within Scott's sympathies, but the heroes, because they must be right, tend to be only tentative adventurers, such as Waverley (the waverer) or outright antiadventurous figures, such as Jeanie Deans in *The Heart of Midlothian,* who passes through many adventures untouched—and who is even a woman.

To put such figures at the heart of an adventure contradicts its spirit, but then Scott could never *approve* the adventurer type. It was Dumas, a less scrupulous mind, who discovered how to replace these unsatisfactory heroes, and thus, from the point of view of genre history, it is Dumas who triumphs.

The list of Scott's imitators in the first three quarters of the nineteenth century is well known. We can ignore Cooper (who will appear in the next chapter) and the English imitators. The best-known names, outside France, are Manzoni and Tolstoy, Sienkewicz, Merezhkovski, Feuchtwanger, Ebers, Hausrath, and Freytag. In France we have de Vigny's *Cinq-Mars* in 1826, and in 1829 Balzac's *Les chouans* and Mérimée's *Chronique du temps de Charles IX,* and in 1830 Hugo's *Notre-Dame de Paris.* These are all imitations of Scott, before the latter's death. Dumas's modification of the genre, which brought it to life again, took another fourteen years. Meanwhile, there was also historical theater (Hugo's *Cromwell,* with a preface inspired by Scott, in 1827, and Dumas's *Henri III et sa cour,* in 1829). And then there was historical painting too.

Marryat and Tolstoy

After Scott, the writer in English who most deserves our attention is Captain Marryat, for the variety of his contributions to adventure as a whole. We have already discussed his *Robinsonade, Masterman Ready.* Several other novels, such as *Frank Mildmay* (1829) and *Mr. Midship-*

man Easy (1836), belong to the picaresque eighteenth-century and Regency romance tradition. Marryat may be called in literary terms a precursor of Scott, in these books, even though in actual date of writing he followed Scott. And then, by the end of the 1830s, when Scott had died, Marryat became a Victorian and wrote *Robinsonaden* and a Scott adaptation, *The Children of the New Forest*.

Marryat nevertheless deserves some attention here, because of his pictures of young-man comradeship in those Regency romances. There is no reason to suppose that Dumas was indebted to Marryat, but in this matter he followed the same pattern. So, from our present point of view (and using the Musketeers story as a category), some of Marryat's work belongs to that category by anticipation. Indeed, Marryat considerably surpasses Dumas in the frankness with which he depicts homosocial desire in male bonding. The only writer of the same period who seems to vie with Marryat in this frankness is Tolstoy. The most vivid examples come from Tolstoy's early writing, of the 1850s, which is partly in the adventure mode: *Sevastopol, The Cossacks,* and a few short stories. In this work, and in the war parts of *War and Peace,* where Tolstoy is again Scott's disciple, he is also his superior in handling these themes.

The root of this love of comrades, both writers tell us, lies in each young man's love of himself, a narcissism that is presented to the reader with a nonironic but self-conscious endorsement by the author. In a variant of *The Cossacks,* for instance, Tolstoy writes: "That people *could* be good and noble if they willed it, Olenin was quite convinced [Olenin is Tolstoy's representative in the story]; his own young soul, he felt, was beautiful, and with that he was content. . . . For my part [the narrator says] I love the amiable inactivity of those young men who survey the scene before them, yet lack the courage to turn their pent-up energies into immediate action. . . . Olenin felt the all-powerful genius of youth was asleep within him, and instinctively followed his impulses."[23] In these early works of Tolstoy, the narrator is usually in love with his young hero (who is himself), and the hero is usually in love with himself.

In this war and adventure work, of the 1850s, Tolstoy explored many aspects of this young man's cult of himself. For instance, in the Sevastopol sketches about his experience of the war in the Crimea, he dwells on the way the young officers there are locked within their own self-preoccupations, even in the imminence of death, and experience every-

23. Quoted in René Fuelop-Miller, *Tolstoy: New Light on His Life and Genius,* 57.

thing in the debased form of "what will impress others." Later, in his horse story, "Strider" (1863), he puts forward a narcissist or dandy theory of love. Serpukhovsky was "handsome, happy, rich, and therefore never loved anybody," and therefore everybody loved him. He, his horse, his mistress, and his coachman were all handsome and superior—the glamour spread from one to another—and so other people were help-lessly attracted to him with a love that commanded and deserved no return on his part.

Tolstoy worked out some brilliant images for this sensibility, notably in the juxtaposition of an older man with a younger man, in which the interest is partly the contrast between them, partly their relationship with each other, but most essentially the revelation that the older man is still the young one, in rougher and gruffer form. ("Decadent" dandies like Oscar Wilde have their own version of this, seen in, for instance, *The Portrait of Dorian Gray*.) Perhaps the most striking example of this occurs in the last of the Sevastopol sketches, in which the younger Kozeltov brother, Vladimir, is described in the most sumptuous, almost cannibal, sensual detail and the older brother is described as faded and coarsened, by contrast. But we realize that he had been just like his brother and still contains that youthful self within him, which can still appear on special occasions. That is the device of the story "Oasis" too, where the contrast is between a middle-aged woman and the girl she had been, while in "Two Hussars" the two men are father and son. (In *War and Peace,* the same thing recurs when Petya Rostov, just before he is killed, is juxtaposed with his older brother, Nikolai, now coarsened and "unpoetic.") These contrasts, though sometimes the author explicitly disapproves the young man's all-mastering love of himself or his reflec-tion, always implicitly enhance that love and induce the reader to share it.

The older brother Kozeltov, an army officer, is described in the first paragraph of "August, 1855." Of his face Tolstoy says, "It would have passed for an attractive one if it had not been for a certain bloating of the flesh and a skin furrowed by deep wrinkles, which, inter-weaving, distorted the features, took away all freshness, and gave a brutal expres-sion." And his character is described in terms of self-love: "His nature had been richly endowed with inferior qualities. . . . His energy was remarkable, but this energy received its impulse only from self-love, although, grafted on this second-rate capacity, it formed a salient and characteristic trait of his nature. . . . Self-love was then the motive force of his most intimate enthusiasms. Even alone in his own presence he was fond of considering himself superior to those with whom he compared himself."[24]

Marryat's autobiographical hero, Frank Mildmay, tells us that even at seven his ruling passion was pride, and "If I have gained a fair name in the [naval] service, if I have led instead of followed, it must be ascribed to this my ruling passion."[25] Kozeltov's self-love is also said to be of a kind especially developed among military men. And Mildmay's is related to his appearance: at sixteen, "my person assumed an outline of which I had great reason to be proud, since I often heard it the subject of encomium among the fair sex, and their award was confirmed even by my companions" (p. 53). Marryat's pattern is the same as Tolstoy's.

The second brother Kozeltov is introduced soon after the older one. "A youth of seventeen years, with black, lively, sparkling eyes and red cheeks, rose with a bound, and having involuntarily pushed against the doctor, said, 'A thousand pardons!' rubbing his eyes and standing in the middle of the room."[26] The stress falls on his naiveté, his unconsciousness, but in him too that is related to self-love. Later we read: "Vladimir Kozeltov, the younger, looked very much like his brother Michael, at least as much as a half-open columbine can resemble one which has lost its flower. . . . As he stood there in his unbuttoned coat, under which could be seen a red shirt with Russian collar; slender, broad-shouldered, a cigarette between his fingers, leaning against the balustrade of the piazza, his face lighted up by unaffected joy, his eyes fixed on his brother . . . one looked away from him reluctantly" (pp. 133–34). But we are also told that Vladimir, having acquired ideas of "culture" from fashionable hostesses, had grown ashamed of his brother.

What we most notice, of course, is not Tolstoy's moral analysis of the young man but his erotic appreciation of him. We also sense, if we know this subgenre, that Vladimir is destined to die. (This is one of the ways in which this variant differs from the Musketeers story. Dumas's heroes don't need to die, because they have not been loved so intensely; their mode is comedy, not lyric tragedy.) Writers in this genre allow themselves such rapture only if its object is shortly going to die. A film equivalent of this is the Australian film *Gallipoli*.

24. Leo Tolstoy, *Sebastopol*, 114, 118.
25. Frederick Marryat, *Frank Mildmay*, 2.
26. Tolstoy, *Sebastopol*, 10.

Turning now to Marryat, we sometimes find a similar pattern of erotic appreciation between young men, but this time it is openly mutual. In *The Privateersman* (1846) the hero, while still a very young man, meets Captain Levee, who is strikingly unlike the "stout, strong-limbed, weather-beaten" captains he has hitherto known. "He, on the contrary, was a young man of about 26, very slight in person, with a dark complexion, hair and eyes jet black. I should have called him a very handsome Jew. . . . He was handsomely dressed, wearing his hair slightly powdered, a laced coat and waistcoat . . . silver-mounted pistols and dagger in his belt, and a smart hanger by his side. He had several diamond rings on his finger, and carried a small clouded cane" (pp. 49–50). Levee offers to take the hero on a jaunt to London. " 'How will you dress?' " he asks him. " 'I think it might be better to alter your costume, now you are going to London. . . . You'll make a pretty fellow, dress how you will' " (p. 58). They order his clothes together.

The hero's relations with women are equally unexpected. Before meeting Levee, he was made slave to the beautiful wife of a wicked old African king and became her boudoir favorite, serving her beauty. "I became very expert, having to rub her hair with a sweet oil, and then roll it up in its natural curls with a quill, so as to dispose them with the most fanciful advantage as to form" (p. 37). Later, in North America, he falls into the hands of Indians and is married by force to a hideous squaw. He escapes her only to fall into the hands of an Englishwoman "more than six feet high, of gaunt appearance and large dimensions: I thought that I had never seen such a masculine creature before" (p. 242). She wants him for a lover, so he runs away, but is recaptured. "When I recovered, I felt a great weight upon my chest, and opening my eyes, found my mistress sitting upon me, and giving orders to the convicts." (p. 249). She attaches a chain and iron ball weighing thirty pounds to his ankle, and when they are attacked by Indians, "catching up the chain and ball in one hand, with her other she caught me round the waist, and carried me into the house" (p. 256).

The man and his friends have sexual relations with women, and he is in love with a moral heroine. These themes are taken seriously by the novelist, and treated convincingly enough, but it is clear that the erotic feeling (that is, the erotic fantasy) runs between the men—the fantasies of delight are homoerotic, those of disgust are heteroerotic. It is also clear that this erotic feeling is a matter of fantasy, insulated from intention and action. It is all intimations of delight or disgust.

In Tolstoy, the erotic sensibility of *Sevastopol* is expressed more subtly but is equally fantasy-like. Even in *The Cossacks,* where there is an important love interest, Olenin is as much interested in Luka, his young Cossack rival, as in Maryanka—he wants to *become* Luka.

I can return to *The Privateersman* to make my final point, which is the realism about war these writers combine with their fantasies about sex. On page 3 we read: "Retreat being cut off, the French struggled with all the animosity and rage of mingled hate and despair; while we, infuriated at the obstinate resistance, were filled with vengeance and a thirst for blood. Wedged into one mass, we grappled together, for there was no room for fair fighting, seeking each other's hearts with shortened weapons, struggling and falling together on the deck, rolling among the dead and the dying." There are comparable passages in *Sevastopol,* for Tolstoy and Marryat were serious moralists as well as erotic fantasists, and the sensibility I have traced in their work is allied to a much harsher wisdom. The most interesting point is perhaps that alliance itself, an alliance forged in the adventure of war. That most male and most gender-specific of all activities selects and realizes certain potentialities of the human imagination and creates the sensibility of adventure.

The Story's Decline

By the last quarter of the nineteenth century, the historical romance had lost status. Dumas, who had in his youth been ranked with Hugo and Balzac, ceased to be taken seriously. Realism had become dominant, and Flaubert was the hero of the world of letters. When *Madame Bovary* came out, Dumas threw his copy on the floor, saying, "If that is good, then everything we have written since 1830 is worthless."[27] The historical romance, in consequence, changed character. The idea of it lost clear outlines, being melted down into the general idea, adventure, and adventure itself lost status, at least among men and women of letters.

Of course, Dumas's story remains popular in some sense, and some of its motifs are useful to contemporary writers. In Kingsley Amis's novels, the hero often finds a saving grace in the masculine comradeship of other young men, which sustains him in his difficulties the way that

27. Hemmings, *King of Romance,* 169.

of the Musketeers sustained d'Artagnan. Just so, motifs from the Robinson story recur in several contemporary writers. But we can only afford to look out for the survival of the stories as wholes.

One way in which the Musketeers story changed was that the history became less important. In Stevenson's hands, for instance, history became more blatantly a source of local color. In his Scottish romances, such as *Kidnapped,* there is still some sense of historical dialectic, but in *Treasure Island* the interest is all episodic and sensational; the Squire and Dr. Livesey take time off from their real lives to go treasure hunting. In G. A. Henty's books the history is perfunctory, and seen entirely from the English point of view.

The factual history that functions as hinterland to the historical romance at its best, comparable to the voyage literature that backs up the *Robinsonade,* can be found in the memoirs of court life and war experience. We can cite as an example the life story of Dumas's own father, who was born in San Domingo in 1762, the illegitimate son of a French noble and a black woman. He was brought to France by his father in 1780, enlisted as a private in the Revolutionary Army, and rose to the rank of general. (Hugo's father was also one of Napoleon's officers, and the poet, like Dumas, remained intensely interested in the Emperor.) André Maurois tells us there were many like General Dumas, mulattoes of noble blood, and they were mostly enthusiasts for the revolution.[28] For instance, he performed heroic exploits that demanded great physical strength as well as courage, and by himself he held a bridge against the attacks of an entire squadron. He was a friend of Murat, another very dashing soldier. But Dumas offended Napoleon during the campaign in Egypt and spent twenty months in jail in Naples. He never recovered his health—he was perhaps poisoned. Thus, much of his life corresponds to his son's themes and plots.

General Dumas died in 1806, when his son was only four, but the latter laid eyes on Napoleon later, in a sacramental moment. The novelist was a man of generous political sympathies, but he conceived a sense of history in which the Napoleonic empire was dominant, as Maurois says. (*War and Peace, Crime and Punishment, Les Misérables,* many of the great novels of nineteenth-century Europe, carry the cult of Napoleon at their heart as part of their inspiration, and there are adventurous elements in each. Napoleonic history is often associated with this adventure type.)

28. Maurois, *The Titans,* 21.

Dumas came to Paris from his mother's home in 1822, when Hugo, Vigny, and Lamartine had just been published. He read Scott and Byron and saw the English actors play Shakespeare. The three English poets seemed to deliver the same message to their French admirer, but Shakespeare was the greatest. "What Dumas found in Shakespeare," says Maurois, "was himself. He, too, possessed the physical energy of the men of the Renaissance."[29] He offered himself to his public as a manifestation of energy.

He was quite radical in politics, in some ways. "Dumas, in spite of his happy exuberance, harbored deep within himself many grievances against society at large, and private enemies in particular."[30] He had been insulted as a mulatto, for instance. And when Garibaldi's revolt broke out, he put his schooner at the command of the rebels and sailed from Sicily to Marseilles to buy them arms. He himself wore a red Garibaldi shirt and received an official appointment. On the other hand, as he himself said, he was friends with all the princes—Bourbon, Orleanist, Bonapartist. Dumas, unlike Scott, could not reconcile opposite values, but he could express all sorts of values with equal zest.

Partly because he cared so little about intellectual consistency and sincerity and turned all his affirmations into rhetorical gestures, he did not come as close as Scott did to winning the laurels of literature. Though in their first years in Paris he and Hugo could appear to be comparable figures, the Académie Française never took Dumas seriously as a candidate. He made his name with historical adventures, while Hugo turned to epic themes and forms. Indeed, like Scott, Dumas undeniably wrote too carelessly, but that was in part because the literary judgment had already gone against them.

In any case, they had created one of the great image-galleries of *potestas*—meaning power in both its official institutional form and in the form of immediate personal violence. *Potestas* is the divinity of the adventure tale, as *Eros* is of the domestic novel. In a story of the Musketeers type, the writer gives examples of every sort of power, from the subtle fencing of a chief minister like Richelieu to a brutal murder done by his hired bullies. The connection between the two, running through all society, is the story's theme.

29. Ibid., 48.
30. Ibid., 224.

5

The Frontiersman Story
The Third Type

From the chronological point of view, one might think, the Frontiersman story should have been discussed before the Three Musketeers type, because the first example, *The Pioneers,* came out twenty years before *Les trois Mousquetaires.* Indeed, Dumas read Cooper's novels with enthusiasm before he began to write in that form himself, and his very popular *Les Mohicans de Paris* was named in allusion to the American writer. There was by then a well-established vogue for seeing a big city in jungle or frontier terms. But before both Dumas and Cooper came, Scott and Scott's Waverley novels, being specimens of the historical type, were subsumed by Dumas and discussed in the preceding chapter.

One difference between the two types was that the Musketeers novel had a dominant mood of exuberant gaiety, especially in Dumas's hands. In the Frontiersman story that mood was replaced by an "epic" dignity, slightly melancholy or stoic. At least this is true of Cooper and of most American writers, who were conscious of writing their national foundation story. (The European writers of Westerns could be more irresponsible because they were more distant from the events.) There *were* un-"respectable" American Westerns, but the phenomena that interest me go with respectability.

Europe acknowledged the dignity of the American writers. Balzac said Cooper was not a romance writer but a historian of America and that Natty Bumppo was more like a great statue than a man (he was a sexless crossbreed of the wilderness with civilization). He believed that Cooper was the only living writer fit to set beside Scott and that his descriptive prose was unique in the way it merged with that great landscape.[1] Dumas was also enthusiastic about Cooper's forests, prairies, and boundless oceans, though he said "absence of substance was well disguised beneath wealth of style."[2] It is clear that both Frenchmen had noticed the "psychological" deficiency in Cooper that strikes us today but that in their time that deficiency was compensated for by something else very exciting.

One way to define that something is as the sublime, understanding that category of aesthetic effect as Burke understood it in his *Treatise Concerning the Sublime and the Beautiful*. In this contrast in aesthetic effects, the sublime has to do with such emotions as awe, fear, dread, and places like mountains, chasms, and ruins, and events like wars, floods, and epic migrations. This kind of effect was the goal of many Frontiersman writers, though in the nineteenth century it was achieved more signally by the American nonfiction writers, such as Dana and Parkman. In the twentieth century, however, in novelists like London, Faulkner, and Mailer, effects of the sublime is one of the things that mark them off from their rivals. (It is interesting to note how often Burke's treatise has been rediscovered in recent years—by Trilling, Jameson, Eagleton—a discovery that must have prepared readers to rediscover adventure.)

Cooper's five Frontiersman stories have a single hero but not a single plot. And of course other writers of such tales had their own heroes. Natty Bumppo had many rivals, for many frontiersmen became famous, in fact and fiction, at more or less the same time. Several biographies were written—for instance, of Daniel Boone. But when Cooper published *The Pioneers* (1823), that novel, like *Robinson Crusoe*, subsumed all the other fictional and factual material before it. Daniel Boone was incorporated into Natty Bumppo almost

1. See George Dekker, *Fenimore Cooper: The Critical Heritage*, 196–200.
2. Dumas, *My Memoirs*, 103.

as completely as Alexander Selkirk was incorporated into Crusoe. But Cooper's novel could not compare with Defoe's story in historical authenticity, or in fictional authority. The *idea* of Natty, diffusely and partially realized over a number of novels, captured the imagination of American and European readers both, but no single plot or text still embodies that idea for us the way *Robinson Crusoe* does.

Nevertheless, we can sketch the outlines of this Frontiersman story hero, and the variables of setting, clearly enough. The frontiersman is a hero who moved between civilization and savagery, in touch with but ahead of his countrymen as they advance their civilization across a continent or across an ocean, across prairies, deserts, archipelagoes, ice-floes. He is their proud precursor, but he is also in flight from them and their civilization; he seeks the consolations of nature and/ or solitude and/or an alien tribal culture. Often he has one true friend, who belongs to another race, as Natty Bumppo has Chingachgook. Some frontiersmen are more the advance guard, some are more the man in retreat; others are equally both, at the same time.

The frontiersman's adventures therefore tend to follow the pattern of the Robinson story rather than that of the Three Musketeers story, to have to do with storms and floods, or prairie fires, or tortures by savages, rather than with the intrigues of court or camp or convent. Book illustrations to Cooper's novels, for instance, show a Natty who closely resembles the pictures of Robinson—dressed in animal skins, both carrying rifle and axe, sighting a prey or resting a friendly hand on a native's shoulder. The Frontiersman story may be said to have taken over from the Robinson story, both in the sense of renewing the topic of white settlement a century after Defoe had introduced it, and in the sense of mythifying the second instead of the first stage in the settlement process—the fight against the indigenous inhabitants of the land. (As we shall see, the Sagaman story may be said to take over from the Three Musketeers type. And there were also waves of renewal within each type's history: the Frontiersman story was revived in France and Germany in the 1850s, again in the 1880s, and in America around 1900.)

Despite that likeness, the frontiersman has more plot contacts with his civilization than the Robinson hero has, his feelings are more divided, and his dealings with civilization are more dialectical. So are his dealings with the other culture. Natty Bumppo is more than once brought to the verge of love and marriage, with women who represent civilization, while in other versions of the Frontiersman type, like the Pocahontas story or the Prisoner of the Caucasus story, the woman is a daughter of the wilderness but the man's relations with her again reflect a dialectic of civilization versus savagery. (In adventure, generally, the savage is superior in dignity and passion, the one more equal to tragedy.) In both cases the erotic has become more important than in the first adventure type, and work has become less important.

Another key relationship the frontiersman has is with a young man of his own race and country, but of superior birth and breeding, who needs to be taught how to live on the frontier: how to live with the wilderness and its animal and native life, which requires a number of skills unknown to city-dwellers (especially to those of the well-to-do classes) and a number of virtues like patience, simplicity, and self-reliance as well as force and cunning and relentlessness. The young man, a member of America's ruling class by birth, must meet the mystery of the continent—a savage mystery, in part—and prove himself against it before he is truly fit to rule. It is an induction, a *rite de passage,* which the old warrior supervises out on the prairie; its spirit is closely related to the *rites de passage* of tribal societies. (This young man is like Scott's young men and shares their fictional weaknesses; the frontiersman is original and, in conception not execution, far superior to Scott's heroes.)

The action of *The Pioneers* takes place after the War of Independence, when Natty Bumppo and Chingachgook are old men living in Templeton, a settlement in New York owned by Judge Temple. The land had belonged to a family called Effingham, but they had fought on the British side during the war and so forfeited the estate. Judge Temple, though by birth a Quaker and not a soldier, represents gentlemanly culture, and quarrels with the "democrats" of Templeton because of the laws he enforces and the standards of taste he upholds. The return home from school of his daughter, Elizabeth, who has been educated to be a perfect American lady, marks the beginning of the action. Love develops between her and a mysterious young man called Edwards who lives and hunts with Natty and his Indian friend, in semi-Indian style, and who is later revealed to be the dispossessed heir of the Effinghams. When they marry, the Temples' ownership of the estate is legitimized, and progress and culture triumph. (Edwards's intimacy with Indians and frontiersmen asserts the claims of the cultured class to own American history too.) But this is at the cost of the old pioneering freedoms: Chingachgook dies, and Natty sets out into the wilderness, away from the settlement, feeling ill at ease where law and order rule and seeking to die in freedom. But this hero proved so popular a symbol of American culture that Cooper was persuaded to revive him and to write about him again and again, at earlier stages of his life.

American literature provides the major case of the Frontiersman adventure, just as the United States provided the major historical case of Europe's frontier. It was by no means the only one, as we shall see, but this country was, and to some extent remained, the white race's land of adventure. That state came into existence, as fact and as idea, during the modern period, when the first adventure novels were being written, and as an idea it was the political product of the forces that found their literary expression in adventure tales. Even Robinson's island was to some degree an objective correlative for feelings about the American promise. The United States was an Enlightenment country, as Henry Steele Commager says, but it was the land of adventure too, for all Europe and even for nations that had no hope of colonizing there.

It was natural that Americans should tell and write adventure tales, partly as a way to define what it meant to be an American. Cooper, and others to a lesser extent, tried to invest such adventures with the dignity of a national epic, though more "alienated" aesthetes, like Edgar Allan Poe, stood for a different and hostile idea of art. But if it was natural that American men of letters should react *against* the adventure tale and try to produce "literature" instead, still some of the best American books have been inspired and shaped by the spirit of the frontier.

The ideas of the frontier and the frontiersman were crucial to America's sense of identity throughout its colonial period, and through its national history up to what we might call its imperial period. Indeed, they still are, and though the myth grows gradually more sentimental and insubstantial with the passing of time, it also gathers meaning and seems to be immortal. Confining the evocative power of that image to the times of F. J. Turner's "Frontier Theory," at the end of the nineteenth century, is as much a mistake as confining the significance of the British Empire to a similar period in British history. In both cases, those were periods of a self-conscious ideology (of the frontier, of the empire), but long before and long after those periods the myth worked powerfully on the general mind, without the blessing of the clerisy or the intelligentsia. It still meant something when President Kennedy spoke of a "new frontier"; it means something when NASA calls space a frontier.

I distinguish two main figures within the composite frontier hero, and two main plots within his story, but in both cases the two are closely connected. The two main figures are the old guide and the young gentleman, and the connection between them develops the theme of Americanism—their relationship is a transaction in becoming American. The old guide, like Natty, *is* America, by virtue of his long years on the frontier, which have filtered the civilization out of his blood, rarefied and purified his links with society. He belongs to the landscape and its animal and savage life, more than to the city and its institutions. The young man, like Edwards, has birth, breeding, and education; he exemplifies the best of American conscience and consciousness. But those very advantages, that refinement, threaten his claim to be an American. He goes to the frontier to be born again, and the mark of his manhood is his acceptance by the old guide. This heroic pair can be found in American novels all the way from *The Pioneers* to *Why Are We in Vietnam?* nearly one hundred and fifty years later. Their names change from Natty Bumppo and Oliver Edwards, via many variations, to Big Luke Fellinka and Randall Jethroe.

The two plots are very like each other. They differ mostly the way nineteenth-century fiction plots generally differed from nonfiction, by relying heavily on a love-romance and an inheritance-imbroglio. In *The Pioneers* (and other novels by Cooper, and novels by R. M. Bird and W. G. Simms, to name some of the earliest) the young man has been deprived of a literal and legal inheritance, and his adventures on the frontier and apprenticeship to the old guide have the (clumsily contrived) effect of winning this inheritance back for him. Along with this property he acquires a highly desirable bride, usually also the object of the villain's lust and the wooing of whom has given rise to many of the plot's peripeteia.

In the nonfictional story (found in R. H. Dana's *Two Years Before the Mast*, Francis Parkman's *Oregon Trail*, and Washington Irving's *Tour on the Prairie*) there is again a young man and an old guide (or recognizable variants thereof), and again the essential story tells how the young man renounces his class privileges, subjects himself to the rigors of the sailor's life (rounding Cape Horn) or the trapper's life (fighting Indians), and satisfies the old guide and becomes a true American. There is no business here with forged wills and wicked lawyers, and the end of the story is not marriage but a return to his home, in both geographical and class terms (which is what marriage meant in the fictional plot). In place of the peripeteia of the fictional plot, the autobiographical writers give the reader a more detailed, episodic, and anecdotal account of the toughening and Americanizing process. Implicitly, also, the psychology of the young gentleman is exposed in a more interesting way by Dana and Parkman than it is by Cooper and Bird. On the whole, the former give a much more convincing picture of the young American gentleman rising to the national and democratic challenge.

The love and law elements in the plot were in fact taken over by this adventure type from the Three Musketeers story. For instance, *Guy Mannering*, the second Waverley novel, is about a property, a disinheritance, a usurpation by legal fraud. Scott's and Dumas's novels are full of such stories, and Scott in particular imagined the legal aspects vividly. The law was one of his greatest interests, and his way to imagine value conflicts and reconciliations. But in the hands of American novelists this plot did not flourish and bear fruit, which gives us an instance of how the adventure types branch off away from each other and how certain plots, or parts of plots, suit one type and not another.

The inheritance plot seems to have been popular enough with Cooper's first readers; it reassured them that this was high-class fiction. But subsequent readers found it less satisfying than the rest of the Frontiersman adventure, which as a whole continued to be popular reading until past the end of the century. Its thematic function seems to have been to satisfy an anxiety in the contemporary book-buying public about legitimacy—the legitimacy of the United States as a nation like the European powers, and the legitimization of the gentleman class as the natural rulers of America.

These are the anxieties hidden within the interest Cooper's readers took in plots like that of *The Pioneers*. Edwards/Effingham is the true heir and, when disinherited by the Revolution, he reacquires the land by marrying the daughter of the new American owners, and deserves it by apprenticing himself to Natty. The property-plot interest died in the course of the nineteenth century, and there is no trace of it in

Mailer's novel. We might explain the death of that interest by the solid establishment of the United States, with an undeniable (if uneasy) gentleman class. But those facts should have made the old guide plot equally out-of-date.

Along with the inheritance plot, the Frontier adventure took from the Musketeers story (in Scott's version, above all) its elaborate and pompous literary styling: the formal prose, the poetic epigraphs, the characterization by "humor," the long introductions and conclusions, full of historical generalizations, and so on. The appeal of this died together with the plot's appeal, and in order to understand it now, we have to understand the caste interests of the readers. The literary novelists of America were telling the Frontier adventure in such a way as to claim the frontier for the gentleman class, claiming it away from the frontiersmen themselves, or at least the "frontier writers." The latter dealt in nonliterary anecdotes and tall tales and southwestern humor and expressed the frontier culture, with its boasting, swearing antinomianism, much more directly than Cooper could or wanted to. The figure Davy Crockett, for instance, made of himself in his political speeches and writings, where he called himself "the Wild Man of the West," had to be overcome by Natty Bumppo, had to be dislodged from his claim to represent the frontier, before the gentlemen of America could feel secure in their position. The pompous style turned the Frontiersman hero into a classical statue, as Balzac said, and gave the adventure epic dignity.

The first two types of adventure also served the caste interests of particular groups. The Robinson Crusoe figure clearly represented the low-church or nonconformist merchant class, and the Musketeers represented the aristo-military class. But the case of the Frontiersman adventure is unusually clear-cut in this matter of caste interest. This type of story demonstrably functioned as part of the ideology of the gentleman class in America and forged an imaginative link between that class and the frontier myth which enables the former to establish a cultural hegemony.

The most striking demonstration of this comes in the careers of two popular politicians, John Charles Frémont and Theodore Roosevelt. Frémont, as a handsome and dashing army officer, led exploring expeditions westward in the 1840s and wrote official reports on them that became best-sellers. Kit Carson, the famous trapper, acted as Frémont's guide, and the two men came to be associated with each other in the public mind, like the old guide and young gentleman in so many adventures. This was an important help to Frémont's political career, which led him to be nominated twice for the presidency, in 1856 and 1864. But even more striking is the case of Roosevelt, who *became* president and who built his spellbinding public persona on his exploits as a frontiersman in the Dakotas and on his friendship with other frontiersmen. All the young gentlemen of the East who had (if only in imagination) gone west and made good as men finally entered the White House in the person of Theodore Roosevelt—and this was in the twentieth century.

Indeed, up to at least 1950, the "woodsman" elements in the Frontiersman story kept the power to please and excite. We can associate those elements with the Robinson story insofar as they had to do with the techniques of survival and the themes of frontier life, alone and far from civilization. But there are great differences. As has been remarked, American writers did not retell the Robinson story, important as that myth was to immigrants and settlers, and the form they did develop had a different historical focus and reference: the Indian wars. When we look at the American writers for description of work techniques, for instance, we find very little of the authenticity Defoe offered us. The principal technique of the American hero, his woodcraft or forest lore, is often highly suspect (as Twain pointed out in his essay on Cooper). It is also used, let us note, principally to track down Indians.

To take a more extreme case, in Robert Montgomery Bird's *Nick of the Woods* (the best of these books) the central debate is over whether whites should scalp Indians when they kill them. The debate is developed step-by-step through much of the book, and the young hero, Roland Forrester, a captain in the American army, is of course horrified by the idea. But the old guide who convinces him to scalp, Nathan Slaughter, has experience on his side. Nathan is, paradoxically, a Quaker by birth and conviction, though liable to periods of homicidal madness caused by sufferings in the wars. The argument for violence is thus ingeniously doubled because of the split in Nathan's identity. In his ordinary, daytime self he is a nonviolent man of religion and will not join his frontier neighbors in anti-Indian expeditions, but at night he turns into a raving Indian-killer. In the first half of the book, when we see the daytime Nathan, Roland the officer teaches him to be manly and ardent and ready to fight, like himself. In the second half, where the other part of Nathan's personality gradually becomes dominant, it is the Indian-killer who shows the captain that war on the frontier must be bloodier than he is ready to admit—uglier than regular armies and military ethics know.

In this Frontiersman story the crucial place of violence in adventure is especially clear. In *Kit Carson's Autobiography* (1856) the modern reader is continually upset by the record of killings (the killing of Indians by the writer and his friends) done with the most meager of motives and of emotional affect. This is the only record we have written by an old guide himself, and he does not have the literary skill, or aplomb, to turn violence into "adventure." Although violence was part of the frontier life, it was barely admitted to the general consciousness, and then in edulcorated form. It took the brilliant boldness of Francis Parkman, in his *Oregon Trail*, to give the love of violence a full place in the adventure story, without a blush or a stammer. On the whole, the nonfictional adventurers avoided the topic. In *Two Years Before the Mast*, violence is always associated with bad men, from whom the writer has distanced himself.

The Robinson story was the dream of starting traditional life, again, from scratch, far from civilization, in some sense purified. The American authors needed a new story—about a life morally *grosser* than the old one—in some ways. They spoke for those who had made the crossing, begun the new life, and found themselves to be trespassing on other people's land and taking their lives—found themselves engaged, in their idyllic newfound land, in war. They wrote, mostly, from the point of view of their racial comrades, though not without a troubled concern about the others. There is a strong pathos in Cooper's portraits of "noble Redskins," while Bird, who in *Nick of the Woods* is so luridly xenophobic, shows a strong feeling for the Indians in other writings.

In his introduction to a later edition of the novel, Bird refers to a hostile review of the first edition by the English novelist Harrison Ainsworth. The latter had objected to Bird's xenophobic depiction of the Indians as bloodthirsty, a depiction that of course justified the violence and vengefulness of Roland and Nathan and the frontiersmen. The details of Ainsworth's charge and Bird's defense need not concern us here. What is important is to see again the self-separation of this adventure type from the parent. Ainsworth was a popular adventure novelist of Scott's school. He spoke for the Three Musketeers type of story, which was more "chivalric" and less grimly realistic about bloodshed—no doubt in part because it was much less close, in date and place and spirit, to the fighting in question. The wars described by Scott and Dumas and Ainsworth were history, or at least legend; those described by Bird were more like news.

The American Frontier Story Told by Non-Americans

The Frontier story, in its American setting, was also told by many Europeans: Captain Mayne Reid in England, for instance, "Charles Sealsfield" and Karl May in Germany, "Gabriel Ferry" and Gustave Aimard in France. Aimard (1818–83) was not a distinguished writer, but he presents an interesting case, in his popularity. The National Union Catalog devotes eighteen pages to titles by Aimard. He went to South America when very young and lived ten years with "savages." He then traveled in Turkey and the Caucasus (lands of adventure), becoming involved in revolutions and conspiracies. When the European revolutions of 1848 broke out, he was back in Paris and joined the "garde mobile." When the new regime was established, he went back to South and Central America and got involved in the trouble at Sonoma in Mexico, which attracted the German adventure writers too.

It was this life-experience that Aimard used to make his stories. After his return to France, he often wrote two or three stories at a time for twenty years. They featured exotic descriptions and were frequently serialized, in *Le Moniteur, La Presse,* and *Liberté.* After the revolution in France in 1870 (in which he again played a military role), Aimard resumed writing, but with less success. He is said to have revived the vogue for Cooper and his subject matter after it had faded in France. Robert Louis Stevenson mentions him as a writer he read much by in Scotland. The *grande encyclopédie* says Aimard's books were "safe": "They do not trouble the heart and they excite the imagination." This was the accolade the moralists awarded to adventure. Adventure was morally safe because it did not trouble the heart, the seat of love.

"Gabriel Ferry" also lived in America, in his case in Mexico and in the 1830s. His *Le coureur de bois* appeared serially in *L'Ordre* in 1850 and later in an eight-volume book form. (He also wrote a *Chasse aux Cossaques,* about the equivalent Russian subject.) This had many translations and adaptations into German, while Captain Reid produced a version in English called *The Woodrangers.* This has a plot quite unlike that of Cooper's American paradigm—it belongs to another subgenre, focused on gold mines and the politics of Mexico, to which we shall return—but one of the heroes, Bois-Rose, is a version of Natty Bumppo. (The main difference is that Bois-Rose will occasionally scalp an Indian, and in general Ferry is closer to Bird in his endorsement of frontier savagery. Like Bird, he was reproved for this in his home country—in his case, Barbey d'Aurevilly was the critic.) He was said to be France's answer to Cooper and to be Cooper's equal in his power to create the Epic of the Wilderness.

On the whole, however, the French Westerns were less remarkable than the German equivalents, and the cultural effect of the latter seems to have been greater. "Charles Sealsfield" (1793–1864, his real name Karl Postl) led an even more adventurous life than the French writers named. Having been a Jesuit priest in Austro-Hungary, he escaped from his order in disguise, made his way to America, and conspired there and in Switzerland with Freemasons and Bonapartists. A much more remarkable writer than Aimard, he gave us one of the few realistic (and grotesque) pictures of the frontier. But these elements in his work made it quite unlike Cooper's, and perhaps for that reason Sealsfield's work was left to one side of the mainstream of Frontiersman fiction.

Karl Postl arrived in America in 1823 and published his first book, *The United States*, there in 1827. Both his titles and his characters' names openly declare his themes, and he used many of Cooper's motifs. For instance, in *The Making of an American* the nobly born Louis de Vignerolles learns from Nathan Strong, the old guide, how to be an American. In *The Indian Chief* (1829) the setting is different (Sealsfield writes first about Georgia, then about Natchez, and then about New Orleans), but the spirit is the same. The action occurs in 1812, the time of the war against England and of Andrew Jackson's victory at the Battle of New Orleans. Tokeah the Indian chief is grim and savage, but noble withal; the hero, Arthur Graham, is very noble and in love with a Spanish beauty, Rosa de Montgomez. (In Cooper's *The Prairie* and some of Marryat's sea stories also, the Anglo-Saxon heroes appropriate the best of the enemy nation—Spain or France—by marrying their loveliest daughters, who are particularly high-bred.)

Sealsfield gives a lot of firsthand detail about frontiersmen and Indians both—much more than Cooper gives—but the surface of his tale is uneven and the form is misshapen. Frontier ideas and frontier habits are mismatched with those of literary convention. Examples are the ghost-story anecdotes of *The Cabin Book* or the frontier humor about elections.

The political ideas are crudely expansionist. In *America: Glorious and Chaotic Land,* Sealsfield tells us that Quakers won't do on the frontier because "they would bend and give in, they would rather put up with anything than fight back, revolt, and strike hard." This is the feeling of *Nick of the Woods,* now expressed in dogmatic form: "We in Texas don't need so much quiet and orderly people, we need restless minds, men that have a noose around their necks and sparks in their bodies, who don't value their lives above a nutshell and are handy with their rifles" (pp. 220–21). Sealsfield compares these men with the Normans, who founded a splendid empire and whose blood makes the Anglo-Saxon peoples still conquerors (a prevision of the Sagaman idea). American frontiersmen "pay no attention to history and value only the present. They are no Hamlets but men of action, and with them world history rolls along ten times more rapidly than in Europe" (p. 69).

In Sealsfield's *Cabin Book* we read: "the high interests of liberty—as well political as religious—urgently demand the separation of Texas from the mother country [Mexico]. So, at least, reasoned our greatest revolutionists. I allow that these reasons would in no way stand the tests of Grotius and Pufendorf—but what would have become of England, what of the world, if professors of international rights had rolled the wheel of the world's history?" (p. 164).

Sealsfield claimed that there was an elective affinity between Germany and the United States, and his books are said to have directly stimulated the large organized migration of Germans to Texas in the 1840s (other writers did similar work). The class affiliation of this migration was variable; what was consant was the love of adventure. The Verein zum Schutze deutscher Auswanderer in Texas (Society for the Protection of German Emigrants in Texas) was founded in Bieberich in 1842; five reigning princes and many aristocrats were among its members. Its aim, which had British government approval, was to build a buffer state to check the expansion of the United States into Mexico. Frédéric Armand Strubberg helped to run the settlement of Friedrichsburg in Texas before he moved on to Arkansas in 1848. His *Amerikanische Jagd- und Reiseabenteuern,* hunting and traveling adventures published in 1857, had great success. Somewhat later writers of German Westerns included Friedrich Gerstaecker (*Fluss-piraten des Mississippis* [River Pirates of the Mississippi], 1848) and Balduin Moellhausen (*Das Mormonen-maedchen* [The Mormon Maiden], 1864).

But the most famous of all was Karl May (1842–1912). The main motif of his frontier adventures, the love between a white man and his American Indian friend, was directly in the Cooper line. Perhaps for that reason May had by the end of the nineteenth century a larger audience for his Western stories (though he had not then visited that frontier) than any other writer in the world.

It is in *Winnetou* that we first meet Old Shatterhand, then a young German working as a tutor in America. Though only a greenhorn (a word May makes play with), he is an expert shot and horseman, is chosen by experienced frontiersmen to become a surveyor for a railroad that is moving west, and wins the friendship of the scouts, who are the aristocracy of the West. (May has a strong sense of hierarchy in manhood, and the young man wins his title by boxing inferior types into submission.) Each episode introduces some new feature of the frontier—grizzlies, buffalo, wild horses, Indians. Shatterhand feels ashamed before the Indians, because the whites are stealing their land; indeed, he wants to become an Indian himself. He becomes the comrade of the huge, bronze, noble Winnetou. The latter's sister falls in love with the handsome German, but it is Winnetou who has his heart.

Westerns were only one of May's interests. He also wrote Easterns, about the adventures of a German by the name of Kara-ben-Nemsi in the Turkish empire. And more interesting than either of these is his work in another subgenre of adventure, to which we must return. But May produced forty volumes of Westerns, translated en bloc into twenty languages and adapted for films and television; and there is still an annual Karl May festival at Bad Segeburg. The magazine *Der Spiegel* has claimed that May had more influence on German youth than any other writer between Goethe and Mann.

That is not implausible if we understand May to stand for all the other writers of Westerns. In *Three Centuries of Children's Books in Germany*, Bettina Huerlimann says that almost every twelve-year-old in Germany knows as much about the Sioux as he does about the original inhabitants of his own country (p. 113). She says even May was remarkably accurate about such matters and reminds us how large a change in German culture this constituted. In Goethe's childhood, no one played at Cowboys and Indians, but nowadays such games are a necessary part of childhood. A 1959–60 questionnaire on the books most popular with

German children gave pride of place to *Leatherstocking, Winnetou, Robinson Crusoe, Treasure Island,* and *Tom Sawyer.*[3] Note that of the five (all adventures) only one was by a German (and that an American frontier-tale), the other four being by English or American writers. Germans do seem to have been more affected by adventure than other peoples, at least judging by literary evidence. Anneliese Hoelder quotes Severin Tuettgers's *Literarische Erziehung* (1931) as saying, "Without the adventure, mankind would never have awakened from the fairytale gloaming of pre-history, and would never have known or altered the face of the earth."[4]

Other Frontiers

There were, however, other white frontiers beside the American, with their own adventure tales. The Russian frontier in the Caucasus, for instance, inspired a number of writers in the first half of the nineteenth century, including Pushkin, Lermontov, and Tolstoy. Also like the American frontier, this one drew foreign adventure-writers, such as Alexandre Dumas, Gustave Aimard, and W.H.G. Kingston (the first two actually visited the Caucasus).

In Tolstoy's short novel *The Cossacks* we can see some close equivalents to the American frontier-tale (though also to the Waverley story, for the Russians looked at the Caucasus the way the English looked at Scotland). In fact, Tolstoy acknowledged the connection in the middle of his adventure by having his hero think of Cooper's tales and how similar his own adventures are. In this story the young man of birth and breeding, Olenin, leaves Moscow at the beginning of the story for the Caucasus, where the Cossacks are fighting on Russia's behalf against the local tribes, called Chechens. Like Tolstoy in real life, Olenin lives in a Cossack household and makes friends both with Russian army officers and with the villagers. Eroshka, an old Cossack guide and hunter, introduces Olenin to frontier life and values; Luka is Olenin's comrade-rival, and Maryanka is the daughter, not quite of the wilderness but of a Cossack wildness. The Cossacks are the frontiersmen, as close in sym-

---

3. Anneliese Hoelder, *Das Abenteuerbuch im Spiegel der Maennlichen Reifezeit,* 26.
4. Ibid., 7.

pathy to those they fight as they are to the Russians they fight *for,* and the tribal Chechens are very like the American Indians, especially in the way the Russians think about them.

Tolstoy's hero, just like Parkman's, for instance, goes to the frontier with romantic ideas about the splendor of nature there, about a rebirth he will undergo. He is, as Parkman is, disillusioned. Nature turns out much grimmer than they had thought, and more disturbing. Olenin falls in love with Maryanka, but she is tempted only briefly by what he, as a Russian gentleman, can offer her. It is the Cossack life that is really glamorous, to him and her—and to Tolstoy. And so both the latter and Parkman *did* find nature and *were* reborn, but in ways that fitted them to become great writers, not children of nature.

Two other stories of the Caucasus frontier, which inspired Russian writers, we can call "The Prisoner of the Caucasus" and "Ammalet Bek," after famous literary versions of them. The first tells how a Russian, held a long-term prisoner in a tribal village, manages to escape with the help of a Chechen (Caucasian) girl. This help is self-sacrificing— in some versions the girl is simply left behind, in others she actually dies. The other story is about a Chechen boy or man hostage who has lived with the Russians long enough to feel himself Russian in important ways. He finally breaks away from his captors, killing a Russian friend as he does so, and joins his own people, only to find that he no longer belongs among them either. (There are Anglo-Saxon variants on both these stories. The latter story was sometimes told about Indian princes educated in England.)

It has often been remarked that the course of Russian history paralleled American history, especially in the tides of migration and conquest. The progress of the Russian frontier eastward across Asia kept pace in many ways with that of the U.S. frontier westward across America. These were the two great tides of white, or Western, civilization, in terms of the numbers involved. There were parallel imperialist heroes in both countries, like Ermak, who led the Cossacks across the Urals into Siberia, and Raleigh, who led the English across the Atlantic into North and Central America. In the early nineteenth century there were comparable rulers and fighters, like Ermolov in the Caucasus and Jackson in America (and the Lawrence brothers in India), and hence there were comparable works of literary adventure—by Tolstoy and Parkman, for instance, in the 1840s—inspired in part by those historical heroes.

Not all frontiers inspired writers equally. The Russian frontier in

Central Asia, for instance, never attracted Russian writers the way the Caucasus did. And the quality of the work inspired also varied from frontier to frontier. The French frontier in North Africa (the Sahara replacing the prairie, the Touaregs replacing the Indians, the Foreign Legion replacing the frontiersmen) became an imaginative focus for French, English, and German writers and later for Hollywood filmmakers. But though the desert seems to have inspired "classical" (i.e., heroic and epic) descriptions of the landscape (Henri de Montherlant in France, Charles Doughty and T. E. Lawrence in England), the adventure story about the North African frontier, as told by Ouida in England and May in Germany, was comparatively crude.

Ouida's novel, *Under Two Flags* (1867), may serve as an example, partly because it had so many imitators. It is very unlike the American frontier novel in a number of ways. For instance, the hero is an English Guardsman when we first meet him, and he does not even arrive in North Africa until page 246 of 806 pages. The first third of the novel is a fashionable-dandy fantasy of the kind that had been popular during the Regency. "Bertie Cecil" is then forced to enlist in a French regiment under an assumed name, because of a high society intrigue, but he remains quite detached from the landscape of the action. Indeed, the whole book continues to be colored by aristocratic titles, and details of fashionable luxuries, and boudoir flirtations. All this could not be less like the world of Natty Bumppo. The hero is neither an old guide nor a young apprentice; he has been prepared for his frontier life by being a Guardsman/dandy/jockey. (Ouida's novel makes propaganda for a more frivolous aristocracy than Cooper is interested in, and is more frivolous propaganda.) Moreover, the character for whom the book is famous is the androgynous young vivandiere, Cigarette, who loves the hero and gives her life for him. There is no equivalent for this in the American Frontiersman story, and only a remote parallel in the Russian frontier stories. (On the other hand, the first scene in which we meet Cigarette—and something in the general conception of the character—may have been borrowed by Kipling for the first scene in *Kim*, for the English in India were seen partly the way the French in North Africa were seen.)

However, North Africa *was* a white frontier, and the Chasseurs d'Afrique regiment Cecil joins is involved in constant skirmishing against the desert tribes, just as the Cossacks are against the Chechens. The hero, moreover, feels himself morally and emotionally on the side of those he fights against. He tells his French comrades, "You are Might, and They are Right" (p. 251). The best of his comrades, indeed, feel as he does about the moral issues. Like the Cossacks in the Caucasus, and like many frontiersmen in American Frontier stories, they admire and sympathize with their enemies, have taken over cultural traits from them, and often resent the city folk of their own race, whose disapproval they feel and on whose behalf they are risking their lives.

This pattern of behavior expresses the dialectic between civilization and savagery important to this genre, which gives it one of its ranges of pathos. On the frontier, and indeed within the circle of war everywhere, the loyalties of fighting men veer away from the ideologies of the governments. (The American Frontier adventure, when in the hands of gentleman writers, is atypical in this regard because it disguises this divergence or mutes this truth.)

It is perhaps worth noting that the novel that largely set the pattern for Ouida's, G. A. Lawrence's *Guy Livingstone* (1857), has episodes in which Ireland serves as the frontier where Englishmen can and must behave like men of empire. Guy Livingstone plays the hero (the adventurer) when the peasantry revolt. In real life such episodes must have been frequent throughout the nineteenth century, and stories about them must have formed part of the anecdotal culture of the English gentleman class in Ireland, but I know of few literary treatments. (Of course, tales of a frontier and frontier behavior only a few miles away would be more disconcerting than tales of Asia and Africa. The facts of such a case would be more difficult to dissolve into adventure feelings.)

There were also many adventures set in other parts of the British Empire. Captain Marryat, for instance, has one set in Canada, *Settlers in Canada* (1845), and another set in South Africa, *The Mission* (1844). The latter is interesting for its introduction of a motif that was to have a long career: the white hunters adopt a native boy, in this case a Bushman, remarkably quick in his intelligence and his feelings, who attaches himself to them—that is, the best of native life transfers its loyalties to the whites. (Henry Stanley the explorer, in real life, adopted such a boy.) Captain Mayne Reid wrote a South African novel, *The Bush Boys* (1856), and there were two partly Australian novels by well-known English authors, Henry Kingsley's *Recollections of Geoffrey Hamlyn* (1847) and Bulwer-Lytton's *The Caxtons* (1849).

On the whole, however, these British Empire variants do not constitute an important subgenre of their own or a clear variant on the American Frontier story. This is perhaps because the Empire thought of itself so little as a frontier, as a place where the British national destiny was enacted. The oceans set a psychic space between the homeland and the colonies. For a long time the people at home thought of the latter, if at all, as empty spaces waiting for settlers to fill and develop them. The one exception was the Anglo-Indian community, and later Kipling's readership. But they then thought of the Empire in terms of the Roman Empire and of consuls and proconsuls, an image very unlike that of the American frontier.

This exception occurred partly because of the extraordinary spectacle India presented of a great and ancient culture subjected to a much smaller but modern power (the East subdued to the West) and partly because of the Mutiny of 1857, the dangers and the triumphs of which seemed, at least to Anglo-Indians, to be the raw material for a work of literature that would be "the epic of the race." Many Anglo-Indian writers did try to give literary form to the English experience in India, but epic was a doubtfully viable form in the nineteenth century—the nearest approach to it was adventure, which lacked literary endorsement. And though one element in what the Anglo-Indians wrote was certainly adventure, they evolved no well-defined adventure form until *Kim* came out in 1904—and that belonged to the Wanderer type.

Perhaps the most interesting feature of English adventures set in India is the way some writers combined stories of the Rajputs with their tales of the English. The latter had admired the romantic military legends of the prince of Rajputana from the beginning of the nineteenth century. James Tod's *Annals and Antiquities of Rajasthan* (1829–32) was a popular compilation of those legends. By the end of the century some writers tried to fuse the two kinds of hero and legend.

There are traces of this in Kipling, but it is carried much further by a writer of the next generation, Maud Diver (a close friend of Kipling's sister), who has heroes of mixed blood, Rajput and English. However, this use of earlier legends is very like the contemporary use of the Icelandic sagas and should perhaps be considered under the Sagaman heading. Both literary strategies had dangerous implications of atavism or racism, for they put a stress on the blood link between two groups of Aryans in both cases: between the English and, on the one hand, the Vikings and, on the other hand, the Rajputs.

Finally, it is worth pointing out that the sea has always been both a frontier and the object of a cult, especially in England and on the Eastern Seaboard of the United States. The sea was the symbol and locus of personal freedom everywhere, and the navy was considered the front line of defense of British political liberties. It is therefore not surprising that many sea adventures have the structure analyzed in this chapter. In such a story, a young man of birth and breeding must make a difficult adjustment to the physical and social severities of life at sea and learns the necessary techniques and wisdom from an old sailor—himself without birth or breeding. We find this story told by Smollett and Marryat and later by W.H.G. Kingston in England and by Cooper and Melville in America.

The American case is especially interesting here, because Cooper's sea adventures are far better than his forest tales, though less famous. Balzac, in his essay on *The Pathfinder,* said Cooper had two great gifts: for *describing* the sea and sailors and for *idealizing* the American landscape. His pilot-hero, in *The Pilot,* is in many ways parallel to Leatherstocking, and Cooper's knowledge of and enthusiasm for sailing is much greater than what he shows for tracking. *The Crater,* a Robinson story with a large element of sea adventure, is perhaps his best single novel. Politically, moreover, Cooper would have liked to see the United States look eastward, toward the ocean and Europe, rather than westward, toward continental empire. The drive west meant both the slaughtering of Indians and releasing the antinomian forces in American society. Both those ideas were repugnant to Cooper. But the public welcomed his Natty Bumppo stories with such enthusiasm that he was induced to write more of them, and so to help fuel the drive to empire.

Melville also resisted the literary role forced on him as an adventure writer, though for different reasons. He felt keenly the split between adventure and literature-or-art (which he conceived more romantically than Cooper did) and wanted to be a great writer, like Shakespeare. But he was first published as a writer of sea-and-island adventures, and his public, via his publisher, pressed him for more of the same. *Typee,* his first book and the most interesting of this group, follows the outline of the Frontiersman adventure roughly, though it combines with that outline motifs from other adventure types. The hero, a common sailor but a gentleman by birth, abandons ship to live alone with a Polynesian tribe on the island of Nukuheva, a sort of frontier where white men meet natives. He represents white civilization to the Typee, and in turn studies their culture. There is the familiar dialectic between the advantages and disadvantages of white civilization. The tribe practices cannibalism, and the young man makes various attempts to escape from them, to return to his homeland. His final success is the climax of the story.

This story differs from the pattern in two important ways, though. The hero does not engage in violence, and he prefers the native culture to his own (except for their cannibalism) because it is a culture of happiness, pleasure, and relaxation. That erotic and hedonistic culture is presented to the reader in glowing colors, while the white presence, both in its military and its missionary form, is destructive. In many ways, therefore, the book is an antiadventure, and this expresses a spiritual rebellion in the author: his calling to write symbolic and poetic narratives under cover of sea adventures, as he did in *Mardi* and *Moby Dick*. But in *Typee* he masked that rebellion by dwelling at length on the natives' cannibalism and the hero's attempts to escape. These stresses brought the narrative line, and superficially the thematic message, back into conformity with the adventure genre—native cannibalism being, from *Robinson Crusoe* on, the ultimate sanction of white imperialism.

Billy Budd, left incomplete at Melville's death, contains elements of the Frontiersman story among the chaos of fragments that compose it. Billy himself is a clear case of the young apprentice to the frontier life— not that he is of superior class and breeding, but he is surrounded with a halo of personal beauty and innocence that has a comparable effect. He turns for training in the mysteries of sea life to various elders, notably the Dansker and Captain Vere. But Melville's other themes and interests cut across any development of the Frontiersman story.

If we ask about factual equivalents for sea adventures, the answer lies close to hand in American writing. *Two Years Before the Mast* is a brilliant evocation of the sea and sailing and shipboard life, which follows the thematic structure of the Frontier adventure. The description of ocean storms and icebergs, and of the movement of the ship, are the nearest thing to epic writing in the nineteenth century. The hero, Dana himself, interrupts his studies at Harvard to sail "before the mast," down the length of the American coast and up from Cape Horn to California (still nominally part of the Spanish Empire). He learns to do a sailor's work and live a sailor's life, and at the same time he sees his nation's manifest destiny to oust the Spaniards and to occupy California, and ultimately the entire continent. The two processes, personal and national, are interdependent, as they are in all the best adventures, from *Robinson Crusoe* on. It is no wonder that the British Admiralty purchased large numbers of *Two Years Before the Mast* for British sailors to read.

As for the land frontier, Washington Irving's *Tour on the Prairie* and Parkman's *Oregon Trail* offer us elderly guides very like Natty Bumppo teaching young men of sensibility. These have some interesting variations on the fictional model—for instance, the frontiersman's erotic appreciation of each other. Parkman's Henry Chatillon is presented to us with discreet stresses on his personal beauty, and there is something similar in Irving's story. Cooper censored much more severely all suggestions of erotic charm in his hero. Sea stories traditionally admitted that theme, under the label "The Handsome Sailor," and we find examples in Dana and Melville, as well as those already cited in Marryat.

In the Russian Caucasus the life of General Ermolov (which fascinated Pushkin) and that of adventure-novelist Bestuzhev-Marlinsky (who served in the army on that frontier after being involved in the Decembrist rising of 1825) may serve as examples of the sources that inspired and informed the fiction writers and their readers. The duel in which the famous writer Lermontov lost his life was a Caucasian adventure. It arose out of Lermontov's mocking another Russian dandy's affectation of Chechen-brave costume. The frontier situation, with its strong suggestions of historical theater, stimulated men to compete against each other in different cultural styles of bravery.

In India also there was a great quantity of adventure anecdote in circulation, in oral and written form. The lives of English women, for instance, were often strikingly different in India from what they would have been in England, and one of the differences was symbolized in the riding whip and the pistol that the Anglo-Indian—woman as much as man—used so much more freely and had to be ready to use against other human beings.

In a story by Sara Jeanette Duncan, a woman returning to India reflects, "Dear old England . . . seemed to hold by comparison a great many soft, unsophisticated people, immensely occupied about very peculiar trifles. How difficult it had been, all the summer, to be interested!" Aboard ship she finds "my own ruling, administering, soldiering little lot . . . acute, alert, with the marks of travail on them. Gladly I went in and out of the women's cabins, and listened to the argot of the men. . . . The look of wider seas and skies, the casual, experienced glance, the touch of irony and of tolerance, how well I knew it and how well I liked it."[5] The story is called "A Mother in India," and its boldest point is that this mother is bored by her own daughter because the latter has been brought up in England and has English limitations.

The Anglo-Indian women were also sexually freer, being much further from the sanctions of family and society, or were thought to be. And then there were books, like Maud Diver's *Hero of Herat,* about the Afghan wars, and the official biographies of the great Indian soldiers, such as Sir Henry and Sir John Lawrence. The lives of the English in India were cast in heroic or adventure form, and they were conscious of it, quite apart from the mutiny itself, which was treated as a would-be epic by Flora Annie Steel in her *Breath upon the Waters* (1897).

Inversions of the Frontiersman Adventure

There were no sardonic inversions of this adventure, as close and careful in their relation to the original as were those of the Robinson story. But we do find elements of irony that are quite unlike those other inversions, in that these are not satirical mockeries by men of letters but protests by frontiersmen themselves or their spokesmen. The point of the satire is that the original form is too literary. This we find in various books by Mark Twain, perhaps especially in *Roughing It* (1872), a compilation of his journalism. He refers scornfully there to that key Cooper concept "the noble red man" and in other places explicitly attacks both Cooper and Scott.

Twain was deeply involved in inverting several of the adventurous types. His *Connecticut Yankee in King Arthur's Court* may be as good an inversion of the historical romance as we have. In *Roughing It* he also mocked the legend of Captain Cook, one of the heroes of sea adventure and a historical equivalent for Robinson. Twain frankly declared himself out of sympathy with Cook, irreverent about his martyrdom. This seems to reflect a big check suffered by the development of adventure mythology.

But it is important to remember the pervasive irony of Twain's writing, which takes the form of self-mockery too and so supports what he makes fun of. His image of himself on the frontier is antiheroic; he stresses his

5. Sara Jeanette Duncan, *The Pool in the Desert,* 9–10.

laziness, boastfulness, cowardice—the way he and many others don't measure up to the frontiersman ideal. "Charles Sealsfield" was a precursor in this satire, and Stephen Crane a successor, in stories like "The Blue Hotel."

A striking contrast, superficially seen, is *The Oregon Trail,* where Parkman describes his companions as a series of clearly distinguished types that make up the hierarchy of frontier life: the hero, the companion, the neophyte, the enemy, and the fool. Of them all, the lowest in the hierarchy is a man Parkman's friends call Tête Rouge, who is the comic butt of all their mockery because he does not measure up to the challenges of frontier life in any way.

Parkman makes Tête Rouge the opposite figure to himself, but Twain presents himself as another such. (One cannot but remember Twain's red hair.) But that means that, however ironic, both were fascinated by real frontiersmen though failures by their standards. Parkman disapproves of Tête Rouge, but admits that he is psychologically useful to the group who make fun of him. They could not have done without him, and Twain implies the same mutual dependence, seen from the opposite side. Thus the inverted adventure belongs with the straight version, both serving the same cultural interests, as it often does in the other types.

Twain was writing at the time of conscious imperialism, when the eyes of Americans were turning abroad. Theodore Roosevelt began by ranching in the Dakotas, but he went on to safaris in Africa and South America and led the United States into its conquest of Cuba and the Philippines. After the Great War there was a revulsion against adventure because of its associations with war, and Hemingway, for instance, associated his name as a writer with that of Gertrude Stein rather than with Roosevelt's, to whom he was surely closer. Hemingway wrote adventures with a twentieth-century coloration, and Faulkner wrote hunting stories. Mailer learned from both of them to make the themes of manliness and violence and adventure and empire central in his work.

Cultural Alliances

The Frontiersman story is primarily in alliance with the cultural themes of the frontier, which means—in American history—the glamorous images of the West, and migration, and the Indians. Within this story (but also outside it), American history is usually seen as a drama of manifest destiny, and later of the American empire. This drama is seen as tragic in part, but inevitable. (This is in contrast to the view of American history that stresses deliberate choices and policies, that focuses on industrialization and economic and political forces—the view I associated before with "civilized values.")

Further allied to the Frontier story is the spectacle of American landscape as enormous and grand, as well as the values of manliness, both in isolation and in comradeship. The crucial human relationship is between the white frontiersman and his friend of another race. Leslie Fiedler drew our attention to this in *Love and Death in the American Novel*, but he interpreted it sexually, viewing the ultimate realities as those of marriage or at least of sexual eroticism. It is possible to read these stories more politically, as having primarily to do with power and force, with *potestas* rather than with *eros*.

Fiedler's erotic criticism is in implicit alliance with the domestic novel, whose principal value is eroticism. That criticism is in the service, therefore, of "serious literature," which makes that genre its pride. There is a hostility between that idea and the adventure tale, and the same alignment of forces in mutual opposition can be seen at much lower cultural levels. Soap operas, for instance, embody the love ideology as much as serious novels do. In soap operas, when a character is told he is ill and withdraws into himself to wait for death, his family is distressed primarily because he won't talk to them about his feelings. One woman tells another, "You know what his problem is? He's a cowboy," meaning that he is trying to be self-reliant. Together they force him out of his stoic withdrawal, fixing him (i.e., fixing the camera and the viewer) with severely loving stares. Being a cowboy is a sin in the soaps. In a Western, talking about one's own feelings is the sin.

More generally, this subgenre is the story of white empire on all continents, and this is so whether it is told in the name of a particular military empire or not, as we saw in the case of India and Russia and France. It is linked to all the other adventures. The stories alluded to by Pushkin, Tolstoy, and others acted on and derived from Russian imperialism. But one of Tolstoy's later and unfulfilled intentions for a novel was to write about a "Robinson Crusoe of the Steppes," the story of a Russian settler moving east, and his friend Sergei Aksakov in effect wrote that story in his *Chronicle of a Russian Family*.

The relevant frontier always lies between white civilization and what is beyond and outside, be that ocean, wilderness, desert, forest, or whatever. Those no-man's-lands and nomads' lands, and their inhabitants, are the great challenge. The story feeds and is fed on all our feelings (guilt as well as glee) about those expanding frontiers, and about nonwhite kingdoms and tribal cultures, and about conquering and being conquered.

Summary and Transition

The first three adventure types have here been linked to nationhood in England, France, and the United States. In fact, these types have had ideological significances that are not so geographically limited, as is suggested by the popularity of each story outside its country of origin. The free enterprise of *Robinson Crusoe,* the glamour of origins of *The Three Musketeers,* and the heroic explorations of frontiersmen are aspects of the nationhood of the West everywhere. But—partly just because mnemonics are important—it seems good to associate each of the three with one particular country.

The other four are equally political but rather different. The Avenger story *did* come to flowering in one historical place and time—post-Napoleonic France—but in an unrelated variant it has been equally popular elsewhere, for instance, in the United States, in both the nineteenth and twentieth centuries, where it expressed the hope that a fiercer and purer authority would arise to punish evil, which would elude the delays and corruptions of constitutional law. This story flourishes generally at the popular-culture level, being only sometimes (in England rarely) taken up by writers who had literary or intellectual ambitions.

The Wanderer story is the type least dependent on a particular place or time. Every nation has to be known through its frontiers, geographical and institutional (and the transgressions against them), and through its various police and military forces, uniformed and plainclothed, public and secret. Reading of spies and moles and double agents, of smugglers and criminals and investigative journalists, of all those with a license to know the secret and to do the forbidden, the reader unconsciously ruminates on the nature of political authority and social morality.

The Sagaman story does have a special national link. Nineteenth-century Germany, in the years of its yearning for nationhood and then of the Second Reich, and twentieth-century Germany, under the Weimar Republic and then the Third Reich, both fed their national pride on images of the Saga heroes. Formally, however, the case is different from the first three types, because the Saga images were incarnate in ancient literary forms, or in poetry and theater, or in Wagner's music dramas or in Nietzsche's philosophy, as much as in adventure tales. In discussing the Sagas, therefore, it has seemed best to stress the atavistic message they carried to all the nations of the West.

Finally, the immensely popular Hunted Man story seems to be, in all countries equally, the way the contemporary reader ruminates on the nature of society. The hunted man represents us all. The man readers identify with is not simply a victim; at several points in the story he is likely to be a hero, a figure of strength, while on other occasions he may be a dangerous maniac or a figure of evil. Thus the various aspects of individual power and individual protest, civic danger and civic security, are revolved in our heads as we read.

One might say that all four of these types have more to do with society than the first three do, and less to do with the state. If viable at all, however, that distinction is no clear contrast but rather a matter of shading. All seven types are eminently political and shape and color our ideas about our own nations, the society and state in which we ourselves live, quite as much as civics textbooks and statistics about voter turnout—as much, perhaps, as biographies of statesmen or serious political novels.

6

The Avenger Story
The Fourth Type

The adventure built around the Avenger figure was popular as written by eighteenth-century "Gothic" novelists before it was given its broader and more modern and political reference in the nineteenth century. The later versions have Gothic features of varying importance, like threats, curses, prophecies, melodrama, and indeed multiple disguises, buried treasure, mysterious signs and codes, and masked identities.

This is somewhat incongruous, because the Avenger story has carried a message that is more liberal, forward-looking, and enlightened, as far as politics goes, than most adventure types. It deals more with the nation-state than with empire (as the Robinson story does) and more with the state than with the nation (as the Musketeers story does). Of course it treats of and in some ways beglamours the exercise of power within the state, but its basic drive is to denounce the agents of injustice and oppression and to mobilize feeling for society's victims.

In the eighteenth-century version, the early phases of the story usually included an innocent young person snatched from a situation of great promise and cast into a dungeon by the machinations of an evil man or men, often wicked barons or mad monks. The middle phases included torture and menace of death and then a thrilling escape (sometimes recapture and reescape). The late phases included the return of a victim, elaborately disguised, and his protracted vengeance.

Such motifs never had much connection with anyone's sense of the real, in the sense of social probability or psychological normality, as Jane Austen pointed out in her inverted Gothic novel, *Northanger Abbey*. But there was a symbolic link between those ruined abbeys or castles and the feudal order that was being contested by the enlightened middle class during the eighteenth century. What made the genre such popular (respectable) reading in the nineteenth century was the adaptation of this machinery to other situations and, most important, to a more contemporary politics. A major feature of that adaptation was the substitution of a young man for a young maiden as victim in the story. (When the Gothic machinery was adapted to the serious domestic novel, as by the Brontë sisters, the victim remained female.)

This substitution happened most significantly in France, where the process began with Eugène Sue (1804–57). He was the son of a doctor of Napoleon and was named Eugène after his godfather, Napoleon's stepson, Eugène de Beauharnais. His father managed to survive the collapse of the empire and found favor under the Bourbons after 1815. (The same was true of Balzac's father, while men like Dumas and Hugo and other writers of mid-nineteenth-century France seem each to have suffered an angry guilt because of family shifts of allegiance. That guilt is a major theme in one of the greatest of Avenger adventures, *Le Comte de Monte Cristo*.)

It is no accident that the Avenger form came to life in France, and in the hands of writers who had had family connections with Napoleon. The many causal connections between history and that literary form will become clear as we examine some of the individual novels, but I can point immediately to the avenging presence of Napoleon himself, while exiled to Elba, and the collapse and flight of the Bourbons as soon he escaped and landed in France for the hundred days campaign. Napoleon hung over France, and all Europe, as a threat, on Elba and again on St. Helena, and even after his death in the shape of his nephew Louis-Napoleon and other Bonapartists.

Eugène Sue wanted to go to sea, but his father insisted he have medical training, so he became a ship's doctor, which he remained until his father died in 1830. Sue then became one of the artist-dandies of Paris. It is another of the incongruities surrounding this story that, in its early versions, it was linked to dandyism. Why that is so will soon become evident.

Sue painted and then wrote—first of all, episodic pirate stories. The episodic form, his biographer tells us, was "the essential armature of the serial novel." He continues with a suggestive phrasing, that in such stories "all life is a life of adventure and *adventure,* promised [or committed] to the storminess of lives especially fertile in tempests and shipwrecks, is no longer limited to its geographical meaning."[1]

Sue played the sportsman dandy as well as the literary kind in the France of the Restoration and, after 1830, that of Louis-Philippe, and soon got into financial difficulty, which exacerbated his radical disaffection. His literary idols were men like Dumas's heroes: Byron, Scott, Cooper, Béranger, but above all Scott, the modern Homer, as Sue called him. Sue imitated Cooper and exchanged mutually flattering letters with the American. In his introduction to *Les mystères de Paris,* Sue says he is going to present Paris to his readers in the same terms as Cooper presented the prairie; because barbarians are lurking in the city of Paris too, if one knows where to look for them. He thus treated French proletarians as an ethnic group, like Cooper's "Redskins," rather than as an economic class. (Balzac also saw himself as depicting Paris in terms of the American frontier, and Dumas, as we know, wrote *Les Mohicans de Paris,* to the tune of a million words.)

Thus Eugène Sue knew several of the adventure types and had tried his hand at more than one. But as he wrote *Les mystères de Paris* he gradually developed a significantly new type of his own. Before beginning his novel, he had read George Sand's socialist fiction and Hugo's *Notre-Dame de Paris* and Balzac's *Le père Goriot,* all of which were highly critical studies of society in one way or another, and sympathetic to the poor. But as an adventure writer Sue believed he had a better right than any of them to deal with the world of the underclass, the world of crime. He announced his ambition to become the Cooper of the social depths: "Everyone has read the

1. Jean-Louis Bory, *Eugène Sue: Le roi du roman populaire,* 103.

admirable pages in which Cooper, the American Walter Scott, has traced the savages' ferocious customs, their picturesque, poetic language, the thousand ruses with the help of which they kill or pursue their enemies."[2]

Such passages show us the close connections between the different adventure stories, and also the way the lines split off from each other—Cooper from Scott, Sue from Cooper. The Gothic subgenre Sue made famous, the Mysteries, became autonomous and strongly influenced even ambitious writers in France, Germany, and Russia (Hugo as well as Dumas, Dostoevsky as well as May). In England too we can see the same form at work in Dickens, but such ambitious and brilliant writers we shall mostly leave to the scholars of traditional literature.

Strictly speaking, one should keep the term "Mysteries" for one particular story in the Gothic group, the analytic portrait of a great city which attracted so many great writers—*Wuthering Heights* is, after all, Gothic without being set in a city. But because that story is so very inclusive, it is also natural to apply the term "Mysteries" to the whole group of Gothic stories. The same is true of the distinction between the Mysteries and the Avenger story. An avenger is not always dominant in a Mystery, as we see in Dickens, but for my purposes the three labels, Gothic, Mysteries, and Avenger, all apply to these stories.

The remarkable thing about Sue's *Mystères de Paris* (1842) was that, despite the distance from which the author viewed the proletariat before he began his famous novel, his attitude toward them gradually became that of a passionate partisan. This was mostly a matter of the enthusiasm his story aroused, but Sue had met and befriended a worker called Fougères in 1841 and suddenly declared himself a Socialist. (Before then Sue's socially critical ideas had been drawn from such reactionary radicals as Joseph de Maistre and de Bonald.) Indeed, the opening of the novel is addressed to a middle-class public, and Sue apologizes for the low life he is going to present to them. But because of the tremendous response to the early installments, he made himself "the poet of the proletariat" and was accepted as a hero of democratic protest, quite widely; John Stuart Mill sent Sue a complimentary copy of his *Principles of Political*

2. Ibid., 247.

Economy. In part three of *Les Mystères,* Sue proposed models of Fourierist social reform outside Paris (describing a model farm at Bouguenval), and in part five there are long lectures on sociopolitical topics. He was praised by the Fourierist paper, *La Phalange,* and by the Utopian Socialists generally, and he was attacked by Marx and Engels just because he was being taken so seriously as a Socialist.

Les mystères de Paris had an elaborate plot or plots, involving characters living at many levels of French society, and revealing a world of crime unknown to the ordinary citizen that yet affects them all. The principal character is an unknown, a man of mysterious origins and identity (finally revealed to be Rudolf von Gerolstein, member of a German reigning family, in exile) who interferes everywhere on behalf of the virtuous and the defenseless and against the powerful and the wicked.

At the age of sixteen, Rudolf had quarreled with his father over the woman he loved and had run away from home. He lost touch with everyone, including his baby daughter, whom he finds again during the novel, as a prostitute in Paris. She was called Marienblume—in France, Fleur de Marie—and is a figure of spiritual purity despite (or because of) her sexual degradation. Her type reappears in many nineteenth-century novels; in *Crime and Punishment* she is called Sonia Marmeladov. Rudolf has imposed on himself the penance of helping the poor and punishing the evil; he appears at many levels of society in many disguises. He is the first of the nineteenth-century superman figures who, Gramsci says, were invented by novelists like Sue and Dumas before Nietzsche developed a philosophy around them.

The several subplots involve each a different socioeconomic class, and most of the characters in one subplot know nothing of the others. But there are links of acquaintance between one person in one group and one in another. There are several large buildings (notably institutions) that turn up in several of the plots. And there are connections between all the criminals. There is an organized kingdom of crime, and at its head is the notary Ferrand, the respectable bourgeois who leads a completely double life.

Rudolf finally drives Ferrand to a grotesque death by satyriasis; he plants in his household Cecily, a half-caste girl who is an incarnation of sex. (Dumas develops that motif in the figure of Haydee in *The Count of Monte Cristo,* and Dickens devises an equally lurid death, by spontaneous combustion, for Krook in *Bleak House*.) Among the good characters, "Le Chourineur" is a reformed burglar whom Rudolf has beaten in single combat and who is now devoted to him. At the end, indeed, he sacrifices his life to save Rudolf's. (This motif too has been much repeated, in milder form; British dandy detectives, from Sherlock Holmes on, have had ex-burglars devoted to them.)

This brief sketch will perhaps have suggested the likeness between Sue's work and that of Dickens (though there is no intention to put the two writers on the same level in terms of literary talent). Dickens also painted great panoramas of city life in which conspiracies of crime play a large part, where the ordinary life is haunted by the horror of what goes on at night and in the fog. He too built elaborate episodic plots, portraying the city as a theater or fantasm in which nothing is what it seems and some people lead totally double lives. There were also German *Kolportage* novels that could be compared. In the literal sense, *Kolportage* and *roman feuilleton* are quite different concepts, but as used by scholars of literature to designate a kind of fiction, they have a lot in common. In Karl May's *Der verlorene Sohn,* the main character is known as the Prince of the Poor—which is one of the titles given to Rudolf von Gerolstein, another embodiment of the same idea.

In *Der verlorene Sohn,* Baron Franz von Helfenstein has murdered his rich kinsman Otto and gotten rid of Otto's two-year-old son, Robert. He has put the blame for the crime on Gustav Brandt, a forester's son, and among people in authority only the kaiser believes in Gustav's innocence. The novel tells the story of Robert's and Gustav's vengeance, which involved the unemployed and debt-entangled weavers, miners, and land workers, of Saxony. May himself had spent eight years in jail and could write about such experience with passion. Like Sue, he links the many characters and subplots via the big institutions of the prison, the hospital, the brothel, and the barracks. And as in Sue's novel, all the kinds of crime turn out to be controlled by one man, the baron—known to his cohorts in the city as Hauptmann (Captain) and to the smugglers in the countryside as Waldkoenig (the Wood King).

The serial version of Sue's novel ran in the *Journal des Débats,* starting in 1842. The response was enormous; some 1,100 letters to the author about it have been preserved. In 1843, twelve magazines in Germany were carrying the story, and in 1844, when the ten-volume edition in book form came out, there were immediately ten translations concurrently into German. It was a case like *Robinson Crusoe:* again there were many shameless imitations. In 1844 alone, in France, there appeared *Mystères de la Bastille, Mystères de Londres, Mystères de Russie, Mystères de Bruxelles, Mystères du grand opéra,* and both a *Petits mystères* and a *Vrais mystères* of Paris.

The Count of Monte Cristo

Probably for reasons of political history, which we have already suggested, it was France that provided the most fertile soil for the seed of the Avenger story, especially in works by Sue and Dumas, and Jules Verne and Victor Hugo. But their work was read all over Europe, even in countries that failed to produce their own versions, at any distinguished level, such as England and America.

There were personal connections between these men. The second and third writers named were friends, Verne being a literary disciple of Dumas and in this genre his direct heir. Dumas might himself be said to be the heir of Sue, but, as in the Musketeers story, he added something to the heritage that transformed and enhanced it. In *The Count of Monte Cristo* (begun in the *Journal des Débats* in 1844, immediately after *The Three Musketeers* ended) the hero, Edmond Dantes, is associated with the fate of Napoleon. He is betrayed at the beginning of the story (by various people, with various motives) and imprisoned for life, and he has been denounced to the authorities as a Bonapartist agent. The story begins in 1814, while Napoleon is in exile on Elba, and Dantes, a young sailor hoping to marry, has innocently taken the exiled emperor a message from Naples and brought a message from him to a man in Paris.

The restored Bourbon government, so recently installed by the Allies, is nervous about a military return by the former emperor, which does indeed occur soon after the trial and imprisonment of Dantes. The official before whom he is taken when accused happens to be the son of the man in Paris to whom Napoleon's letter is addressed. He condemns Dantes so that the letter may be destroyed and all memory of it suppressed. Thus, in various ways, extrinsic, incidental, and yet historical, Dantes is associated with Napoleon's cause, in the minds of the book's characters and in the minds of its readers.

There is, moreover, a more essential moral and imaginative association with Napoleon as avenger, which could be expounded as follows: At the beginning of the story, Dantes is a pure, proud, ardent, ambitious soul who becomes sinister, dangerous, inflexible, and indifferent to ordinary feelings as a result both of his enemies' actions and of his subsequent immense wealth and power. His development could therefore remind readers of Napoleon, as his situation could remind them of other political radicals and revolutionaries in post-Napoleonic Europe, when the novel was published. For instance, Napoleon's nephew and heir, Louis-Napoleon, was a friend of Dumas's. (It happens that the two men visited Elba, and the nearby island of Monte Cristo, together.) Later, of course, Louis-Napoleon became Emperor of France. Just as strikingly, Dantes's betrayers rise to wealth and position in the France of the Restoration and Louis-Philippe and become symbols of the sordid greed, moral compromise, complacency, and hypocrisy of which the latter regime was generally accused.

Dantes becomes a different kind of symbol of pride and power. He too represents the corruption of French society, but in a brilliant and energizing way. He escapes from his dungeon in the Château d'If by a brilliant coup; thrown into the sea as a corpse tied up in a sackcloth bag, he cuts himself free in the water and swims to safety. Finding a buried treasure with the aid of an ancient map, he returns some years later to France, unrecognizable and having taken the name Count of Monte Cristo, and so wealthy as to be omnipotent. He engages in secret and elaborate machinations to bring about the ruin of his former enemies and enlists the sympathy of their children against them. The novel becomes a drama in which high-principled and rebellious youth denounces and destroys middle-aged, middle-class compromise; memories of the Revolution shame the realities of the Restoration. This was the message of much of the approved literature of France in and after the middle of the nineteenth century. One can cite Stendhal's novels as associating their young heroes with the figure of Napoleon, and Balzac's as depicting the newly moneyed class as corrupt and disgusting.

Volker Klotz says that Dumas's novel outdoes Sue's in three ways: first, the hero carries this extra charge of excitement from his association with Napoleon; second, his double identity as both Dantes and Monte Cristo lets him represent both ordinary France and the exotic Orient;

and third, his motives and actions are more authentic because they are less moralistic.[3] We might add two things: unlike Rudolf von Gerolstein, he is of low birth, a self-made man, and he is innocent when condemned.

Klotz also points out the compressed-spring action-and-reaction of injustice and then vengeance, imprisonment and then self-liberation, as well as the contemporaneity of the plot machinery—Monte Cristo has a private yacht and uses the telegraph system, and he and his enemies make use of significantly modern methods of self-aggrandizement and aggression. This is one point that distinguishes this adventure type from the Musketeers story. Dantes becomes ubiquitous and omnipotent, just as the new forms of communication and transport were; the main railway lines from Paris to Orléans and to Rouen were opened in 1843. He is a "liquid" hero, like money and electricity; his power flows everywhere, anonymously.[4] This is a new hero, called into being to defeat the new dragons of bourgeois capitalism. His self-regeneration has its parallels in the literarily respectable *Bildungsroman,* but there such changes are only psychological—the hero is merely the central character. In an adventure, the change of regeneration makes the man into a real hero.

Monte Cristo is recognizably a modern god. He dies in his island prison and then is born again in the sea. He returns from no one knows where and declares, "Vengeance is mine!" He raises a sunken ship for Morrel; he makes Villefort's daughter appear to die and rise again; he acts secretly on his enemies, who seem to suffer from "acts of God." Morrel's family fall on their knees before him. He is always hearing himself praised, and by people who do not know he is the person to whom they are referring.[5]

Figures of power belong not to the novel proper but to the adventure, to the *roman feuilleton.* The *feuilleton,* a literary supplement to newspapers, born in 1800, took to printing fiction in the 1840s, and some of it, like Sue's and Dumas's, had political overtones. The *Revue Indépendante,* with which George Sand and Pierre Leroux were associated, loved *Les mystères de Paris.* Many of these writers—Sue, Dumas, Sand, Lamartine—took part in the 1848 revolution, and that has been called the *feuilleton* revolution.[6] Thus, when we scorn the *feuilleton* and put

3. Klotz, *Abenteuer-Romane.*
4. Ibid., 65.
5. Ibid., 71.
6. Bory, *Eugène Sue,* 320.

our faith in art, we are likely unconsciously to be abandoning our faith in positive change and heroism, or so the German theorists of adventure argue.

Captain Nemo and Other Avengers

In Jules Verne's novel *Twenty Thousand Leagues Under the Sea,* Captain Nemo is driven to his vengeance by the memory of some mysterious wrong done to him and his people by a foreign empire. This leads him to conduct a private war against that country's shipping in his submarine, the *Nautilus.* Like the Count of Monte Cristo, the Captain has acquired enormous wealth from hidden treasure he found under the sea; and in Verne's world, as in Dumas's, wealth immediately brings social and political power. Again like the Count, there is a mystery about the Captain's origin, and throughout the book Verne keeps that secret even from the reader.

He had originally intended to make Nemo Polish, and the foreign empire Russia, the target of most liberal indignation in nineteenth-century Europe. But the Russian government got wind of his design during the story's serialization and officially protested to the French government. (Turgenev was involved in the negotiations as an intermediary.) Such an incident gives us a sense of how popular Verne's work was and of how much power went with his kind of popularity. In the event, he decided to keep the secret of Nemo's origin right to the end of that book, and when the character reappeared, in *The Mysterious Island,* it was revealed that he was an Indian prince who had lost his kingdom to the British by fighting against them in the War of Independence of 1857.

Thus this Avenger hero was linked to two of the oppressed nations of the nineteenth century, Poland and India, and two of the wicked empires, Russia and England. However, Verne makes the point that the British are in India as the agents of progress and that Nemo was fighting fruitlessly, tragically, against history, whereas the Russian government was seen by European liberals as the enemy of progress. So the two were not completely aligned. But still the figure of Nemo expressed an indignation at England's oppression which was to be developed further in later Verne novels.

Nemo was also linked to Napoleon, just like Dantes, though in a more purely symbolic way. The major clue to his identity throughout most of *Twenty Thousand Leagues Under the Sea* is that the initial letter "N" is stitched, stamped, carved, or otherwise worked into the various surfaces of the *Nautilus,* and "N," in nineteenth-century France, suggested Napoleon.

Verne's *Mathias Sandorf* (1885) is again an Avenger story; the background is a Hungarian revolt against the Austrian Empire. It is dedicated to the memory of Dumas, Verne saying that he had tried to make Sandorf the Monte Cristo of his series *Les voyages extraordinaires.* (Dumas's son wrote in reply that Verne had been a better literary son to his father than he himself had been.) Sandorf is a Hungarian noble who is also a scientist and engineer. He owns iron and copper mines and is absorbed in his experiments, but he also leads a band of freedom fighters and so is betrayed to the government by a group of greedy villains who are interested only in his money. The story tells how Sandorf disappears into the sea and is presumed dead for fifteen years. He returns under the name of Dr. Antekirrt to revenge himself on his enemies, who have grown rich and respectable on the fruits of their crime. (Just as in *The Count of Monte Cristo,* the sons and daughters of those enemies gather around him.) He now owns an island called Antekirrta, an independent state of which he is the enlightened and scientific despot. Everything there works by electricity, silently and invisibly. The adventurous element of physical danger and heroic prowess in hand-to-hand fighting is therefore embodied in two acrobats, extraneous to the story's themes and barely attached to the plot. (This is another case of the literary decadence we often find in Verne.)

Thus Verne followed Dumas in giving the Avenger adventure a hinterland of liberal politics, a liberalism expressed not only in sympathy for oppressed nations or classes abroad, but also in scorn for the corruptly successful at home and a thrilled admiration for criminal-heroes.

The Mysteries

In what we call the Mysteries novelists, there is a structure of feelings and topics that parallel the structure in Verne and Dumas. In Hugo's *Les misérables,* published in 1862 but partly written in 1848, there is a good deal about Napoleon, and in Balzac's *Comédie humaine* the chart of French society is like that of *The Count of Monte Cristo.*

This larger Gothic form, the Mysteries, proved extremely attractive to talented and ambitious writers as well as to the mass readership, up through the 1860s. This subgenre therefore invites us to examine the relations between adventure and literature in nineteenth-century Europe more closely than we have done up to now.

At this point, however, we must distinguish between the Mysteries and the Avenger stories. The former often included an act of vengeance but were rarely dominated by an avenger figure. The Mysteries of Sue and Dumas were Avenger adventures, because in each the whole action is dominated by a single, protracted act of vengeance. But that is not true of Dickens, Balzac, and Dostoevsky, whose Mysteries *include* adventure and avengers, but also many other things.

We can begin a little earlier than the publication of Sue's novel and approach the form via the interests of those who read it and wrote it. This will explain the link between the story and the apparently incongruous dandyism of its early writers. Mysteries often expressed an interest in low life and/or the sporting life, on the part of both writer and reader. Such an interest was "aristocratic"—that is, it featured people of title and was alienated from middle-class moralism, domesticity, and "respectability." It was part of the dandy persona that attracted men of sensibility as well as men of fashion in Regency England and Restoration France.

This persona was attractive to writers all over Europe, but it was believed to be English in origin. Jockey clubs, for instance, had an English atmosphere, and so did boxing matches, boxing being a sport watched by many and practiced by some in fashionable society. Consequently, the disreputable eating and drinking places where pimps and pickpockets as well as gamblers gathered became places of fashion that were of interest to readers as well as to sportsmen, and an interest in crime stories became part of literary sensibility.

Several of the early writers of Mysteries were sportsmen-dandies to some degree, notably Eugène Sue and Edward Bulwer-Lytton (usually referred to as Lytton), both of whom were friends of the leading dandy in both England and France of the 1830s, the Count d'Orsay, himself a minor man of letters. Perhaps the most famous dandy novel was Lytton's *Pelham* (1828), which was said by the *Revue des Deux Mondes* to have become the textbook on the subject of English manners for all Paris. In London the future prime minister, Disraeli, attributed his own social success to his application of the lessons *Pelham* taught. Disraeli remained both a good friend of Lytton's and his comrade in politics, as Dickens was in literature.

Dickens and Dumas, quasi-dandies themselves, were friends with Sue and Lytton, who were fully so, and those were the four great names of early Mysteries writing in England and France. All of them displayed something of the flamboyant antibourgeois dandy style, in clothing, manners, opinions, and in their novels. This dandyism was a complex phenomenon. One of its great heroes was Byron (*Pelham* owed a clear debt to Byron), and it brought with it Byron's type of political radicalism and literary ambition. Byron had made a famous radical speech in Parliament defending the weavers of Nottingham, and in 1838 Lytton made a famous speech defending the black workers of the West Indies. And Byron's demonic heroes, like Lara and Manfred, were precursors for the avenger heroes of the Mysteries.

Later Mysteries writers, such as May and Dostoevsky, were not dandies in most senses. But they did share one set of the earlier writers' interests: they were great readers of the daily newspaper and/or attenders of criminal trials—passionately, if ambivalently, concerned about anyone accused. George Augustus Sala said of Dickens, "What he liked to talk about was the latest new piece at the theatres, the latest exciting trial or police case, the latest social craze or social swindle, and especially the latest murder and the newest thing in ghosts," and Philip Collins, who quotes Sala, adds that Dickens morally preferred "the criminal regulars of sensational fiction—thieves, swindlers, and murderers—[to] such favorite civil offenders as heartless seducers, rapacious landlords, greedy moneylenders."[7] Few of his novels end without a gallows or a jail, disgrace or sudden death, and the same is true of the other Mysteries authors.

A lesser subgenre, comparable to the Avenger story and also to be counted in the Mysteries group, is sometimes called the Newgate Novel, after the famous London prison. In such a story the hero is a criminal. He or she is either the object of a chase/search or a representative victim, or the story is a study in the motivation of crime.[8] One of the first of these to achieve both a wide circulation (every copy was sold on the first

7. See Philip Collins, *Dickens and Crime*, 1.
8. See James L. Campbell, *Edward Bulwer-Lytton*, 39.

day of publication) and some "respectability" was Lytton's Highway-
man novel, *Paul Clifford* (1830). This had a radical flavor because the
author asked the reader to see parallels between the criminals he was
describing and figures in high society. (One trick he employed was to
give his subjects suggestive nicknames. Gentleman George, for instance,
suggested George IV himself.) The plot included an abducted child, a
double identity, long-hidden family secrets, and a judge who condemns
his own son to death. But the author was also making a serious and
well-informed attack on the penal code of the time. During the 1830s,
Lytton belonged to Lord Durham's circle of "philosophical radicals"
and corresponded with John Stuart Mill and William Godwin. (In fact,
Godwin was part responsible for *Paul Clifford*. He suggested that Lytton
write a new version of Gay's *Beggar's Opera*.)

This type of story has something in common with *Les mystères de
Paris,* which was to follow it a little more than a decade later, in theme
as well as plot. Lytton went on to write other Newgate Novels, of which
probably the most famous was *Eugene Aram* (1832). In this story the
criminal hero is a gentle scholar who is driven to commit a murder quite
against his character by a poverty that prevents his pursuing learning.
But there is a philosophical theme involved in this, as well as the familiar
political theme. According to Lytton's interpretation of the case (the
novel was based on fact, and other writers had other interpretations),
Aram had convinced himself by reading Bentham's philosophy of utili-
tarianism that a crime that advanced the general good was ethically
justified. A crime based on such a motive is of course Dostoevsky's
subject in his *Crime and Punishment,* one of the greatest of Mysteries
from a purely literary point of view.

The Newgate Novel was extremely popular in the 1830s in England.
Another famous title was Harrison Ainsworth's *Jack Sheppard* (1839).
But the genre came under severe attack on aesthetic, moral, and sociopolitical grounds, as part of the general attack on Regency and dandy
ideology. Such novels were thought to enlist the reader on the side of
criminals, against the law and against respectable society. One could say
the genre fell victim to the new moral and political mood that established
itself in England at the end of the 1830s and that we can call Victorian.
It was a mood Carlyle expressed in a polemic against Lytton in particular, and in his attack on dandyism in general, in *Sartor Resartus*. Lytton
wrote a pamphlet in self-defense entitled *A Word to the Public,* in 1847,
but he wrote no more crime novels.

At the end of the 1840s Lytton turned to domestic fiction with his three-part novel, *The Caxtons,* and settled down to satisfy the new tastes. But through his collaboration with Disraeli in politics and Dickens in literature, he continued to exert an influence that was in some ways anti-Victorian. Like Dickens, Wilkie Collins, and Charles Reade, who constituted something of a group, Lytton was anti-Evangelical, hostile to the religious movement that became so powerful a component of Victorianism. The Mysteries and their kind of adventure were popular but not quite respectable reading in Victorian England, and that helps explain their literary obscurity even now.

The greatest figure in English literature who needs to be mentioned in connection with Mysteries—one who might be called a Mysteries novelist—was Charles Dickens. He began to publish in the 1830s, with *The Pickwick Papers.* We find Mysteries elements already in *Oliver Twist* (1837–38), which shows a fascination not only with brutal crime, in the story of Bill Sykes and Nancy, but also with the idea of a kingdom of crime, in Fagin and his school for thieves. Another important Mysteries element is the dramatization of the institutions of the workhouse and of poverty and misery. The melodrama plot elements, such as the abducted child who is to be restored to his family at the climax, are also typical of Mysteries.

Through Dickens's work, the city of London became as much a Mysteries city to its citizens as Paris became through the work of Sue and Balzac, and St. Petersburg became through Dostoevsky. Indeed, the word belongs to Dickens by right of historical precedence. His *Nicholas Nickleby,* which has a heartless bourgeois villain like Ferrand, and *Barnaby Rudge,* which has vivid scenes of popular riots, also in fact preceded *Les mystères de Paris.* The resemblance between Sue and Dickens was seen as soon as the French Mysteries began to appear. An article on Dickens by J. Milsand in 1847 compared the two writers and said that the Englishman had invented the genre in which the Frenchman was writing.[9] George Eliot said in 1856 that only Dickens's humor saved him from Sue's aesthetic and political weaknesses of sentiment.[10] Other writers, such as Dostoevsky, were deeply impressed by both men and took much the same message from both.

The difference between the two, and the reason Dickens is not *neces-*

---

9. J. Milsand, *La Revue Indépendante,* March 1847, pp. 161–91.
10. George Eliot, in *Westminster Review,* July 1856.

sarily to be called a Mysteries writer, is that he organized the same fictional elements in a different way. His fiction is not, for instance, primarily adventurous, nor does a single angel-demon avenger dominate the scene in his fiction, as Rudolf von Gerolstein and the Count of Monte Cristo dominate their novels. (If there had been such a figure he would not have been a count or a prince.) Oliver Twist and Barnaby Rudge, Nicholas Nickleby and Martin Chuzzlewit, are victims or naifs, and the same is true of David Copperfield and Little Dorrit. There is often both an angel and a demon in a Dickens novel, but they are not fused into a single figure. The dominating presence in a Dickens novel is Dickens. Later the novels grow more thematic, as the titles *Dombey and Son* and *Bleak House* suggest, but none is dominated by single acts of vengeance. (Perhaps it is significant that the story of Edwin Drood, which *was* to have been so dominated, as far as can be judged, was called *The Mystery of Edwin Drood.*)

Thus the title of Mysteries writer is not obligatory for Dickens because of the profusion of other kinds of material in his novels. But several of them have some of the excitements of adventure, and he has the serial structure so reminiscent of Dumas, Sue, and Dostoevsky. Indeed, Dickens was more of a Mysteries writer than Dumas in his enthusiasm for criminality and for the monstrous in crime. He has the great institutions of oppression (the prison in *Little Dorrit,* the school in *Nicholas Nickleby,* the court in *Bleak House*). He has the hypocrites, like Pecksniff and Chadband, and he has the money monsters, like Merdle and Boffin.

Perhaps most important, he has the elaborate plot, or set of plots, with action proceeding on a series of social stages totally separate from each other and yet connected. Philip Hobsbaum says that though Dickens's plots vary from novel to novel, the theme is always "an attack upon a System that refuses to take account of human needs."[11] The other Mysteries have this kind of theme, and the typical narrative device of a person pursued to discover his or her secret. *Bleak House* offers a vivid example in the flight of Lady Dedlock, a complex pursuit in which several pursuers prey on each other.

This pursuit is a crucial device in a Mysteries novel (early worked out in Godwin's *Caleb Williams*) because the reader also is hurrying after the fleeing figure, picking up clues, full of pity, horror, foreboding, disgust with the pursuers, but still determined to grasp the secret. And

11. Philip Hobsbaum, *Reader's Guide to Charles Dickens,* 149.

this emotional ambiguity is the essence of reading *The Count of Monte Cristo* and *Crime and Punishment* and some of Balzac and Hugo. In Hugo we think above all of *Les misérables,* which was published in the same year as the Dostoevsky novel, and of the long pursuit of Jean Valjean by the detective Javert. But whereas Valjean is a criminal forgivably and almost accidentally, in Balzac's *Comédie humaine* we find a criminal who has been described as crime itself—Vautrin—who is yet a member of the police.

The Mysteries side of Balzac's work shows itself early in *Le père Goriot* (1834–35). All Paris is epitomized in the Pension Vauquer, where the main characters have rooms; in the young Eugène de Rastignac, eager to conquer Paris; and in his relations with old Goriot's high-flying daughters. Balzac gives us the Mysteries' vivid contrasts of social level, the shameful links between them, the perilous insecurity of those on high, the grinding misery of those below, and above all the secret power of crime, embodied in Vautrin. He is omnipresent and omnipotent. Jailed after the events of *Le père Goriot,* he returns in other novels, murders, disfigures himself with vitriol to disguise himself, finally becomes chief of police.

All these stories, which include some of the greatest fiction of the nineteenth century, could be called Mysteries, and so linked to adventure. And as such, especially in England, this sort of writing was held to be inferior. "Thackeray to a certain extent seemed to have beaten Dickens 'out of the world,' " says Walter Phillips in his study of "sensational fiction." "The realism that became ascendant with *Vanity Fair* was in a sense 'high-brow' fiction. Having therefore the suffrage of the best reviews and of solid, conservative folk," Trollope, George Eliot, and Thackeray stood in superior opposition to Dickens, Reade, and Collins.[12] The latter were called "sensational novelists," and that phrase could label another subgenre, parallel to the Avenger and Newgate stories—except that these writers are nowadays recognized and honored by the men and women of letters.

Conclusion

The adventure of the avenger remained very popular throughout the nineteenth century, especially among readers who had radical convic-

12. Walter C. Phillips, *Dickens, Reade, and Collins,* 23.

tions about the situation treated. One example, popular in the United States, was R. M. Bird's play *Oralloosa, the Last of the Incas,* about a seemingly loyal Indian at the Spanish court in Peru who turns out to be an Incan prince by birth and bent on revenge against the European usurpers. (Another of Bird's plays was *Caridorf; or, The Avenger.*) Ethel Voynich's novel *The Gadfly,* extremely popular with radical readers though never taken seriously by literary critics, is another example. This was set in Renaissance Italy and had a bastard for its Avenger hero, but it was widely taken to represent contemporary political situations symbolically.

No doubt the American book with an Avenger hero most famous with literary readers is Melville's *Moby Dick* (1851), in which Captain Ahab seeks revenge on the universe at large and focuses his anger on a giant white whale, forcing the crew of his whaling ship to pursue it against all common sense and reason—and comes to his death by so doing. The political reference in this is less clear. Though the ship and the crew represent democratic society, Ahab seems to belong to another world of meaning. Melville's sympathies were more metaphysical than political; they were above all literary. This means that his book is more impressive as a work of Romantic art but less authentic as an adventure. Only the very last chapters, describing the battle between the whale and the ship, have the quality of real adventure, though it seems likely that Melville intended the whole work to have that character. It is difficult to believe even in the sea as long as Ahab has center stage.

We may associate France with this adventure type, though not so predominantly as we associated it with the Musketeers story. The fit is not so tight, because Dumas's focus here is on the state not the nation, and on modernity not history, and the state and modernity are international categories. However, wherever it may be set, this story is full of political references, and it helped define and body forth the liberal imagination of the Western world. If it is slightly different from the first three types, it points forward to the last of my seven, the Hunted Man, for as we have noted, the excitement of pursuit is always ambivalent, and most hunters are also hunted at some point.

The fact that the vengeance adventure's historical hinterland prominently featured Napoleon and other Bonapartes was no doubt one reason why British writers—at least those at the respectable level—did not write the story. (Here again we must distinguish between the Avenger story, and the Mysteries and the Gothic. The latter two categories *did* flourish in England, in various forms.) England had led the fight against Napoleon and engineered the status quo that replaced him. It seems to have looked to writers as criminally foolish a game to play with the idea of Napoleon in nineteenth-century England as to play with that of Hitler was to seem in twentieth-century America.

Dumas's novel was, however, widely read in English, and deeply felt. An interesting analysis of its influence is found in James Joyce's auto-biographical novel, *Portrait of the Artist as a Young Man* (1916).[13] As a boy, Stephen Dedalus, we are told, pored over a ragged translation of Monte Cristo every evening. "The figure of that dark avenger stood forth in his mind for whatever he had heard or divined in childhood of the strange and terrible" (p. 62). The reading thus organized and energized various psychic materials in Stephen (who had been "insulted by life" and confusedly needed a revenge). He acted out and reinforced the story's themes by building himself a model of Dantes's cave and then by associating houses and landscapes near his home with those Dumas described. One cottage became Mercedes's house. "Both on the outward and on the homeward journey he measured distance by this landmark: and in his imagination he lived through a long train of adventures, marvellous as those in the book itself. . . . He became the ally of a boy called Aubrey Mills and founded with him a gang of adventurers in the avenue" (p. 63). Within this gang, Stephen imitated the demeanor of Napoleon. This example must stand for many others, which we pass over because their interest is not sufficiently political.

Only at the very end of the nineteenth century did such writers as Conrad and Conan Doyle overcome that inhibition and begin to use the figure of Napoleon—or at least Napoleonic history—the way other historical subjects were used. In France, by contrast, the figure of Napoleon was too potent and many-sided to be exiled for long. It became possible to mention him on the Paris stage after 1830 (because of the part Bonapartists played on the winning side in the revolution of that year), and in 1831 Dumas put on a play, *Napoléon Bonaparte*. (Dumas was in some sense a Bonapartist by birth.)

Napoleon was also a stimulus in other literatures. He is, in quite different ways, a powerful presence in both of the two great Russian novels of the 1860s, *War and Peace* and *Crime and Punishment*. He is the enemy of Russia, symbolically as well as literally, in the war Tolstoy describes, and he is the inspiration for Raskolnikov's aim to become a superman, in Dostoevsky's novel.

13. James Joyce quotations below are from the 1964 edition of *Portrait*.

However, there were also other historical figures—among contemporaries—who were evoked for readers as they read tales of vengeance. There were all the great liberal martyrs, the prisoners and exiles of the Russian, Austrian, Turkish, and British empires, and of Spain and France and Germany. Famous names like Mazzini and Garibaldi, Marx and Engels, Kossuth and Herzen, through all the others from Ireland, Greece, Poland, Hungary, and so on—their fates could all be seen as mirrored in that of Edmond Dantes, the Count of Monte Cristo.

We note, for instance, the importance of the image of prison in so many versions of this story. It had origins in Gothic literature (the ruined abbeys where mad monks chained up their victims in their cells), but it had also the historical origin of the Bastille and other such institutions. The lack of such a symbolic building in England and America is perhaps one thing that made them less fertile ground for this story. But it is also notable that the storming of Newgate in *Barnaby Rudge* is described with horror and that the French Revolution scenes in *A Tale of Two Cities* are at best ambivalent.

The taking of the Bastille by revolutionary forces remained one of the greatest symbolic events of history during the one hundred years that followed. Silvio Pellico's book *Le mie prigioni,* his account of his various imprisonments by the Austrian government for his work on behalf of Italian unity, was quite popular throughout nineteenth-century Europe. The story of national unification (above all, Germany's and Italy's) joined the story of national liberation (the liberation of Greece/Poland/ Serbia/Hungary from the Turkish/Russian/Austrian empires) to make the substance of the liberal political myth of the century. (Edmond Dantes's co-prisoner in the Château d'If, the Abbé Faria, who gave him the treasure map that made him rich, wrote a book in jail on the theme of Italian unity and freedom.)

The story had, then, strong liberal affiliations, which helped make it culturally respectable long after it became clear that men of letters would give it no high literary status. It was part of the liberal imagination. Any young man jailed on political grounds, whatever he had done, symbolized that drama—for instance, Fabrice in Stendhal's *La Chartreuse de Parme.* Before committing any crime or receiving any punishment, young people could powerfully imagine themselves avenging on society the wrongs of its victims.

In the twentieth century, by contrast, at least in America, there have been a notable number of Avenger stories with conservative overtones.

A hero representing middle-class morality, when pushed too far by the forces of anarchy, violence, organized crime, and sexual perversity, takes up arms and destroys them. We have seen many such movies in the 1980s, with heroes played by Charles Bronson, Sylvester Stallone, Clint Eastwood. There are fictional equivalents in John D. McDonald's work, especially his Travis McGee stories; and in Robert Parker's novels Spencer plays a similar part. This was not without precedent in the nineteenth century (especially in the United States, again). Taking the law into one's own hands is a theme that has been very attractive to both writers and readers (in part because of the thrill of sacrilege that accompanied it). The "regulators" of the Southwest, about whom Charles Sealsfield and Friedrich Gerstaecker wrote, were avengers.

As for the variables, it is easy to see that the Avenger story favors scenes in which old or not-young protagonists act—men who have a long history of injury and injustice with which to explain away the cruelty of their vengeance. As is usual with the protagonists of adventure tales, women were late to appear among the nineteenth-century avengers, but when they did (Lytton's *Lucretia,* Mrs. Maxwell's *Lady Audley's Secret,* Lydia Gwilt in Collins's *Armadale*) they brought a thrill of greater horror. The same is true of nonwhite avengers. Indians and Chinese begin to appear at the end of the nineteenth century in stories directly about the mutiny or in Collins's *Moonstone,* and in stories by Conan Doyle or about Dr. Fu Manchu. In novels like *The Klansman,* black avengers appear in the fiction of the American South. At the very beginning of the twentieth century, John Buchan gave British readers an African avenger in *Prester John.* Perhaps these figures, or the political nightmares from which they derive, are what provoked the crop of white-conservative Avenger stories in this century.

7

The Wanderer Story
The Fifth Type

A dventures have been told or written around wanderer figures, in some loose sense of adventure and wanderer, from the beginning of story-telling. We, however, are interested only in modern Wanderer adventures that were written in the period after 1700 and that tell tales that have some political bearing, like the types already described. For our purposes, therefore, we are confining adventure and wanderer rather narrowly and strictly, rejecting certain tales lest our argument lose coherence and cogency.

Part of what we mean by "political" is the sheer excitement of travel, concentrated in our period in the phrase "round the world." In the late twentieth century the idea of travel in space has perhaps replaced that earlier excitement of world travel, but perhaps not. The excitement was not just a matter of the modernity, danger, or rarity of such travel; it was also a matter of circumscribing and compressing by one's own movement the whole planet on which we live. This is a political feeling, because it is so much the mark of privilege, so much more accessible to some classes than to others, but also because it is part of the triumph of humankind over the environment. To travel around the world, and even to read about such travel, made one a progressive.

What are typical cases of Wanderer adventure of the modern kind? Two examples, by Defoe and Verne, are the early eighteenth-century *Captain Singleton* and the late nineteenth-century *Les enfants du Capitaine Grant*. In the first, the protagonist finds himself the leader of a band of sailors making their way across Africa from the east coast to the west; he meets danger and difficulty from savage tribes and wild animals, from jungle and torrent and desert, but he triumphs. He goes home with a fortune, spends it in England, and in the second half of the story becomes a successful pirate, sailing around the world and making another fortune. In *Les enfants du Capitaine Grant,* a Scottish sea captain named Grant has disappeared in South America. His young children, under the protection of a Scottish nobleman with a yacht, go in search of him, beginning where he was last seen and traveling from South America eastward across the Atlantic to Africa and, having traversed that continent, to the islands of the South Seas and on to Australia, across sea and land along a line of latitude. The enormous scope of this wandering, the intoxication of the distances covered, is one of the things that make these exemplary Wanderer adventures. But other features have more to do with character and courage.

When Captain Singleton lands on the coast of Africa, he writes, "It was here, that we took one of the rashest and wildest, and most desperate Resolutions that ever was taken by Man, or any number of men, in the World; this was, to travel over Land through the Heart of the Country, from the Coast of *Mozambique,* on the east-Ocean, to the Coast of *Angola* or *Guinea,* on the Western or *Atlantick* Ocean, a Continent of Land of at least 1800 miles; in which Journey we had excessive Heats to support, unpassable Desarts to go over, no Carriages, Camels or Beasts of any kind to carry our Baggage, innumerable Tigers, Lizards, and Elephants; we had the Equinoctial Line to pass under, and consequently were in the very Center of the Torrid Zone; we had Nations of Savages to encounter with, barbarous and brutish to the last Degree, Hunger and Thirst to struggle with; and, in one Word, Terrors enough to have daunted the stoutest Hearts that ever were placed in Cases of flesh and blood" (p. 58). This is a typical menu of the Wanderer adventure, and as much of a plot as we usually find.

In most cases, as in the Captain Singleton and Captain Grant stories, the reader's interest is divided between the seas and lands described, with their flora and fauna and human societies, and the ancient and modern forms of transport employed, with their various delays and delights. (*Around the World in Eighty Days* is the single title that best suggests these pleasures, but the actual story omits too much of the best that such adventures can give and pushes the type to the verge of self-caricature.) The sense of movement, the sense of geography, gives a sense of power—the power of the individual reader, which is recognizably a shadow of the power of imperial cultures.

This is as true of nonfictional wanderings as it is of fictional wanderings. We can turn back to Dumas for a definition of that power: "To travel is to live in the full meaning of the word; the past and the future are swallowed up in the present; one fills one's lungs, takes pleasure in everything, holds all creation in the hollow of one's hand."[1] This definition is in the first of Dumas's many books of travel description, a genre he helped make popular. That account of Switzerland, *La Suisse: Impressions de voyage II,* was his best-selling book before *The Three Musketeers.* It is of course the travel book which is the most natural twin to this adventure type. The travel book took on new life at just the same moment in the nineteenth century as several of these subgenres, and of course responded to the new facilities for travel after the Napoleonic wars. The first of the Murray series of British Handbooks for Travellers (also about Switzerland) came out just when Dumas's did. And most of the great popular writers, like Dumas and Dickens, and some of the more literary authors, like Châteaubriand and Stendhal, practiced this kind of writing.

In the generation after Dumas, Jules Verne wrote a number of Wanderer adventures. Three of the most notable, *Michel Strogoff, La machine à vapeur,* and *Mathias Sandorf,* are set in three of Europe's great empires—the Russian, the British (in India), and the Austrian. Their plots and themes have a good deal in common, as Jean-Yves Tadié points out. Each one is about the empire's political troubles, each features a pursuer who is himself pursued, each has a trio of characters at its center (a man and woman couple, and their adver-

---

1. Alexandre Dumas, *La Suisse: Impressions de voyage II,* 24.

sary), and each grants only minor importance (compared with other Verne books) to machinery.[2] They therefore constitute a recognizable variety within the Wanderer adventure.

The special feature of Verne's adventures is the scientific explanations the author offers at every point. These occur in all his stories. In *Twenty Thousand Leagues Under the Sea*, for example, we find a chapter with the characteristic title "Everything by Electricity" and this passage: "You know the composition of sea-water. In a thousand grams, one finds ninety six and a half hundredths of water and about two and two thirds hundredths of sodium chlorate; then, in small quantities, magnesium and potassium chlorate, magnesium bromate, magnesium sulphate, and calcium sulphate and carbonate. You see then that sodium chlorate is there in a notable proportion. Now, it is this sodium which I extract and from which I compose my elements" (p. 119). The science is made exciting by its function in a new mode of movement—the submarine—in *modern* transport.

We can take *Michel Strogoff* as our main example of Verne's Wanderer stories. Verne had originally called it *The Czar's Courier*, but the Russian embassy in Paris asked him to change the title (as it had also protested over Captain Nemo), and the subtitle became "Moscow–Irkutsk"—the stretch of 5,523 kilometers the hero has to traverse. The story begins, like a Musketeers story, in the imperial palace in Moscow. The czar has a secret mission of the highest importance that must be performed at top speed, which he entrusts to Michel Strogoff. There is a vivid description of the different landscapes of the Russian Empire, the different climates and crops, and the various languages and costumes and tribal cultures.

There is also emphasis on the means of transport Strogoff employs, especially the indigenous ones, like the tarantas. Along the way he acquires a companion, Nadia, and an enemy, Ogareff. Finally he falls into the latter's hands and is blinded by him, after which Ogareff assumes Strogoff's identity and travels under his name. But despite his disability, Strogoff becomes the pursuer instead of the pursued. (This playing with identities and roles is a feature of several adventure types: d'Artagnan assumes de Wardes's identity in order to sleep with Milady, and Oppenheim and Buchan later take it to extremes.) Strogoff must now be led everywhere by Nadia, but he travels on

2. Tadié, *Le roman d'aventures*, 72–73.

after Ogareff and at the climax of the story reveals that he has his sight after all, and triumphs over his enemy. In such a story the standard literary ingredients of adventure—danger, suspense, surprise, horror—are blended with the specific spices of the Wanderer subgenre, geographical, technical, and political.

Twain and Kipling

Two other examples of the genre in English, more brilliant from a literary point of view, date from the end of the nineteenth century and the beginning of the twentieth: Mark Twain's *Huckleberry Finn* and Rudyard Kipling's *Kim*. In both an Irish orphan boy travels across a large portion of America/India, and the storyteller depicts the geography and the social varieties in vivid color, putting the protagonist in close contact with other-racial experience. In one the representative of that experience is a black ex-slave, in the other it is a Tibetan lama. The white protagonist is a boy, not a man, and that was true of Captain Grant's children in the Verne story, though Defoe's hero had been a man. One sign of the aging of the adventure genres is the substitution of children for adults, both as readers and as protagonists.

In these two stories the means of transport are again old as well as new, and there is a preference for the old means—rafting down the Mississippi, mountaineering in the Himalayas. "Kim had all a plainsman's affection for the well-trodden track, not six feet wide, that snaked among the mountains; but the lama, being Tibetan, could not refrain from short-cuts over spurs and the rims of gravel-strewn slopes. As he explained to his limping disciple, a man bred among mountains can prophesy the course of a mountain-road, and though low-lying clouds might be a hindrance to a short-cutting stranger, they made no earthly diffurence to a thoughtful man. Thus, after long hours of what would be reckoned very fair mountaineering in civilized countries, they would pant over a saddle-back, sidle by a few land-slips, and drop through forest at an angle of forty five on to the road again. Along their track lay the villages of the hill-folk—mud and earth huts, timbers now and then rudely carved with an axe—clinging like swallows' nests against the steeps, huddled on tiny flats half-way down a three-thousand-foot glissade; jammed into a corner between cliffs that funnelled and focused every wandering blast; or, for the sake of summer pasture, cowering down on a neck that in winter would be ten feet deep in snow" (pp. 231–32). These old ways of living, and of traveling to see these lives, test individual manliness, while the railways and river steamers display national power.

The boys in both books are in their early teens. Huck runs away from the foster parents who look after him in his Mississippi town and floats down the enormous river with the runaway slave, Jim. Both Huck and Jim get involved in a series of escapades along the way that represent the comic and the tragic sides of life in the South before the abolition of slavery. Kim, who has even less parenting, leaves Lahore when a Tibetan lama, seeking a legendary river mentioned in a story about Buddha, passes through. Kim himself goes seeking the secret of his birth with a couple of half-understood anecdotes, but he also gets involved, by members of the British Secret Service in India, in foiling a Russian plot to foment an uprising. Huck and Jim are running away from pursuers, and Kim and the Lama are actively, if fantastically, seeking a revelation, but the two couples are alike in the legendary or dreamlike character of their traveling—its evasion of the reality principle as their readers know it. The dream, however, is rooted in empirical facts and skills, as in *Robinson Crusoe*.

Huck tells us, "When it was beginning to come on dark, we poked our heads out of the cotton-wood thicket and looked up, and down, and across; nothing in sight; so Jim took up some of the top planks of the raft and built a snug wigwam to get under in blazing weather and rainy, and to keep the things dry. Jim made a floor for the wigwam, and raised it a foot or more above the level of the raft, so now the blankets and all the traps was out of the reach of steamboat waves. Right in the middle of the wigwam we made a layer of dirt about five or six inches deep with a frame around it for to hold it to its place; this was to build a fire on in sloppy weather or chilly; the wigwam would keep it from being seen. . . . Every night we passed towns, some of them away up on black hillsides, nothing but just a shiny bed of lights, not a house could you see. The fifth night we passed St. Louis, and it was like the whole world lit up" (pp. 69–70).

Huckleberry Finn and *Kim* describe somewhat shorter journeys than *Captain Singleton* and *Les enfants* and do not have the round-the-world feeling. For that reason, for classification they can be subsumed by the first titles. Of course they have other virtues and are, as complete wholes,

just as fine examples of the Wanderer adventure, not to mention their
purely literary merits.

Because of the literary tradition I have described, there can be no clear-
cut beginning point for the Wanderer tradition, as there is for the
Robinson story or the Musketeers story. We find travelers like Kim and
Huck even in the oldest folktales. But the authors who are the best
examples of the Wanderer adventure writers—in a way equivalent to
Defoe and Dumas in the earlier cases—would be Twain and Kipling,
because in their hands the Wanderer story is both charged with the
excitements of empire in the modern sense and achieves a striking
literary success.

That is most true as applied to Kipling, who publicly allied himself
with British authority in India (though we should remember that he was
only the bard of the Empire's master class, that he was quite alien to
them in many ways). Twain is often thought to have been anti-imperialist
because of his satires on the American overseas imperialism of the first
decade of the twentieth century, the last decade of his life. We should,
however, remember Twain's racism with regard to the American Indian
and that he had always been the bard of progress in the crassest sense,
celebrating America as the mother country of modernity. In any case,
the excitement of empire expressed by the Wanderer adventure cannot
be construed as an approval of empire (or progress). That excitement
can go with many kinds of judgment. The crucial thing is the rendering
of certain feelings sharply and perceptively enough to communicate
them to others.

Both *Kim* and *Huckleberry Finn* are gentle and playful adventures
and, by comparison with, say, Verne's or Defoe's work, subtle and
sophisticated works of literature. The most important single aspect of
that subtlety is that both authors turn their backs on the historical forces
they serve: in Kipling's case the British administration in India, and in
Twain's case American material and moral progress in the years after
the Civil War. They take for granted the splendor of those achievements
and ask our affection and amusement for the alternatives—the other and
the past. In their company we move backward in time as we move
onward in space. In Twain's case it is the recent American past we visit,
the South before the Civil War; the war is assumed to have redeemed the
old evils and aroused new energies, practical as well as moral. In
Kipling's case it is the "immemorial" panorama and pageant of Indian

life, barely touched by modernization. In both cases the reader (con-sciously or not) is always measuring the distance between his or her here-and-now and the gigantic diorama being unfurled before him. He is invited to nostalgically and sentimentally prefer the past, but if he wants to be reasonable and serious he will also exult in his own condition and cherish its values the more for his visit away from them.

For instance, Jim and the Lama represent two kinds of nonwhite experience—nonwhite culture and knowledge—palatable to the white race. The white boy rises superior to his companion—inferior in wisdom, no doubt, but superior in vitality, which is the value adventurers care about. These stories differ from those by Defoe and Verne in that they are not so set on instructing the reader—they offer insights rather than information—though they have a strong factual interest. They are also by talented artists in language, and yet (because of the equivocal relations Twain and Kipling, being adventure writers, had with the literature of their time) they escape the crippling category of "literature and not adventure." That category circumscribes, for instance, Thomas Mann's *Felix Krull* and limits its potency as adventure. Twain and Kipling wrote not for literary critics but for readers who hoped to find truth and value in adventure.

The Melodrama of Wandering

Elaborately plotted melodramas that half-belong to this adventure type appeared in France and Germany in the nineteenth century too. One example is Karl May's *Das Waldroeschen* (1882–83), which was sub-titled "Die Verfolgung um die Erde" (The Pursuit Around the World). Covering the years 1850–67, it describes an attempt to usurp the fortune of a rich Spanish family, the Rodrigandas, by replacing the true heir, Mariano, with another male child. This is foiled by the efforts of Karl Sternau, a German doctor and frontiersman in the American West, and his pupil Curt Helmers. In the background are major figures from German and Mexican public life: Benito Juarez and the ill-fated Em-peror Maximilian, Bismarck, and Kaiser Wilhelm I. (This variety of the Wanderer adventure was often linked to Mexican history.) May com-bined a faith in liberal and progressive values with a sentimental enthusiasm for the Kaiser and the Prussian Junker class. Curt Helmers is born into the middle class but is able finally to join the aristocratic Prussian army, and this is a sign of hope for Germany.

May insists on the moral superiority of the prairie and its people; Karl Sternau foreshadows Old Shatterhand. (Many Germans believed in their close cousinship with the frontiersmen, believed that Natty Bumppo, for instance, had a historical German prototype, Johann Adam Hartleben, born in 1743 in Edenkoben.) But the scope of this story is worldwide. Among its many episodes is one involving Arabs in Dayla, where May follows a narrative of English explorer Richard Burton. However, May does not follow Burton in his enthusiasm for Islam, substituting instead the ordinary Western allegations of slavekeeping and sexual immorality.

Books like May's also differ in form from those we have looked at so far. The plots as well as the themes of *Kim* and *Huckleberry Finn* could be called modern—frankly episodic and lighthearted. The moments of melodrama are designated as belonging to the other, the background— to the past in the South, to the Indians in India. The protagonists, who represent us, pass on, detach themselves, leaving the melodramas behind. This story of May's is essentially melodramatic, and that fact is related to its Mexican material.

From 1850 on, there were several novels by French and German authors about Mexico, and most focused on the historical French attempt to set up a new regime there, to replace the Spanish one. After various other attempts, Napoleon III landed French troops in Mexico in 1862, and in 1864 Maximilian von Hapsburg was named emperor, to be deposed and shot three years later. This was a story that dramatized in real life Europe's fantasies of imperialism—conscious imperialism in the French style (eagles and fanfares, an army and a court) as distinct from the English style, which proceeded steadily (before 1876) under the stolid appearances of commerce and Christianity.

Napoleon III's initiative had been preceded by an attempt by his friend Count Aimé Raousset de Boulbon, to build himself a kingdom in Mexico. Boulbon, born in 1817, first left Europe for Algeria, where he tried to buy himself enough land to set up an independent state there. Then, after attaching himself to the fortunes of Louis-Napoleon in France, he set off for Mexico. In San Francisco he joined forces with Charles de Pindray, who had raised some North American troops, on a commission from the government of Mexico, to defend Mexico against the Apaches. But Boulbon attempted a coup d'état and was arrested and shot, at the age of only thirty-five.

Some facts of Mexican history were dramatized in various ways by "Gabriel Ferry" in *Le coureur de bois*; by "Sir John Retcliffe" in *Puebla: Oder der Schatz der Ynkas*; and by "Frederic Armand" in *In Mexico*. These are all examples of *Kolportage* adventure, according to the May scholars' classification, and I am using "melodrama" here as equivalent to *Kolportage*. These stories don't fit neatly into our seven-part taxonomy; they cut across our categories because their subgenre was not much practiced in England. (Charles Kingsley's *Westward Ho!* may be the most similar English novel, with its elaborate episodic plot and far range of settings, but the central story is quite different.) This topic, and the formal devices that went with it, were largely alien to the respectable Anglo-Saxon mind. It is probably significant that among these writers at least "Retcliffe" (his real name was Herrmann Goedsche) was a professed hater of England and admirer of Napoleon III who wanted his country, Prussia, to emulate France in military adventurism.

Of these *Kolportage* writers, the most relevant to our Wanderer category is Karl May. His more famous but less interesting Westerns and Easterns are called by German scholars *Reiseromanen*, travel novels, which is close to Wanderer adventures. From our point of view, the Westerns are of the Frontiersman type, but the Easterns could be fit into the Wanderer category. Unlike the Westerns, they are deeply involved with German espionage in the Ottoman Empire, and we shall see that espionage is a cultural ally of the Wanderer tale. They are, however, less interesting examples of that genre than his *Kolportage* novels, such as *Das Waldroeschen*, which goes all around the world and is in a sense historically dialectical.

Volker Klotz points out that the *Reiseromanen* of both East and West had settings that were point for point the reverse of contemporary Germany and so gave their readers the easy thrill of escape. (He makes an interesting comparison between these stories and the zoos and museums recently opened to the general public in the nineteenth century: nature in unnatural arrangements, history in frozen potpourri—a mild and public surrealism. Kim's adventures, we might recall, begin from the museum in Lahore, which was in biographical fact Kipling's father's.) By contrast, the *Kolportage* novels, going to and fro between Germany and abroad, raised questions rather than offering escape. They made the homeland seem adventurous and the abroad seem familiar.[3] They therefore offered a more dialectical experience.

3. See Fritz Martini, *Probleme des Erzaehlens in der Weltliteratur*, 162, 163, 167.

The Wanderer as Literary Myth

The wanderer is the archetype of all adventurers, if you study adventures out of historical context, as literary myths. Indeed, it has been argued that all literature is the story of a quest. One need not accept that argument: "all literature" can be boiled down or essentialized in more than one way; but certainly one can think of many stories that include a good deal of traveling, literal or spiritual, from the *Odyssey* and the Old Testament book of Exodus on, via the medieval quests and the Spanish romances and the French *romans précieux*. The Wanderer label promises both the form and the content of all adventures: both the episodic form, its only bounding line a deferrable climax and natural limits like birth and death; and the interest content—the geographical descriptions, the sense of travel and change, social panorama, and social criticism.

Pure myth cannot, by definition, have much content of any current affairs kind. Looking for strictly mythical wanderers, we find, for instance, the Wandering Jew and the Flying Dutchman, around whom so many legends have been woven. From the point of view of the social function of adventure in the modern world, especially in its relation to white empire, these are somewhat peripheral. The more they belong to literary myth, the less they belong to social myth.

It happens that these two topics attracted some of the writers of adventure. Both Eugène Sue and Pierre Féval wrote Wandering Jew stories (Féval also wrote a *Mystères de Londres,* after the pattern of Sue's Mysteries) and Captain Marryat wrote a Flying Dutchman tale, *The Flying Ship.* But none of these books is as successful as others of their authors' work, either as adventure or by literary criteria.

But certain combinations of adventure and realistic fiction deserve to be considered. The most famous variety, from the history-of-literature point of view, is the picaresque story, built around the picaro, a type of story popular in much of Europe from the late sixteenth century to the late eighteenth.

The picaro story was attractive to Defoe, whose *Colonel Jack* and *Captain Avery* fit into this category, as do his books about remarkable female picaros, *Moll Flanders* and *Roxana,* and, as I have argued, as would *Robinson Crusoe* itself if one gave equal attention to all the parts of both volume one and volume two.

But both the self-conscious picaresque and the literary-mythical quest should be set somewhat apart from the books we discuss here, as not being modern adventure in our sense. The picaresque was the closer to the categories we are discussing. It contained socially and morally realistic episodes, antiromantic in reaction against the Spanish romances, and thus parallel in tendency with Defoe. But the difference between it and his adventures is the respectability and self-respect of the latter's narrators; Moll Flanders the thief, and Captain Singleton the pirate, either are, or sound as if they are, always climbing the social ladder, always making money, keeping their accounts, and raising their expectations. And this self-respect is not unrelated to the self-respect of the writer and of the adventure form.

The picaro, on the other hand, is essentially disreputable. One of the most famous of these stories was translated into English in 1622 as *The Rogue* and referred to as "The Spanish Rogue"; this was Mateo Aleman's *Guzman de Alfarache*. Several of Defoe's protagonists *ought* to be rogues, judging them by their deeds, but reading their narratives you have to find another category for them. They seem to see themselves as, or he presents them as, respectable businesspersons. They belong to a modern world, in which "rogue" can be applied only to people beyond the pale, to reckless roistering outlaws.

Because literature is called to resist the clichés of the moment, including those of respectability, the picaro-rogue has persuaded many men of letters to weave stories about him. The picaro is literature's idea of an adventurer. Such stories provide an opportunity for satirical description and analysis of various social classes and national types. The actual adventures serve as part of the social criticism. For instance, if the rogue robs a rich mansion, we see its various rooms from a robber's point of view; the same is true if he seduces a nun in her convent or is seduced by a fine lady in her marital bed. But if these episodes dramatize the rogue's roguishness, his externality to the social scheme, rather than virtues of courage and endurance, they will not be adventures as defined here.

Michael Nerlich discusses this subgenre in its later nineteenth-century and early twentieth-century form.[4] He deals with Charles de Costers *Uelenspiegel* (1867), Romain Rolland's *Colas de Breugnon* of 1913–14 (which is also the date of Gide's *Caves du Vatican* and of Thomas Mann's *Felix Krull*), Mann's *Joseph* (1933–38) and his brother Hein-

---

4. Michael Nerlich, *Kunst, Politik, und Schelmerei.*

rich's *Henri IV* (1935–38), and Gide's *Thésée* (1948). Nerlich says these are all disguised images of the artist as laughing rogue. The idea is explained by his subtitle, "The Return of the Artist and Intellectual into the Society of the 20th Century." He says they are not real picaros; from our point of view, they are not real adventurers.

In these books the episodes are too firmly restricted to the function of illustrating the author's moral view, or too clearly a part of an ambitious literary enterprise. The adventures don't seem real enough. The sense of literary or intellectual aspiration inhibits the thrills of fear and love for the hero that derive from reader identification and are proper to adventure. Take, for instance, *Felix Krull*. Obviously, that must be called an adventure in some sense, but Mann's literary personality, his fiction's imaginative ethos, is the epitome of all the qualities that alienate the reader from adventure in its simplest and most essential sense.

Kim and *Huckleberry Finn* are not picaresque in Mann's way, nor are they like the others Nerlich discusses, because of their mixture of social irresponsibility with various kinds of respectability. In *Kim* one can see that the idea of the Secret Service allows the reader to be on both sides of the moral question at once—indifferent to ordinary responsible behavior but *more* responsible than those who abide by those standards. In *Huckleberry Finn* there is something comparable in Huck's (and Twain's) duplicity about the slavery question: Huck's apparent corruption and real innocence in that regard.

Other Cultural Forces

There are more familiar classifications that coincide in part with that of the Wanderer—for instance, thrillers and espionage and private eye fiction, insofar as they send their protagonists traveling, whether geographically or just socially. (Western novels don't seem to offer much variety, or indeed much depth of social observation.) Then there have long been literary stories that have journalists as heroes—notably, at the end of the nineteenth century and the beginning of the twentieth, stories by Stephen Crane and Richard Harding Davis and Ernest Hemingway. Their work is certainly Wanderer adventure.

As this would suggest, the biographies and autobiographies of journalists, spies, detectives, con men, and mercenary soldiers provide much of the raw material, the factual anecdote, that belongs to this type, the hinterland to the fictional adventures, which arouses our interest and compels our assent. Examples include Vincent Sheean's and William Shirer's autobiographies. (Historical *studies* of these types, insofar as they exist, do not seem to constitute a factual equivalent; they are too intellectualized.)

Another factual equivalent for the Wanderer story is the achievement of mountaineers, climbers, hikers, and so on. In *The Challengers: British and Commonwealth Adventure Since 1945,* Ingrid Cranfield discusses adventures in mountains, caves, the poles, flying, gliding, and swimming. It is worth noting that the people involved have in common with fictional adventurers of this type an enthusiasm for the latest equipment, and also that there is a social structure to the group. They are predominantly public school and military in background, as their names and nicknames make clear. Some 80 percent of them are men, and the women are usually unmarried.

The books they write are often autobiographical. Perhaps especially close to fiction is the type of book nowadays published by the central figure in a television program featuring climbing, diving, or flying feats. Two French examples are Christian Brincourt's *La face cacheé de l'aventure* (Brincourt has run such a program on French television since 1971) and Alain Bombard's *Au-delà de l'horizon,* whose program has the same name.

So far, with the other adventure types, I have suggested a link between each adventure hero and one particular nation, though in the case of the Avenger story that link was tenuous. In the case of the Wanderer tale, it does not seem appropriate to suggest such a link, but one can point instead to two seemingly opposite social frontiers, especially the property of empires: the huge central city and peripheral untraveled lands. Such wanderers as the journalist and the spy are plausible heroes for this subgenre because their work can plausibly send them to either frontier— or shuttling to and fro between the two. They are not frontiersmen, because they move not so much in a literal legal frontier as in these metaphorical ones, where the moral and social criteria of civilized life break down under stress of one kind or another.

Thus the Wanderer adventure plays an important part in shaping the modern white consciousness, the self-consciousness of white empire. We (at least those who read boys' books) have all been imaginative adventurers from the beginning, because of our reading. And this too is a political fact. It is part of what both sides of the confrontations feel when "East" meets "West" or "North" meets "South," or white meets nonwhite. The whites have a heritage of expanding conquering consciousness that is also tied to nonpolitical ideas and images (the images of adventure)— that is, politically unselfconscious. The nonwhite feels the other's heritage.

Thus, by and large, Third World people do not go on adventures. Ingrid Cranfield's account of adventures shows that the largest number of adventure heroes come from the United Kingdom, and the smallest from Third World countries in the Commonwealth. As climber Chris Bonington says in his *Quest for Adventure,* "Adventure as we know it today is a very recent phenomenon. The concept of climbing mountains or sailing small boats just for the fun of it could only come to those with sufficient wealth and time to indulge their whims. . . . Comparatively few people from the Third World play the adventure game" (p. 12).

But Bonington himself describes the basic satisfaction of climbing as involving "the hot heady spice of risk. . . . It means pitting one's ability against a personal unknown and winning through . . . taking one's life literally in one's hands" (p. 11). So adventure in this sense continues to excite and challenge long after it seemed to be outdated. In *The Last Secrets,* a book of the 1920s, John Buchan listed the last great challenges to man, from seeing Lhasa to exploring New Guinea, and he concluded that all the really great mysteries had been solved. But Ingrid Cranfield in 1976 was saying how many "last great journeys" had been undertaken since the concept had seemed outdated, in 1945, and she even cited a sixteenth-century adventurer, Martin Frobisher, who had set off to seek the Northwest Passage because, even then, that seemed "the only thinge of the world that was left undone."

The adventurer type and career is well exemplified by Alain Gerbault (1893–1941), who was born into a wealthy industrialist family in France and prepared to enter one of the *grandes écoles* of that country. Small for his age, he made himself a tennis champion when young and went on to be a pilot during the war, and then a sailor. Though a French patriot, he loved England and English poets—Kipling, Masefield, Shelley—and recited their poems aloud in storms at sea.[5] He was one of those for whose benefit Gide and his friends tried to introduce English adventure into French literature.

5. Eric Vibart, *Alain Gerbault,* 53.

Gerbault was excited by reading Jack London's *Cruise of the Snark,* a true story of the author's sea adventures, and when he heard an Englishman say that no Frenchman could have done what London did, that crystallized Gerbault's ambition to prove him wrong. Gerbault became a national hero when he sailed alone from Nantucket to Gibraltar in 1923, and he declared, "I nurtured my great project in order to prove that the spirit of adventure had not died in France."[6] Such adventurers and their national audiences are closely linked. One might say that an adventurer's audience *is* a nation, and that that is one definition of a nation. (Thibaudet, it will be remembered, said literary adventures are written for a race, not for a reading public.) Most adventurers have sponsors, often among big industrialists if not from the armed services, and they have direct links (i.e., nonliterary links) to publishers and the media.

But like many adventurers, Gerbault was in revolt against his civilization, and from 1925 on, when he reached the South Seas, he became more and more a partisan of the natives of those islands and a critic of the French administration. We shall recognize a likeness to his British precursor, Robert Louis Stevenson. Gerbault intervened in politics there and got into trouble. He wore native costume and danced in native ceremonies, and he rejoiced in Europe's adoption of the sun cult, as a sign of the decay of white superiority. In his *L'empire du soleil,* Gerbault said he aspired to be another Kim, another "little friend of all the world."

The wanderer does not seem, then, to embody any one nation's self-consciousness as demonstrably as the other adventure types we have studied, but—more important for our argument—the wanderer does seem to embody the feelings of the imperial citizen about the empire he belongs to. This is not necessarily a directly political consciousness, but it usually tends toward that. The most vivid case, no doubt, is that of *Kim,* where for most of the book the reader delights in the sheer color and variety of the Indian scene and the adventures of the Tibetan lama and the Anglo-Indian boy. But finally, as the goal of all this adventuring, as the only satisfactory conclusion, Kim's destiny to be a Secret Service agent and a servant of the British Empire looms up.

As our quotations showed, in Kipling's hands geography itself, or what Buchan calls topography, becomes an imperialist form of knowl-

6. Ibid., 69.

edge that feeds a lust for possession and power. One cannot say quite that about *Huckleberry Finn,* or even *Captain Grant* perhaps. But surely even in Twain's novel the majestic power of the Mississippi ultimately belongs to the American empire and swells the heart of every American reader, and all the motley pageant along those banks, and all the laughter, accrue to the same imperial cause, the same sense of greatness.

There are also aspects of literature, and of the sociology of literature, that relate to this Wanderer subgenre. Many writers (and painters and artists in other media) think of themselves as adventurers of this type. An obvious example is the "tough guy" writer like Hemingway and Mailer. Mailer, who set out to imitate Hemingway, has said that he has always expected one day to have to take to the hills with a gun. Then there are adventurer writers like T. E. Lawrence and the other desert writers of England and France, and the sailor and mountaineer authors. But there are also less obvious cases. It is not possible really to make sense of a career like George Orwell's except by seeing him as in part an adventurer—a wanderer—his social criticism deriving its authority from his experience as wanderer and his continuing stance on the very edge of society. And even D. H. Lawrence, whose actual wanderings must be called domestic, those of a married man, aspired to be an adventurer. His career too makes sense only when one takes that aspiration seriously.

As for sardonic reversals of this genre, we can turn to Stevenson in such works as *The Ebb Tide* and *The Beach of Falesá,* or to Conrad. From *Almayer's Folly,* his first novel, to *Victory,* Conrad presents us with a series of wanderers who come to grief—and to imaginative grief too, for they come to a sordid rather than tragic end. *The Secret Agent* and *Under Western Eyes* are his versions of the espionage novel. Conrad is perhaps the greatest or the archetype of adventure-reversers, and that accounts for his great and sustained literary prestige. He has been the literary establishment's hit man in its feud with adventure.

Twentieth-century literature has been full of later Conrads, from Malraux to Maugham to Le Carré, but in most (and indeed in Conrad himself) the sardonic note is subverted by the romance it offers to limit. Pierre Mac Orlan put the point as a generalization in *Le petit manuel du parfait aventurier.* The twentieth-century wanderer is just as romantic a figure as the nineteenth-century version, except that the contemporary excitement attaches itself more to the sordid.

As for the variables, the early examples of *Moll Flanders* and *Roxana* show us the flexibility of the Wanderer subgenre, its availability to women protagonists. However, their stories show only elements of wandering, and the later record shows a huge preponderance of male protagonists. The adventuress, as we have seen, has been given a less serious story to tell, something closer to scandal or mere pornography. As for the individual versus the group, the wanderer usually feels alone, but in fact he usually has companions. Singleton has the group he leads, and later his comrade, William; Huck has Jim, Kim has the Lama. In the literal sense of individual and group, the alternatives seem to be blurred, but the feeling of solitariness is important.

Wandering is an element in many other adventures, as adventure is an element in many kinds of fiction. Travel is the simplest, most pervasive, and also the blandest and least challenging, kind of adventure. Most people's adventures come when they are traveling, and most travels have a spice of adventure in them. Wandering is simply a more spontaneous and planless—more adventurous—form of travel. It falls far short of being cast away on a desert island or killing a man in a duel.

Travel literature is an enormous category, still lively today and recurrently attractive to writers of talent and literary ambition—take, for instance, D. H. Lawrence and Evelyn Waugh in the 1920s, and Paul Theroux today. Both the panorama of things described and the detachment of the describer please the reader. It is in this guise that we can encounter and acknowledge facts of political and economic life that we find it awkward to name (except to denounce or repudiate) in our own society. We are willing, as we travel, to see things as colorful, not as black or white, right or wrong. This is another of the functions of adventure, and especially adventure of the Wanderer kind.

8

The Sagaman Story
The Sixth Type

The Sagaman type of adventure, unlike the other types, is named after a precursor, and that earlier genre—the Saga—is associated with a premodern society. So here, more definitely than elsewhere, we see adventure writers seeking a source of energy in the past. Indeed, stories of this type ask readers to move imaginatively to and fro between their present modes of being and those very different ones, as a way to acquire strength.

The reference is primarily to the Icelandic sagas of the thirteenth century, but that should not entirely exclude the other Norse and Teutonic stories that go by that name. All the sagas, and particularly those about the Nibelungen, written in the same century in Austria, inspired and fascinated later writers, above all in imperial and postimperial Germany. Friedrich Hebbel called the Nibelungen legends Germany's national epic, and the partial parallel between that country's use of the *Nibelungenlied* and England's use of *Robinson Crusoe* and France's use of *Les trois Mousquetaires* is half the interest of the Sagaman story for us.

However, it is most of all modern writing that concerns us, and adventure not epic. We approach the Sagaman story via writing in modern languages, and so the Icelandic sagas have a preeminence, because of their record of stimulating modern writers, in England as well as in Germany. The elements of homely realism in their art, and their political enthusiasm for freedom and "equality among gentry," seemed less dangerous and more familiar than the Romantic politics and eschatology of the *Nibelungenlied* (such as the idea of the Twilight of the Gods). This was especially true for writers in English, and after Wagner had set the latter to music.

What are the main elements of the Sagaman story? Their pattern has been variously analyzed, but in *The Icelandic Family Saga*, T. M. Andersson speaks of an Introduction (including a genealogy), a Conflict (between two men, two groups, or a man and a group), a Climax (someone gets killed, usually the hero), a Revenge (including a feud) and a Reconciliation (often involving the law), and an Aftermath.

Two examples are the sagas of Egil and of Grettir. In both, the main character is brave and powerful, of forceful and imperious temper—a leader, but quarrelsome and difficult to get along with, partly out of meanness, partly out of integrity. There is a succession of semi-independent episodes, some much more relevant to the main plot than others but arranged roughly in alternation. In some we see the hero's fortunes (or those of his family and party) rise, and in others we see them sink. They rise because of all the hero can do for others (for the king, in Egil's case) and because powerful men intercede on his behalf. Each sinks in a series of defeats and disasters, leading to his being outlawed and finally killed.

Andersson's word "revenge" reminds us how much this adventure type has in common with the Avenger type, and we have seen that the latter had something in common with the Musketeers story. The differences between the three are fairly clear, in their range of political and imaginative reference—for instance, the importance of certain local and historical color in this case; and in the saga readers' going back and forth between past and present. But it is appropriate to stress here that these differences are a matter of date as much as of inner truth, that they are extrinsic as well as intrinsic. In other words, each adventure story has a limited life span, the life being in part dependent on the urgency of the politics to which it corresponds, and the limit being determined by the number of its repetitions and by the consequent fading of its appeal to both readers and writers. (The one exception to this, the seeming immortality of *Robinson Crusoe,* can no doubt be explained by the way the educational system institutionalized that story. That, after all, is the explanation for the immortality of "literature" too.) Thus, the Avenger story partly replaced and continued the Musketeers story, and was in its turn replaced by the Sagaman story.

As for the original saga hero, two types are usually distinguished: the handsome, blond, lighthearted, and lucky, like both Thorolfs in the *Egil Saga,* and the dark, embittered, and sarcastic, like Egil and Skella Grim. (Grettir is red-haired and freckled—an anomaly, but another opposite of blondness.) Both types end tragically, however, and for both loyalty between men is the essence of life, which only fate can destroy. Sometimes it is primarily loyalty between leader and followers, sometimes mutual loyalty between equals (as in the *Sworn Brothers Saga*).

Women also play a part in some sagas, and unusually powerful parts for the adventure genre, as the stories of Gudrun in the *Laxdale Saga* and Hallgerda in the *Njal Saga* show. They are powerful agents of *eros,* but also of *potestas,* powerful for their dynastic ambitions and strength of will. They stand out as strong compared with the heroines of medieval romances, who are more passive and pathetic, and in contrast to the women of the Musketeers story, who are less convincing as women of power. In the *Laxdale Saga* the four-person central drama tells how Gudrun has her husband, Bolli, kill the man she loves, Kjartan, resulting in a bitter feud. Gudrun and Kjartan are strikingly gifted people, natural leaders, and strongly attracted to each other. She married Nolli, Kjartan's best friend, thinking that the latter was going to remain in Norway, out of her reach. When he returns, her love turns to jealousy and hatred. (She plays the part Brynhild plays in the Ring legend, Kjartan plays Sigurd's part, and Bolli plays Gunnar's.) The women may be said to predominate.

Nevertheless, it is worth noting that when Halldor and other of Kjartan's brothers come to avenge his death on Bolli, Gudrun meekly goes out to wash her linen in the brook. As a woman, she can take no part in actual fighting, and this means she does not act in the central action. The Sagas are notable for the concrete detail in which they describe weapons (both types and individual swords or axes, which sometimes have names) and fights. Particular strokes are given with particular weapons, and the wounds inflicted are described. Women are limited to casting spells, egging their men to quarrel, and betraying them, as when Hallgerda (out of some long-hidden grudge) at a crucial moment in a fight refuses her husband a lock of her long hair to make a new string for his bow. The psychological interest of the women's roles is great, but when some modern scholars see them as more central to the stories than the men, they seem to forget the importance to the Icelanders of the actual fighting.

What is most striking about this type of adventure is the frankness of the violence, which is committed by the hero as much as by the villain. This is a physical violence in single combat: Egil bit through the windpipe of his antagonist, and Grettir (when the berserk Snoekoll sat unsuspecting on his horse with a shield in front of him) suddenly kicked the shield up so that it broke his upper jaw, and the lower jaw fell down and at the same moment pulled Snoekoll off his horse and cut his head off. Although such violence cannot compare in destructiveness with the explosions described in Verne's or even Defoe's novels, it more directly confronts the reader with a moral challenge.

The contrasting moral virtue of the saga heroes is political independence. In the *Egil Saga* the main hero, his father, and his grandfather all refuse to attend the court of Harald Fine Hair, the first king of a united Norway. They refuse to become his noblemen, preferring to remain semi-independent rulers of lands on the periphery of the kingdom. Indeed, this is true of all the Sagas, in that Iceland as a whole was a settlement of landowners who fled from the establishment of Harald's suzerainty. Their political ideology is therefore rather like the frontiersmen's and the opposite of that of Dumas or Scott, which glorified the establishment of the nation-state. (Scott at least had a strong feeling for what that establishment cost, but still he recommended the sacrifice.) The Icelanders were men who refused to belong to a nation-state and who crossed the seas looking for new and free land. In this they were precursors of the great white migration, and notably of the early Americans, but they were of the landowning and servant-employing class, and therefore congenial to the aristo-military class of nineteenth-century Europe, who fed their dreams on the revived sagas.

The Popularity of the Sagaman

The nineteenth- and twentieth-century Sagaman adventures differ from other adventures in their archaizing and atavistic character, their looking backward to so much earlier an age. Its historicalness "justified" the story's more savage style of virility, and the story itself gave the justification of history to the imperial nations at the end of the nineteenth century. Of course, the Musketeers story could be described as doing that too, especially the way Scott wrote it, for he does justify his violence. (Dumas, however, does not seem to have any qualms about fighting or any need to make a moral issue of it.) But that story's violence was, as depicted, romantic rather than savage, and at least by the time the Sagaman story became popular, the Musketeers type had lost all power to challenge its readers morally.

It is worth noting that the Sagaman story is often tragic, ending in the death of the hero and of the hopes invested in him—the end, one often feels, of all scope for his kind of virtues within society. The Musketeers story, and most other adventure types, are comic rather than tragic. It does not seem plausible to attribute the switch in the character of adventure simply to premonitions of the Great War, but it fits in with other signs of moral despondency and fear in the imperialist period before 1914. We should remember that this was also the period of pacifist idealism inspired by Tolstoy and Gandhi; public opinion, some people thought, had developed past the point of tolerating armies or war or patriarchy. The ugliness of Saga adventure was in part a denial of that idealism.

There were, however, signs of a strong interest in the Sagaman story long before the end of the nineteenth century. Scott, for instance, was a direct precursor of the enthusiasm for that story. His novel *The Pirate* included saga material and took some of it from Defoe. (Again the familiar few names recur. Why? Because adventure constitutes a tradition, just as literature does. It is an imaginative world, evolving but continuous, despite the differences between the types.) But the strength of Scott's work was the way his mind achieved viable compromises between the modern imagination and older forms. He wanted not to change the modern mind but to give it energy and flexibility by opening it to the past. The Saga adventure, as revived a generation or two later, was a more emotional endorsement of the virile prowess of the past in defiance of the present—at least, defiance of its liberal-moral consensus.

The first translation of the sagas into English, and so the beginning of the cult, seems to be in the first volume of Hakluyt's *Voyages* (1601) and thus contemporaneous with the first stirring of the other adventure types in the Renaissance mind. This passage was a forty-page translation of Arngrim Jonsson. Then there was a fragment in Bishop Percy's *Reliques of Ancient Poesy* in 1763, and then came Scott's abstract of the *Eyrbygga Saga,* published in 1814, the year of *Waverley.*[1]

In the mid-nineteenth century there came translations by G. W. Dasent, of primarily antiquarian appeal, and then, in the last quarter of that century, a revival of ordinary fictional interest, not accidentally contemporary with the efflorescence of imperial pride and anxiety, in England and the rest of Europe. The Sagas reflected the iconography of the Anglo-Saxon empire of the nineteenth century, showing its race and caste pride, in a reassuringly small and remote mirror. The Teutonic racism that developed so gradually but strikingly in, for instance, the American historians of the nineteenth century—from Prescott and Motley to Parkman and Adams—found the Sagas just to its taste. (The Anglo-Saxons are still more masculine than other races, these historians said, and their primitive politics is the source of our great institutions.)

Eric Magnusson and William Morris began their series of translations from the Icelandic in 1869 with *Grettir the Strong* and continued for a quarter of a century. Edmund Gosse made an epitome of the *Egil Saga* in 1879, and Paul du Chaillu wrote a historical work, *The Viking Age,* in 1889–90 (in which he claimed to give scholarly proof for the popular idea that the English descended from the North Teutons) and a historical novel, *Ivar the Viking,* in 1893.

Paul du Chaillu (1832–1903) may serve us to represent the ideologists of Sagaman adventure. He wrote first about Africa and was widely known as "the gorilla hunter" because he aroused late nineteenth-century Europe's fascination with the big apes. In that capacity he was a precursor of Edgar Burroughs and the Tarzan story, but then his attention turned, while living in America, to the Vikings. "In America he had seen immigrants from the north countries and had been impressed by their physical perfection and almost epic qualities of appearance and character," says his biographer.[2]

---

1. R. B. Allen, *Old Icelandic Sources in the English Novel.*
2. Michel Vaucaire, *Paul du Chaillu, Gorilla Hunter,* 220.

Du Chaillu himself explains, "While studying the progress made in the colonization of different parts of the world by European nations, I have often asked myself the following questions: How is it that over every region of the globe the spread of the English-speaking people and of their language far exceeds that of all the other European nations combined? Why is it that, wherever the English-speaking people have settled, or are at this day found, even in small numbers, they are far more energetic, daring, adventurous, and prosperous, and understand the art of self-government and of ruling alien people far better than other colonizing nations?" These questions led him to study the Vikings, and to declare that contemporary England and America drew their strength from that ancestry, because, "all the nations which have risen to high power and widespread dominion have been founded by men endowed with great, I may say terrible, energy; extreme bravery and the love of conquest being the most prominent traits of their character. The mighty sword with all its evils has thus far always proved a great engine of civilization."[3]

England became the most powerful colony of the North Teutons, du Chaillu explained, and then waxed more powerful than the mother country, just as nowadays she sees America taking over from herself. However, "The impartial mind which rises above the prejudices of nationality must acknowledge that no country will leave more a glorious impress upon the history of the world than England. Her work cannot be undone; should she today sink beneath the seas which bathe her shores, her record will forever stand brilliantly illuminated on the page of history."[4] Thus the interest in the Vikings, and the writing of a modern Viking saga, is closely linked, for this Frenchman, with the world triumph of the Anglo-Saxons.

This interest was thus quite international. Germany and Scandinavia were special cases, because of their closeness to the historical source. But some of the writers and thinkers of the United States were also strongly influenced, as the case of Thorstein Veblen shows. The idea of society depicted in the Sagas was an important criterion for Veblen in his sociology of contemporary America and Europe.

Then G. Stanley Hall's *Adolescence* (1904) pointed out that the period of individual development (a concept Hall largely invented) corre-

3. Paul du Chaillu, *The Viking Age*, vii–viii.
4. Ibid.

sponded to the period of migrations in human history—a time of upheavals for both the race and individual, which naturally gave rise to myths and sagas, with their tales of battle and heroic leaders. Hall's seminal work focused the attention of a large audience on adolescence as the most interesting phase of life and associated it with the Sagas. And Theodore Roosevelt, in his famous lecture of 1899 on "The Strenuous Life," contrasted Americans, descended from and still themselves "stern men with empire in their brains," to the Chinese, long content to rot by inches in ignoble ease and therefore defeated by nations who have not lost "the manly and adventurous qualities." If America had avoided the Civil War, said Roosevelt, it would have saved hundreds of thousands of lives and hundreds of millions of dollars, but Americans would have shown themselves weaklings, unfit to stand among the great nations. "It is a base untruth to say that happy is the nation that has no history," he declared, reminding us of Dumas's ideas about the historical novel.[5] The adventures of the past explain the greatness of the white nations now, especially *some* white nations, and their greatness depends on renewing that tradition of adventure.

These speculative ideas were put into practice from the beginning, in a number of cultural projects, especially aimed at boys. (Adolescence was at first treated as, in effect, a male phenomenon.) When Robert Baden-Powell's *Scouting for Boys* (1908) appeared, it extolled the *rites de passage* practiced by African tribal cultures like the Zulus and the Swazis and set out frankly to imitate them.[6] The aim of the scouting movement was that English and American boys should also be trained to manliness and not allowed to drift into becoming poor-spirited wasters, "soft, sloppy, cigarette-suckers."[7] Reversion to tribal culture, and the reading of adventures, including the Sagas, was an important part of those projects.

Meanwhile, such novelists as Jack London, Frank Norris, Theodore Dreiser, and Stephen Crane created adult fictional heroes who reverted atavistically to the savagery of Berserk Vikings. Examples are Crane's story "The Blue Hotel," Norris's novel *Moran of the Lady Letty*, Dreiser's *The Titan*, and London's "Call of the Wild." This last was published in 1903 to immediate acclaim and remained popular for at

5. Roderick Nash, *The Call of the Wild*, 82.
6. See J. A. Mangan and J. Walvin, *Manliness and Morality*, 201.
7. Ibid., 203.

least thirty years. It was the story of a tame dog taken to the wild north and lost and gradually reverting there to being a wolf. The story ends with the dog "leaping gigantic above his fellows, his great throat abellow as he sings a song of a younger world."[8] This is, of course, an allegory of human atavism occurring under the influence of the savage North and enthusiastically recommended.

Countries that considered themselves highly civilized, and overcivilized for conflict with their enemies, took consolation in the promise that their men would "revert" atavistically, in time of war. The next step was to see men taking on the qualities of noble animals—lions, bears, wolves—as a result of hunting them. Faulkner shows the bear in that light in his story "The Bear," and Hemingway shows the lion in "The Short Happy Life of Francis Macomber." In both cases the reader is asked to see and feel what the animal sees and feels, reverently. The animal is more authentic than the men who confront it. And the climax comes in *Why Are We in Vietnam?* when Mailer's hero tries literally to inhale the breath and the spirit of a dying wolf.

These works push their effects to the verge of self-caricature, but in O. E. Roelvaag's *Giants in the Earth* (1927) we find the saga hero adapted to modern mores, even adjusted to marital relations. Roelvaag's book is a composite work, including both the heroic story of Per Hansa, who triumphs as a pioneer on the prairie, and the antiheroic story of his wife, Beret, who goes mad under the stress of their life there.

Per Hansa sees what he is doing as founding a new land, like the Icelandic saga heroes: " 'Good God!' he panted, 'This kingdom is going to be *mine!*' " (p. 35). The second volume is titled "Founding the Kingdom." The other men in his settlement are seen in saga terms, one as a giant, another as a comic. But most striking are the passages where Per Hansa, the saga hero, is presented to us—adapted to a gentler modern ethos, to the beautiful rather than the sublime. "There were moments when he felt confident that he would live to see the day when most of the land of the prairie would be taken up; in such moods, there was something fascinating about him; bright emanations of creative force seemed to issue out of his square, sturdy figure; his whole form became beautiful, the lines of his face soft and delicate; whenever he spoke a tone of deep joy rang in his words" (p. 127). We are told that he is then irresistible even to his wife, who is in some ways deeply

8. Nash, *The Call of the Wild*, Introduction.

opposed to him, and that he seems to caress everything he touches. At the same time, Roelvaag saw his characters, and himself, in saga terms. His Norwegian home, we are told, stood stark and unprotected against the skyline, while behind it loomed the iron mountains of the coast. "A gloomy, desolate scene—a perilous stronghold on the fringe of the Arctic night" (p. xii). This is the saga landscape.

The spread of the Viking cult, and more generally the spread of the idea of their descendants' superior vitality and virility, was studied by the French philosopher of imperialism, Ernest Seillière, in a series of works, mostly between 1880 and 1920. His attention was focused on Germany, but also on France, where he traced the history of what he called Germanism (the theory that the French were German in origin) back to François Hotman's *Franco-Gallia* of 1574. A next step came in the eighteenth century when the Comte de Boulainvilliers invented a *feudal* Germanism, claiming that the aristocracy of France, as distinct from the lower classes, were of Teutonic and all-conquering stock, devoted to freedom and rebellious against kings, like the Icelanders. The count was protesting in the name of the French nobility against the dominance of the royal court at Versailles under Louis XIV. His book was published only in 1727, after that king's death. In the early nineteenth century the similar ideas of the Comte de Montlosier had some influence, and then came the better-known Comte de Gobineau, whose racial theories were received with enthusiasm by Wagner and his circle in Germany.

De Gobineau claimed Viking ancestry for his class, and for himself in particular. In 1879 he wrote *L'histoire d'Ottar-Jarl, pirate norvégien, conquérant du pays de Bray en Normandie*, in which he claimed to descend from this Ottar-Jarl, who was, like du Chaillu's Ivar the Viking, a semidivine son of Odin. Seillière traced the imperialist passion in the politics of many European nations, but also in their aesthetics and general philosophy. The ideas of racism and empire carried the image of the Viking like an emblem or a figurehead.

Works and Ideas Inspired by the Sagas

Germany was the country most responsive to the sagas' inspiration, but just for that reason it did not express that inspiration primarily in the humble form of the adventure tale. German literary intellectuals took an interest in the sagas all through the nineteenth century, following up the work of the Romantics. The *Bibliography of Comparative Literature* of 1950 has a chapter on sagas in which nearly all the titles are in German and run primarily from the 1850s to the 1920s.

The most famous individual case is that of Wagner, who apparently as early as 1843 carried a copy of Jacob Grimm's *German Mythology* everywhere with him. But of course other writers and artists were also interested in the same material. It was in 1843 that Wagner wrote *Der Nibelungen-Mithus* and a prose version of *Siegfrieds Tod* (later titled *Die Goetterdaemmerung*), and he finished the Ring cycle of music dramas in 1852. But besides Wagner, Henrich Dorn wrote a Nibelung opera in 1854, and Friedrich Hebbel a *Nibelungen* trilogy of plays in 1855–62.

Meanwhile, the political and military unification of Germany was proceeding under banner slogans like "blood and iron" and the consciously archaic, not to say atavistic, leadership of Bismarck. The two projects were closely connected. Germany imagined itself, in its national and imperial form after 1870, in saga-like terms. Statues of Teutonic warriors who defied Rome were erected, as were statues of Bismarck that made him seem comparable.

In the next period the important publisher and publicist Eugen Diederichs used the sagas to define a mystical version of German nationalism between 1900 and 1930. It is no accident that he began publishing a big series of Sagaman adventures in 1911. From 1912 on, his journal *Die Tat,* and his writings and speeches were major sources of ideas about specifically German religion, education, and art—which meant also pre-Christian and pre-Enlightenment kinds. In 1919, for instance, Diederichs gave an address commemorating those who died in the war, in which he began by greeting the green grass, the woods, Brother Wind, the clouds, Sister Sun, and so on, and he recalled his first Teutonic solstice ceremony, building a fire on a mountain, in 1904.

Diederichs's solemn exhortation was not adventure in the sense of hairbreadth escapes and narrative suspense, but it did celebrate the grander themes of saga adventure, taken as tragedy or religion. In a *Die Tat* essay of 1927, titled "Religion und Tragik," one of Diederichs's writers claimed that the Germans were like the Greeks in being tragically and not dogmatically religious, that they experienced life through heroic stories, and that such peoples were singularly free in mind and feeling even when constrained in action, compared with, say, the English.

Diederichs's group were very interested in dance and theater, and the epic and mass theater of pre-Nazi Germany often used saga-related themes.

The Nazis continued the trend begun under Bismarck. In their school textbooks, even *Robinson Crusoe* was said to be Nordic, in the central character's defiance of fate and his "Germanic" resourcefulness. Campe's version of the story was recommended for children to read, though it would be better for boys to read *Die Hoehlenkinder,* by a real German, or, better yet, Blunck's *Urvaetersage.*[9]

In Germany, saga adventure became philosophy in the work of Nietzsche, and music-drama in the work of Wagner—art and thought of the most ambitious and prestigious kind. This is not the place to discuss those two men at length, but it should be said that in Nietzsche's case what is relevant is not just his fascination with figures like "the blonde beast" and ideas like beyond good and evil, and the death of God, but his epistemology. One may surely say that Nietzsche found ultimate reality in the verb and not the noun, and in the verb of action not the verb of being. This is adventurous philosophy.

As for Wagner, one must point to the ideology of anti-Semitism in Wagner himself, in such Wagnerians as Houston Stewart Chamberlain, and in Wagner's Nazi heirs. Nothing is more central to that ideology than the idea that the Germans are, through all the centuries, a saga people, adventurous and heroic, their wisdom unconscious blood-knowledge, while the Jews are the opposite, a rootless and overcivilized people of ideas, of overdeveloped consciousness. The supreme German hero is Siegfried.

But it was not primarily through adventure novels that this ideology was spread in Germany, and so from this point on we shall concentrate on English-language saga adventures. R. B. Allen lists fifty-seven English-language novels of some note that were directly modeled on the sagas, most from the last quarter of the nineteenth century or the first of the twentieth.

He does not pay as much attention to the numerous writers for boys, such as J. F. Hodgetts, a professor of literature, who wrote *The Champion of Odin* (1885) and other titles for the *Boys' Own Paper.* Hodgetts was racist in the familiar bluff style; he said English boys were too straightforward to like the tricky Greek gods, while the Norse gods would appeal directly to their own Teutonic impulses.

9. Christa Kamenetsky, *Children's Literature in Nazi Germany.*

Two of Allen's fifty-seven are by R. M. Ballantyne (*Erling the Bold* is the better known of the two), one is by John Buchan, one is by Rider Haggard, one is by Scott, and one is by Charles Kingsley (*Hereward the Wake*, of 1866). I single these titles out because their authors are notable in the history of adventure in other ways. Kingsley wrote a book about the rise of the Teutonic race, titled *Heroes*; he inherited from the Carlyle of *Heroes and Hero-Worship* the calling to give Victorian England contact with the saga world and its virtues.

Kingsley's Hereward defines himself as a Viking and a Berserker, though at other times he is "just a boisterous lad"; the two concepts blur into each other. At the end, Hereward is said to have been the last of the old English, while the first of the new English is an agricultural squire (a way of linking past and present taken further by Kipling). Among other of Allen's titles, in some way remarkable in themselves, are Allen French's *Story of Rolf and the Viking's Bow* (1904), E. R. Eddison's *Styrbiorn the Strong* (1926), and, above all, Julian Corbett's bloodthirsty but powerful *Fall of Asgard*.

The plots of these stories vary, but the ideology is consistent and usually very plain. The preface to French's *Story of Rolf* states: "The sagas reveal the characteristics of our branch of the Aryan race, especially the personal courage which is so superior to that of the Greek and Latin races, and which makes the Teutonic epics (whether the Niebelungen Lied, the Morte d'Arthur, or the Njala) much more inspiring than the Iliad, the Odyssey, or the Aeneid." He associates this personal courage with "the prominence of law in almost every one of the Icelandic sagas."[10]

We have already referred to G. A. Lawrence's *Guy Livingstone,* which suggests the connections between these stories and the unofficial morality of English public school life. The novel is largely a document of Regency dandyism, but it uses the imagery of Vikings and Berserkers and delights in atavistic reversions. The narrator, a weak boy at school who needed Guy Livingstone's protection, adores him for the rest of his life and reflects that no one in adult life receives such undivided admiration as a schoolboy hero. He connects this with premodern modes of feeling and relationship. "The prestige of the Liberator [Daniel O'Connell] among the Irish peasantry comes nearest to it, I think; or the feeling of a clan, a hundred years ago, towards their chief."[11] This expresses, in

10. Allen French, *Story of Rolf and the Viking's Bow,* ix.
11. George A. Lawrence, *Guy Livingstone,* 21.

concentrated form, the atavistic attraction of leadership and implicitly of violence.

Many historical novels were written for children in the mid-nineteenth century, and many of those were about saga heroes—for instance, the Kearys' *Heroes of Asgard* (1857) and G. W. Dasent's *Tales from the North*. These stories appealed to the experience of adolescence, especially as undergone in the English and American boarding schools that prepared future rulers of the Anglo-Saxon empire. We saw an example of this in *Guy Livingstone*, and another is Thomas Hughes's *Tom Brown's Schooldays*, especially as that was sometimes understood. Tom Brown was to his frail and clever friend, Arthur, as Guy Livingstone was to the narrator of that novel, and he is as fine an example of courage, toughness, and force; but he is subdued to the Victorian ethos (represented by his headmaster, Dr. Arnold of Rugby), not the Regency.

The Thomas Hughes novel, however, could be read in a non-Arnoldian way, as something close to a Sagaman story. So when it was published in 1857, it was welcomed by, among others, Fitzjames Stephen, who wrote an appreciative essay that was published in the *Edinburgh Review* in January 1858. Stephen treated the story as a truthful representation of public school life but brushed aside its Christian pietism to point to a pagan ideology and a brutal training in "manliness" that lay beneath. The paganism is Teutonic. Stephen, for instance, described the boys' celebration after winning a house match as being like a carousal in Valhalla, and the intention of his comparison is primarily to enhance the school ethos. Mentioning this in his essay "Social Darwinism and Upper Class Education in England," J. A. Mangan agrees with Stephen that Social Darwinism was what the public schools taught.[12] The Sagaman adventure was a way of teaching the values of Social Darwinism.

The climax to the series of school-life stories in England came with Kipling's *Stalky and Co.* This is a climax both in intellectual interest and in its embrace of the "savage" ideology we are studying. Kipling wrote it in reaction against Dean Farrar's famous *Eric; or, Little by Little*, which tried, like Hughes's book, to introduce Christian values into a school-life story. Kipling used frankly "tribal" and "anthropological" language to describe his boys' behavior. An important symbol is a West African drum that belongs to one of the boys, and the drumming has the same significance for them as it had for the tribe that made it. In

12. Mangan and Walvin, *Manliness and Morality*, 135–59.

contrast, there is no Christian symbol, and even the patriotic symbol of the flag is desecrated if explicitly appealed to or expounded. It must be kept out of sight and worshiped in dumbness.

The Story's Historical Function

One attraction of the Sagaman adventure was clearly its image of passions and actions that are simpler and stronger than educated white men at the end of the nineteenth century felt capable of, passions and actions that they believed came more easily to their national and class enemies. We can find an early example of this even in one of the Robinson stories, Ballantyne's *Coral Island,* when the boy Jack is intoxicated with battle and reverts to a primitive fierceness. Other striking examples come in Rider Haggard's novels—for instance in *King Solomon's Mines,* where mild Sir Henry, forced to fight, turns into a Berserk Viking and then is an equal and comrade to the Zulu warrior-giant, Umslopogaas. This last is an important phenomenon in himself.

Both Winston Churchill and Graham Greene have mentioned the importance of the figure of Umslopogaas in their fantasy life as boys, and Haggard attributed his stories' popularity to the Zulu's presence within them.[13] In *Nada the Lily,* the most impressive and bloodthirsty of those stories, Umslopogaas runs with a wolf pack—an atavistic fantasy that Kipling took over in *The Jungle Book.* Haggard apparently drew this figure from a real axe-wielding Zulu warrior whom he knew in Africa in 1876–77, and Umslopogaas lived long enough to hear of the novels in which he appeared and to declare that Haggard ought to pay him half the take. (The relationship between the two was like that between Tolstoy and the giant Cossack from whom he drew the Eroshka of his *Cossacks.*) There is a complementary relationship between the Zulu warrior and Allan Quatermaine, the white hunter, which extends the contrast between the two sides of Sir Henry and energizes many of these tales. Quatermaine is physically unimpressive and emotionally inexpressive. Dry and prudent, he does not belong in the company of such heroes as Umslopogaas and Sir Henry. But he is the master of the situation in the stories in which he and the Zulu both appear, just as the

13. Margery Fisher, *The Bright Face of Danger,* 207.

white man is always the master in his dealings with all savage and heroic races, because the white man is always potentially savage as well as civilized.

Haggard develops a theory of this atavism, and of how much the denizens of England have forgotten, sheltered as they have been, of nature and their own deeper nature. His characters who have lived adventurous lives abroad feel very out of place in England. (Cecil Rhodes and Kipling said they felt this; it was a widespread feeling in the imperialist epoch.) And this theory becomes a premise of adventure writing from this point on—you find it in Kipling and Buchan and Edgar Rice Burroughs, for instance. Kipling offered his readers subtler versions of the reassurance Haggard offered, and Burroughs (in his Tarzan stories) offered much cruder ones.

A connected idea is the cult of the North, which around this time begins to attract adventure writers in preference to the South. A major instance of this is William Morris, to whom I shall turn in a minute, but two other cases are John Buchan and Norman Mailer. These are two barely compatible names, Buchan being so prim and British in his language, Mailer so gross and American, but as exponents of northern adventure they have something in common. Buchan's *Sick Heart River* (called *Mountain Meadow* in England) and Mailer's *Why Are We in Vietnam?* both make a mystic cult of the Arctic Circle and its animal and vegetable life, and its mysterious relation to the rest of the earth. Within the Arctic lies the end of the quest for the protagonists of both novels, the ultimate secret.

There is a cult of the North that is part of the saga cult. *The Pied Piper of Dipper Creek* (1943), by T. H. Raddall, includes a story called "North." Raddall, who later became a major historical novelist in Canada, was in a sense first discovered by Buchan, who wrote a foreword for that book, comparing the writer with Scott, Stevenson, and Kipling. "North" begins humorously but ends mystically, describing "a hard bright quality of spirit that the North itself provides. . . . I knew it then, the secret of the North, the knowledge that could come only from a wrestle with its mysterious power. . . . The old Vikings knew. They'd learned a bit of the lesson with that stark mythology of theirs, and acquired enough of the elixir to make them masters of the world in their time" (p. 78).

Raddall says, "I don't mean any militaristic nonsense" (p. 79), but we need not believe him too implicitly. His book was published during the war, and it behooved him to dissociate himself from the Nazis. "I mean that a strong-limbed race like ours, having the arts of metal and all that goes therewith, moving into the North and making it their own, are bound to receive an infusion of soul that will make them superior to any other on earth. . . . The strong ones, the keen ones, have been pushing steadily north. . . . The storm and sunshine, the harsh land and the cold sea, the flaming aurora and the keen stars wheeling about the Pole, the thrill of flight and the brute power of the pack—these are the booming bass notes, and the half notes and minor harmonies" (p. 79).

This cult of the North is not a necessary part of every Sagaman adventure, but the two go together. Himself an enthusiast for the Norse mythology, C. S. Lewis has written about William Morris as a celebrant of northernness. He also sees Morris in other ways that relate him to our argument. Lewis says Morris was not a medievalist, as he has been called, but a sagaman—that is, more spiritually remote from us. "Other stories have only landscape: his have geography," the life of the land (which we might call the cult of the land). He calls Morris a pagan and the most irreligious of our poets—meaning, of course, not Christian.[14] Moreover, Lewis suggests that Morris's *Well at the World's End* was inspired by Haggard's *She,* written ten years earlier, and he sees Haggard as a mythopoeic imagination. This shows us a map of the literary tradition cognate with the one being drawn here, and quite unlike the usual one.

One connection between this literary taste and its contemporary politics is pointed to in Haggard's dedication of his Sagaman novel *Eric Bright-Eyes.* He dedicates his story to the Empress Frederick of Germany, whose husband had just died, because the emperor, who was like Eric in his death, had been interested and fascinated by Haggard's tales in general, and this one was about "a hero of our Northern stock." (In the introduction, Haggard describes Iceland as a republic of aristocrats where "men of heroic strength" performed deeds "worthy of that iron age," and he told how he himself had visited Iceland to study the sites named in the sagas.) The Emperor Frederick was the first to inherit the throne of a united and imperial Germany. Had he not died so young, he would have ruled it through much of the time that his son, the famous Kaiser, actually did. Haggard offered his stories to feed the imperial imagination, English or German. And it seems clear that many nine-

14. C. S. Lewis, *Rehabilitations*, 39, 42.

teenth-century intellectuals also—such as Leslie Stephen and Max Weber—derived some of their self-styling, however fantastic, from such
reading.

This was a period of high-culture atavism, and Haggard wrote some
of the most evocative of such adventures. His novel of 1887, *Allan
Quatermaine,* is dedicated to his son "and to many other, unknown
boys" in the hope that it will help them develop toward "the highest rank
whereto we can attain—the state and dignity of English gentlemen."
They will reach that dignity by going through the fires of savagery in
their imaginations as an initiation.

The introduction to *Allan Quatermaine* is an extraordinary repudiation (supposedly written by Quatermaine) of nineteenth-century liberal
England. He, Quatermaine, must go back to Africa despite having retired
to England. "No man who has for forty years lived the life I have, can
with impunity coop himself in this prim English country, with its trim
hedgerows and cultivated fields. . . . He begins to long—ah, how he
longs!—for the keen breath of desert air; he dreams of the sight of Zulu
impis breaking on their foes like surf upon the rocks. . . . Ah! this
civilization, what does it all come to?" (p. 14).

He has tried to learn the refined ways of those "children of light," his
countrymen, but he can't because he believes that "in all essentials the
savage and the child of civilization are identical" (p. 14). This was, of
course, what many people were saying then—for instance, Freud's
cultural teaching could be read as a corroboration. "Civilization is only
savagery silver-gilt" (p. 15). England will fall back into barbarism, as
Egypt, Greece, and Rome did. More than that, in emergencies we even
now fall *gratefully* back on the nineteen parts out of twenty in us that
are still savage. "Civilization should wipe away our tears, and yet we
weep and cannot be comforted. Warfare is abhorrent to her, and yet we
strike out for hearth and home, for honor and fair fame, and can glory
in the blow." He longs to return to Africa, to Nature, the universal
mother. "I would go back again where the wild game are, back to the
land whereof none knows the history, back to the savages, whom I love"
(p. 17). This is atavism at its blandest.

Even more clearly, and paradoxically, William Morris seems to have
found in the sagas themselves a monitor for his self-regeneration. In
1873, the year he set off for Iceland for his second visit (he made the
pilgrimage, like Haggard), he wrote his friend, Mrs. Coronio: "I very
much wish not to fall off in imagination and enthusiasm as I grow older;

there have been men who, once upon a time, have done things good and noteworthy, who have got worse with time, and have outlived their powers; I don't like that at all. . . ."[15] It was Iceland that was to save him. His Pre-Raphaelite friends, Rossetti and Burne-Jones, mocked him for his love of the North—they preferred Italy and the South. But Morris seems to have found in Iceland and the sagas the infusion of imagination and enthusiasm he needed. By then, the North was the place of adventures, the South was the place of amorous dalliance. His envoi to his translation of the *Eyrbygga Saga* in 1869 thanked the poem for freeing him from the spell of fear, and his preface to the *Volsunga Saga* states: "This is the great story of the North, and should be to all our race what the Tale of Troy was to the Greeks."[16] He is saying about England what Hebbel said about Germany, that this was our *Nationalepos.*

Much of Morris's career was spent in a search for such strength of inspiration. Early he called himself a "dreamer of dreams, born out of my due time," and asked, "why should I strive to set the crooked straight?" (1868). And the prologue to his *Earthly Paradise* begins, "Forget six counties overhung with smoke; Forget the smoking steam and piston stroke." He is going to forget reality, turn away from contemporary industrial England, to tell the tale of how men once sailed off to find the earthly Paradise. But then he decided to reembody the heroes, and not merely to dream of them. It was in 1870 that he began to study Icelandic and "turned to the North," and his turn to Socialist politics was a continuation of the same enterprise, insofar as it was a search for strength and sternness in place of dreams and beauty. In other ways, of course, there remained a severe conflict between socialism and the saga sensibility.

Morris is of interest to us because of that conflict. Jack London presents the same phenomenon, of an enthusiastic Socialist who propagates images of masculinist violence and dominance, which we usually associate with the opposite political persuasion. But Morris seems the subtler and stronger mind, and he certainly enjoys more prestige as a spokesman for a humanist socialism. It therefore seems well to examine one of his Sagaman adventures in a little more detail.

The House of the Wolfings depicts a Gothic society on the point of succumbing to the imperialism of Rome. Morris solicits all the reader's

15. William Morris, *Collected Works,* 10:ix.
16. Morris, *Selected Writings and Designs,* 15.

sympathies for these people and yet implies a pride of race, caste, and gender in them. This race/tribe are tall and comely, gray-eyed, and tanned with a ruddy and cheerful hue, while their thralls/slaves are shorter and darker and more crooked of limb. "Merry was the folk with that fair tide, and the promise of harvest, and the joy of life. . . ."[17] But they make sacrifice of enemy prisoners and a maiden of their own kindred, and there is a continual current of masculinism—"a man, a glorious creature with a gleaming helm on his head."[18]

This shows a similarity between Morris's saga feeling and that of London (and Haggard and Kipling), and something even more blatant is suggested by his depiction of Thiodolf, the hero. His hair was dark and curly, "his forehead was high and smooth, his lips full and red, his eyes steady and wide-open, and all his face joyous with the thought of the fame of his deeds, and the coming battle with a foeman whom the Markmen knew not yet. . . . He was a man well-beloved of women, and children would mostly run to him gladly and play with him . . . a man that knew not bitterness of soul."[19] This must surely strike anyone who has seen photographs of Morris as a self-portrait, full of self-love.

The House of the Wolfings was published the year after Haggard's *Allan Quatermaine,* and there are striking similarities. War is the dominant event for both writers. The plot simply transposes an anthropological analysis of this society into narrative form. Many ceremonies are described; blasts of the great war-horn, assemblings in the Roof, and at the Hill of Speech, and at the Thing-Stead. The story of the Folk, including its past and future, is told in a series of speeches, both in prose and in verse, by messengers, spokesmen for the Wolfings and other kindred, and by those possessed of second sight.

There are two series of events in present time, closely intertwined. One is the advance of the Romans, and of the battles that ensue between them and the Markmen; weapons and armor are described in some detail, and so are actual combats between individuals, as in the sagas— though Morris, like Haggard, also describes the strategy and tactics of battles. The other revolves around the insistence of the woman called the Wood-Sun that Thiodolf wear a hauberk of chain mail woven by the dwarfs that will protect his life. This is a self-flattering fantasy of erotic

17. Morris, *Collected Works,* 14:9.
18. Ibid., 34.
19. Ibid., 55.

pathos. The Wood-Sun is immortal, being of the gods' race, and she has long loved Thiodolf. But the hauberk, granting him invulnerability, also cuts him off from his Folk and—since he is their leader—means that they will all be defeated. In the last great battle he takes it off and is killed, but he is happy to die for and with his people.

There is some suggestion that the gods are growing jealous of men, because of their powers and because of the beauty of the love men bear each other. This goes with Morris's socialism harmoniously enough, as does his picture of the Romans as city men who have sacrificed their civic freedom to become a great imperial power. But in other ways the society of the Folk is, from our viewpoint, strikingly dominated by pride of race, caste, and gender. And this is a story that Haggard or Kipling might have written to glorify that society.

Kipling's aunt and uncle Burne-Jones were great friends of Morris, and as a child Rudyard heard many stories from the latter, including a story fragment that he tells us he could not make sense of until he finally realized it came from a saga. In fact, though Morris spent years translating and imitating the sagas, it was Kipling who devised a politics that harmonized with that source. The enthusiasm for those stories was much more appropriate to him politically, though his literary expression of that enthusiasm was more oblique than Morris's. Kipling's atavism shows itself most clearly in *The Jungle Books,* where the law of the jungle is shown to be the origin of human law and where the different species of animals seem to represent different tribes or nations in hierarchical order. Morris more blatantly feeds our Fascist tendencies.

Later British and American Writers

John Buchan can be said to be a twentieth-century heir of both Kipling and Morris, but he differs in a way that is perhaps unexpected. He wrote appreciatively about Morris, and one of his best books, *The Path of the King* (1921), clearly derives from Kipling's *Puck of Pook's Hill.* The first story in that collection, "Hightown Under Sunfell," is a Viking saga adventure as seen by a small boy. In the later *Man from the Norlands* (1936) the Haraldsens are a modern family but devoted to the sagas, father and son. In time of battle, the former swings an axe, like their Viking ancestors, and the latter goes berserk. This story would logically reach a Wagnerian climax in which their Great House would be engulfed in flames and their family wiped out. But the writer backs away from that ending, as he backed away from tragedy and melodrama in general. His political temperament, wrongly called Fascist, was very mild, and he wrote adventures, not sagas. For that reason, Buchan belongs in the Hunted Man category of adventure, not the Sagaman category.

As well as reassuring the Anglo-Saxon readers of the superiority of their race and the naturalness of their world dominance, Sagaman adventures enabled them to slip the yoke of Christian and genteel values, to imagine themselves as creatures of force, splendor, and savagery. This was a drive generally felt at this time. (One sees it clearly in Richard Jefferies's *Bevis*, though it is not expressed in saga form there.) The contradiction between those qualities and traditional moral values was covered by the word "evolution." We used to be savage, and now we are civilized, but we can revert whenever necessary; thus we are really both at once. This idea clearly relates to Nietzschean ethics, the philosophy most closely related to adventure in all its forms.

I mentioned earlier the American naturalist writers, London, Norris, Crane, and so on, who depicted contemporary poverty, savagery, and death with a lurid "realism" that turned their stories into something like Symbolist dramas. This literary enthusiasm ran parallel to the taste for saga stories, and the two supported each other. Another way to describe the history of adventure is to say that around the beginning of the twentieth century the naturalist writers took up the Frontiersman story again, to tell it with a new, grotesque imagination and different sympathies, including a strong feeling against civilization and the cultured class. (The saga hero, like Natty Bumppo, embodied an independence and a virtue that had flourished in the past, it was thought, and that they felt the need of in the present time.) Thus in Jack London's *Sea Wolf* (1903) Humphrey van Weyden, a literary critic, is carried out to sea by Wolf Larsen, the Sea Wolf of the title. Weyden has a soft hand. "Dead men's hands have kept it soft. Good for little else than dish-washing and scullion's work," says Larsen in disgust. Weyden passes into a state of "involuntary servitude" to Larsen until his muscles harden and his manly pride swells enough for him to fight.

This could be called a version of the Natty Bumppo story, but emotionally dark, especially because the reader is forced into the unfavorable role. He has to identify with Weyden (a reader is a kind of literary critic) while the writer identifies himself with Larsen. When the woman of the story, though a poet, hits Larsen with a seal club at a moment of crisis, Weyden thinks: "Truly she was my woman, my mate, fighting with me and for me as the mate of a caveman would have fought, all the primitivism in her aroused."[20] This sort of thing is unimaginable in Buchan. It is also unimaginable in Cooper, or indeed in any frontiersman story. But similar things can be found in Crane and Norris, and it is closely related to the contemporary taste for saga stories, whether originals or modern imitations.

Frank Norris's novel *Moran of the Lady Letty* is also full of Viking imagery, reversions to Berserker fury, and women warriors. We see the political reference of this widespread literary rhetoric in Norris's essay "The Frontier Gone at Last" (1902), where Norris draws connections between the American frontier and the Norsemen's conquests. Norris says that Americans had always relied on having a frontier to the west of them, that the frontier was their romance and poetry, "the firing line where there was action and fighting, and where men held each other's lives in the crook of a forefinger."[21] But so had the English, in the old days. For the Anglo-Saxons, Norris says, England had been that frontier, and Hengist was the equivalent of the Apache Kid. (This is close to what du Chaillu said.) After conquering Britain, and as long as the Atlantic barred the way farther west, the impulse to expand was forced to turn east, in the Crusades.

An interesting extrapolation of the saga enthusiasm, which confirms this connection to the actual British Empire, was the feeling for Rajput legends among the British in India. The Anglo-Indians were necessarily the most consciously imperialist of all the types of English, and they admired and loved the martial races (the nonpolitical races) under their rule—for instance, the princes of Rajasthan, whom they saw in Viking and knightly terms. A compilation of Rajput legends and history, by the Englishman Tod, *The Annals and Antiquities of Rajasthan* (1829–32), was very popular in India.

One novelistic expression of that feeling was Maud Diver's *Far to Seek* (1921), one in a series of novels about the interactions of Indians with the English. The young hero, Roy, has the blood of two virile races mingled in his veins because he has an English father and a Rajput mother. The latter trains his imagination by telling him "folk-tales of

20. Jack London, *The Sea Wolf*, 236.
21. Nash, *The Call of the Wild*, 70.

East and West; true tales of crusaders, of Arthur and his knights, of
Rajput Kings and Queens, in the far off days when Rajasthan—a word
like a trumpet-call—was holding her desert cities against hordes of
invaders, and heroes scorned to die in their beds" (p. 5). Roy's carriage,
we are not surprised to be told, betrayed innate pride of race, and in
time of battle men like him are half English gentlemen, half savages.

Tod's book is described by Diver as "that grim and stirring panorama
of romance and chivalry, of cruelty and cunning; orgies of slaughter and
miracles of high-hearted devotion" (p. 92). Diver's novels were, in her
day, like those legends, intended to inspire an aristocracy and to reconcile aesthetes and humanists (the readers) to the military caste: "Poet
and Warrior; the eternal complements" (p. 93). Roy finds that Rajasthan,
"this strong, unlovely region of rock and sand, of horses and swords, of
chivalry and reckless daring, irresistibly laid siege to his heart" (p. 164).
This can remind us of another imaginative locus to the British imperial
imagination, though not literally part of the Empire—Arabia. (A series
of writers—for example, Richard Burton, Charles Doughty, T. E. Lawrence, and Freya Stark—have written brilliantly about that desert landscape and Arab warriors.)

In the nineteenth century and the early part of the twentieth, then,
there were plenty of Sagaman stories and related forms. But in the
second half of the twentieth century, has this form disappeared? Even
recently, there has been a subgenre of adventure stories about organized
crime that employ many of the motifs of the Sagaman type under
different names—for instance, stories of Mafia feuds, such as *The
Godfather*. Here again the world is organized into "families" that are
banded together with other families and against still other families—
with one man on each side as supreme chief, and the happiness of
individuals (typically, in Romeo and Juliet love affairs) sacrificed to the
interests of the whole. This is an example of how the adventure types
live on in our own time, though somewhat disguised.

9

The Hunted Man Story
The Seventh Type

The Hunted Man adventure story is often included in the more amorphous "thriller" category as a subgroup. That is appropriate. The idea of being hunted is an important part of most thrillers, perhaps of most adventures, at some point, and if some thrillers contain a lot of other material too, the Hunted Man story has exerted a certain hegemony over the rest.

We can distinguish two kinds of Hunted Man story: the conservative and the liberal. The first is the British thriller of the kind written by John Buchan; the second is the American kind written by Raymond Chandler. Because there are innumerable varieties of such stories, in this case one is bound to feel more arbitrary than in dealing with the other types. But Buchan's and Chandler's stories have interesting parallels, and I claim that both are liberal, Buchan as much as Chandler, because they promise the reader that the unaided individual can take on large organizations and conspiracies that are subverting the state or the nation and can triumph over them. This is an exhilarating message, and in some sense a democratic one, even though the hero works against the institutions set up by and for citizens. These heroes, making modern society work despite itself, are brothers to Robinson Crusoe and d'Artagnan, energizers of the readership.

The Hunted Man adventure type differs from its immediate precursors among the adventure types, most notably from the Sagaman story and the Musketeers story, in that it is assertively contemporary. The setting is modern, and reference is made to names and events that sound like the news in one's daily paper. The weapons used are often of the latest kind, and the writer then shows off specialized knowledge about them. The ways of getting about are likely to include the fastest of cars or planes, submarines or diving equipment. (In this and other ways, this type is close to the Wanderer type.) Hunted Man stories are also assertively contemporary in their language and feeling, assertively unlike old-fashioned or pompous styles of narrative or dialogue.

Even a political conservative like John Buchan has for his most famous hero a "new man," in London from South Africa, Richard Hannay, who talks with a colonial drawl, resonant of the veldt, the wide-open spaces, and the fast-growing new cities. And T. E. Lawrence pointed out the sense of speed and simplicity, "as of a stripped-down athlete," that Buchan's narrative techniques give. The American writers, such as Raymond Chandler and Ross Macdonald, are not as simple as Buchan stylistically, and their plots can be labyrinthine, but in their own brilliant ways they certainly give an acutely "contemporary" feeling.

The protagonist of this adventure type is, superficially, an anti-romantic figure, who sees himself as ordinary. He may have adventurous experience *behind* him, but no desire for any more. He wants, allegedly, to be an ordinary person, but he has a greater than ordinary capacity for action—with his fists, his guns, his cunning, his connections to other men of force, keepers or breakers of the law—and a greater than ordinary sense of responsibility. Sometimes he is, or has been, a detective or an attorney; sometimes he is strictly a private citizen. In any case, he is effectively alone when he stumbles across a clue, an inexplicable incident, which leads him to find other clues, and ultimately to unravel a puzzle, a plot, a conspiracy. And at the heart of the conspiracy he finds a social monster, an organization, sometimes totally illegal, sometimes apparently respectable, that threatens the life of his city or his nation.

Following these clues, piecing together the scattered truth, he attracts the attention of the organization and himself becomes a hated man. From this point on, everyone he meets, even old friends, are likely to turn out to be agents of the conspiracy, corrupt and treacherous, either out of weakness or out of malevolence. Houses, streets, office blocks, familiar to him and of a type familiar to the reader, become sinister. And this transforms the familiar adventure properties, like creakings in the dark, bludgeonings from behind, drugged or poisoned food, windowless basements, and instruments of torture; they become charged with meaning, with ultimately political significance.

One thing that distinguishes this kind of adventure is that so much attention is given to the enemy, who can be (to take examples from the movies) a form of organized crime (*The Maltese Falcon*) or a plot within the military (*Seven Days in May*) or a giant corporation (*The Parallax Affair*) or, most popular recently, the nuclear power industry (*The China Syndrome* or *Silkwood*). It is thus a type especially congenial to the liberal imagination, replacing the Avenger story, which has now fallen into conservative hands.

We can take Buchan's *Thirty-Nine Steps* (1915) as our exemplary case. It was the first of Buchan's books to sell in large numbers, though he was by then well established as an author, and it set the pattern for his later thrillers. When it begins, Richard Hannay (who became so popular he returned as the hero of the author's later stories, like d'Artagnan and Natty Bumppo) is growing bored with London and England. Like Allan Quatermaine, he has been spoiled for life in England by his experience of freedom and adventure in Africa.

Unlike Quatermaine, a hunter, Hannay is said to have been an engineer, like some of Kipling's early heroes. But neither engineering nor any other technology plays any significant part in Buchan's imagination. His heroes are clubmen—all of them successful in various power fields, perhaps most typically in law or politics. What they have in common is the habit of command, the habit of success, though their fame is usually limited to a small circle. The names of many of them are "not known to the general public."

Hannay is rescued from his tedium by an appeal from a stranger, a man who happens to live in the same building, who has stumbled across a plot by the German government to steal the defense plans

England and France are drawing up together. (Buchan became a thriller writer by grace of the war. He wrote this story, which is very unlike most of his earlier production, immediately after the outbreak of war in 1914, though it is of course set some time earlier.) When this man is killed, Hannay decides to take over his mission and disappears from his flat in disguise, with Germany's agents in pursuit of him.

The date of France and England's top-secret meeting (and therefore of the planned theft) is known to Hannay, and this gives him (and Buchan) a fixed number of days to play with, in which Hannay must elude capture and persuade the British government to believe his story. Hannay hides first in Scotland, and assumes a number of disguises, each involving one other character, in clearly marked-off episodes, titled "The Adventure of the Road Mender," "The Adventure of the Political Candidate," or whatever. Back in England he makes contact with Sir Walter Bulivant, a reassuring figure of authority in the government, but it is still Hannay who must defeat the enemy, largely by penetrating a series of devilish disguises by its agents. He breaks a number of laws in the name of a higher law, makes a number of hair-breadth escapes, inflicts heavy punishment, and masks heroic virtues with humorous self-depreciation.

Cultural Connections

Buchan believed in and worked for the British Empire, and it is easy to show, or at least to argue, a connection between his adventures and imperialism. This is of course an exceptional case. Most thrillers have no overt political message, and the covert message—that individual men must be ready at all times to take over the function of enforcing law and order—can be blended with quite a number of different politics. Such writers as Raymond Chandler and Ross Macdonald are implicitly very liberal, quite apart from the quasi-anarchist message carried by all adventure.

Of course there are right-wing adventures of the Hunted Man type, in which the conspiratorial forces unmasked turn out to be (until recently) Soviet espionage or the KGB. It is my impression that these have less prestige and can count as a variant on the dominant ideology. One example would be the James Bond stories. This reminds us that another variable is the status of the central character, who may be, as he is in the Bond stories, an agent himself. A third variant is that the conspiracy is sometimes the work of some rich man or family, not of a corporation. All these variants, however, use parts of the main story and reinforce our feeling of its shadowy and potential presence.

As my examples suggest, the Hunted Man adventure is popular with contemporary readers and writers, but it is not new, for it has attracted them for nearly a century. The first of the Buchan series came out more than seventy years ago and seemed to be a book of and for that moment—the outbreak of the Great War—but the form has proved durable. That was of course a right-wing adventure, as defined above, since the conspiratorial force was the national enemy. But this was not always the case in Buchan's stories. In *Three Hostages* the conspiracy was rooted in the diseased brain of an evil genius.

The voice Buchan invented for his main hero in *Thirty-Nine Steps* was South African, but strikingly like the American and later the British voices used by most heroes of this story type: "I had just about settled to clear out and get back to the veldt, for I was the best bored man in the United Kingdom."[1] He is a disengaged appraiser of civilized life from outside: "It struck me that Albania was the sort of place that might keep a man from yawning" (p. 12). This was the role appropriated by colonials and Americans visiting London, but they also play it in their homelands (a good literary example is Christopher Newman in Henry James's *The American*). Says Hannay: "I vowed I would give the Old Country another day to fit me into something; if nothing happened, I would take the next boat for the Cape" (p. 12). Hannay, it will be apparent, is not really so reluctant to have an adventure as I said the heroes of this story type claim to be—but then *they* aren't really, either.

In the beginnings of Chandler novels the hero sets himself apart from society in the same way—or rather, to the same effect—as Buchan's hero does. *The Big Sleep* (1939) begins: "It was about eleven o'clock in the morning, mid-October, with the sun shining and a look of hard wet rain in the clearness of the foothills. I was wearing my powder-blue suit, with dark-blue shirt, tie and display handkerchief, black brogues, black wool socks with dark blue clocks on them. I was neat, clean, shaved and sober, and I didn't care who knew it. I was everything the well-dressed

1. Buchan, *Thirty-Nine Steps*, 12.

private detective ought to be. I was calling on four million dollars."[2] The humor is implicitly aggressive. This man is ready to step beyond the limits of civic order. But the implicitness itself implies that the aggression is under control—the control, ultimately, of a civic conscience like Hannay's.

At the beginning of Chandler's *High Window* (1943), Marlowe is summoned to the home of rich people in Pasadena. "From the front wall and its attendant flowering bushes a half-acre or so of fine green lawn drifted in a gentle slope down to the street, passing on the way an enormous deodar around which it flowed like a cool green tide around a rock. . . . At the end of the walk, on a concrete block, there was a little painted negro in white breeches and a green jacket and a red cap. He was holding a whip, and there was an iron hitching ring in the block at his feet. He looked a little sad, as if he had been waiting there a long time and was getting discouraged. I went over and patted his head while I was waiting for somebody to come to the door."[3] Chandler invites the reader to join Marlowe in this minimal gesture of independence and skepticism about wealth and respectability, a gesture that promises, just because it is minimal, that the independence will be acted out.

Chandler's *Little Sister* (1949) begins: "The pebbled glass door panel is lettered in flaked black paint: 'Philip Marlowe . . . Investigations.' It is a reasonably shabby door at the end of a reasonably shabby corridor in the sort of building that was new about the year the all-tile bathroom became the basis of civilization. The door is locked, but next to it is another door with the same legend which is not locked. Come on in— there's nobody in here but me and a big bluebottle fly."[4] Shabbiness, even the sordid, is an important feature of Marlowe's ambiance, and not, of course, of Hannay's. But Hannay is fond of wearing "ancient" tweeds and "disreputable" flannels, and he claims he cannot understand the respectable middle classes. In the same way, Marlowe is unlike Hannay in his rudeness to women and his overt sexuality, but we soon realize that he is deeply chivalrous. At the end of the first conversation in *The Little Sister* the indignant lady blushes and says softly, " 'I think you're very nice—really' " (p. 28).

Buchan gave all his interest as well as sympathy to the individual hero,

---

2. In *The Raymond Chandler Omnibus*, 3.
3. Ibid., 321.
4. In *The Second Raymond Chandler Omnibus*, 19.

but there are writers of this story type who are fascinated by the organization the hero defies, and in their stories the latter's adventures occur largely inside the organization, uncovering the conspiracy step-by-step. Such stories are sometimes set inside large business concerns, and even more often nowadays inside national intelligence agencies. One of the first of these was Somerset Maugham's *Ashenden; or, The British Agent* (1928). The most famous single name in writing of this kind today is John Le Carré, and the theme of the most contemporary examples is evoked by the word "mole," first used by Le Carré in *Tinker, Tailor, Soldier, Spy* (1974).

In this case the line of separation between fictional and nonfictional treatments of the theme is particularly thin. The fascination of Le Carré's books and other such novels is exactly the same as the fascination of the investigative journalism about Burgess and McLean, and then about the Third Man, and most recently about the allegations of Peter Wright in *Spycatcher*. But it is not confined to that subject-matter; another such topic is the men of Britain's Arab Bureau, before and during the Great War.

In *The Illicit Adventure*, H.V.F. Winstone says, "I set out to tell the story of the Arab Bureau, to write about those men who dreamt their dreams dangerously in the openness of day, whose faith 'sold them into slavery,' a splinter group who fought their own way within a larger conflict, fashioned their own ends and devised their own strategy."[5] These were actual men whom Buchan knew and admired; he drew some of his heroes from them. But the interaction of fact and fiction went both ways—Winstone sees the men he describes in literary terms, and they saw themselves that way. Lieutenant Gerard Evelyn Leachman was "all the heroes of Rider Haggard, the *Boys' Own Paper,* and the North West Frontier rolled into a single frame; lithe, fearless, and belligerent" (p. 430).

Later Winstone says that our men in the Syrian desert were "reared on the precepts of Empire and service, yet questioning creatures, inclined to the High Toryism of the Milner and John Buchan brand, devotees of the Round Table, somewhat Francophobe, and decidedly clever" (p. 81). The most famous individual among these men, T. E. Lawrence, became Buchan's close friend and was protected by him in the years after 1918.

Because their world stood beyond the law and at the frontiers of

5. H.V.F. Winstone, *The Illicit Adventure*, xi.

civilization, it belonged to the realm of fantasy, of adventure, however undeniable its facts. No one knew what to believe about what was happening, or at least how to interpret it, and so they lived morally on personal style and vitality, as adventurers do. Their archetype has to be the double agent who deceives one or both of his masters. The distinction between reality and fantasy becomes unstable in such a life; that is why it has always been easy for men of letters to ignore adventure tales and adventures, which undeniably do partake of fantasy. But when one realizes how much reality is defined by civilized consensus and how much of fact as well as feeling that excludes, one is tempted to call reality just the most brilliant of fantasies.

Thus the men of the Arab Bureau spied on each other much of the time. Winstone describes how he came to see through the official version of their work. "I began to look afresh at the policy-makers and their henchmen, at the soldiers and agents, spies and camel-dealers, at the travellers and explorers and their guides and contacts." He began to move, one might say, from the Buchan to the Le Carré point of view: "In the end I came to the conclusion, remarkable though it may be, that these two bodies devoted a larger part of their energies to spying on each other and countering each other's schemes, than to undermining the activities of the enemies of imperial Britain in the east."[6] This is the sort of nonfictional material that reinforces the message of the Hunted Man adventure.

Themes and Parallels

Two themes introduced by Buchan seem to have had a good deal of influence on subsequent writers of the story. One is the idea that a very narrow and fragile partition separates ordinary life from violence or barbarism. This idea had of course been exploited by Dickens and Balzac and the writers of the Mysteries. But Buchan gave it a fresh, contemporary focus; for him the locus of fear in London was not so much a slum alleyway at night as Picadilly at noon. When Graham Greene wanted to express the insecurity about life the Second World War had taught us, he

6. Ibid., xi, xii.

said it proved that Buchan had been right. (Greene often wrote Hunted Man stories himself, but he gave them a burden of highbrow ideas.)

The second motif is parallel in the domestic sphere. Buchan shows us people so cleverly disguised as to be unrecognizable even to those who have scrutinized them before. The fascination of disguise had been exploited before—notably by Kipling in *Kim* and by Conan Doyle in the Holmes stories. The different focus Buchan gives is to insist on the psychological mechanism of the deception—the disguised man cannot be recognized if he is *thinking* himself to be someone else—to a remarkable and indeed implausible degree. The hero of *Thirty-Nine Steps* repeatedly stares the villains in the eye and yet cannot be sure they are the men he met before. This device obviously plays with an extreme sense of insecurity in the reader.

One of Buchan's disciples was Agatha Christie (not of course in the purely detective parts of her oeuvre), who carried both these motifs to an extreme in her remarkable novel *At Bertram's Hotel,* at the end of which the whole social world in which the action took place is revealed to have been a deception. Dozens of people, working for years in a well-known London hotel, are alleged to have been all playing a part. But the sense of unreliability in ordinary appearances is everywhere in twentieth-century adventures, even in writers who seem unlikely to have learned anything from Buchan. For instance, in Ross Macdonald—where half the relationships with which the story begins turn out to be false at the end—husbands were really brothers, nextdoor neighbors were really long-lost sons, deadly enemies were really lovers, and so on.

Though I distinguished the detection from the adventure in Christie's work and dismissed the former as much less relevant, detection always has an indirect connection to adventure, even in the detective fiction of British women writers. We see this in a seashore scene in Dorothy Sayers's *Have His Carcase:* " 'I wonder,' said Harriet to herself, 'whether I ought to be able to deduce something or other about the state of the tides' " (p. 10). Harriet is not at this point engaged in a case; she is merely flexing her intellectual muscles, which are the muscles Sayers's readers too must employ in order to appreciate what they read.

Having duly deduced something, Harriet says to herself, "Perfectly simple, my dear Watson." She is acknowledging her most famous precursor and the tradition in which Sayers writes. A different precursor she might have cited was the mass social movement of the Boy Scouts, whose members were taught to read signs in the same way. And their direct reflections in detective fiction are Conan Doyle's Baker Street Irregulars and Buchan's Gorbals boys. This widespread zeal for detection and zest in looking for clues expresses a taste for seeing life as an adventure—that is, seeing it as it is lived on the borders or frontiers of civilization—of which a striking case must always be the literal frontier, national or imperial.

Despite the parallel or cousinship between the British and the American writers I am pointing to, they are of course significantly different. The writer most obviously similar to Buchan is the English Geoffrey Household, whose *Rogue Male* (1939) is described by the publisher, plausibly enough, as the most exciting novel of adventure since *Thirty-Nine Steps*. Like that precursor, *Rogue Male* is told in the first person, and the voice is that of an English gentleman adventurer. It was obvious to any observer, the hero says, that he was no politician: "I might perhaps have sat for an agricultural constituency in the south of England, but . . ." (p. 7). This could be one of Buchan's English heroes speaking. In another of Household's books the hero is, like Richard Hannay, a mining engineer.

In *Background to Danger* (1937) and *The Mask of Demetrios*, published the same year as *Rogue Male*, Eric Ambler began a series of in some sense left-wing thrillers. But his central character, Latimer, is as much the English gentleman as Household's or Buchan's.

Like Ambler's and Buchan's, Household's books are called "classic thrillers," which probably alludes to their gentlemanly class ambiance. But there is a significant difference between them, in the later writer's greater stress on terror, pain, and cruelty, which is connected with his interest in entrapment and entombment. Neither of these features is found in Buchan; they are prominent in the much cruder writer, Dornford Yates, who is cruder both as a writer and as a thinker.

Related English thrillers include the stories, very popular in their day, about Raffles (by A. E. Hornung) and those about the Saint (by Leslie Charteris). Here, as in Buchan, we have a gentlemanly hero, who gets involved in adventures by night and in disguise. He too breaks the law in the name of a higher law, and sometimes even assists the police when they are at a loss. One difference is that Hannay and his friends and equals, British or American, are in no sense thieves; another is that they are linked to the political themes of their day.

In the post-1918 stories of Yates and "the Sapper," about Richard Chandos and Bulldog Drummond, each with his band of friends, there are only rare political allusions, which are of a pitiful crudity. But the real difference is the brutality of the fighting. Buchan's imagination is from every point of view, favorable and unfavorable, more refined than theirs. It is also interesting that whereas there is something of the dandy in the first two writers, and something of the rogue in the latter pair, Buchan avoids both forms of 1920s stylishness. This made him seem old-fashioned at the time, but by now his adventure type seems the more durable.

A more blatant but still interesting contrast lies between *Thirty-Nine Steps* and the very popular French thriller *Fantomâs,* published in Paris just four years earlier, in 1911. *Fantomâs* was written by Marcel Allain and Pierre Souvestre, two hack writers commissioned by a publisher to produce something that would sell. The title character is a master criminal whose identity is revealed only gradually. He has no psychological or social plausibility, and he strikes the imagination only by the scale and savagery of his crimes, especially in sequels to the story. (In one he puts sulfuric acid in the perfume atomizers of a department store; in another he introduces plague rats into an ocean liner.)

Just before writing *Fantomâs,* and at the very beginning of his career, Allain had written an article titled "Nietzsche and Sports" for a Paris magazine. Nietzsche was in vogue in Paris at that time. Maurice Leblanc, creator of the character Arsène Lupin, has also been associated with Nietzsche. Lupin, another of the popular criminals of fiction then (Leblanc was twenty years older than Allain), has been described as a Parisian Zarathustra, a hero of the will to power. And the authors of a recent study of these books agree; they also compare Lupin, like de Gobineau, with a Norman pirate and a Viking.[7] Clearly this is a long way from Buchan and from the Hunted Man thriller—closer in fact to the Sagaman thriller.

Fantomâs was extraordinarily successful. Thirty-one sequels were written, and five films were made from it in 1913 and 1914. Fantomâs as a character cannot be said to develop, but his legend becomes more elaborate with time: he has a beautiful English mistress, Lady Beltham, and a mysterious daughter, Hélène; and he is pursued by a master detective, Inspector Juve, and an enterprising reporter, Jérôme Fandor.

In the original story there are hints that Juve is really Fantomâs, and this is typical of the several motifs that link this story back to Sue's

7. Antoinette Peske and Pierre Marty, *Les terribles,* 63.

Mysteries, and its progeny like *Les misérables* and *Le père Goriot.*
Rudolf von Gerolstein had a mysterious daughter, and the detective-
criminal link is as strong (and much more interesting) in Hugo and
Balzac. Fantomâs is shown, on covers, brooding gigantically over Paris,
like a cruder Monte Cristo.

This story has little in common with *Thirty-Nine Steps,* but it is
interesting to consider in this context for its proof of the popularity of
the crime thriller, and even more for the favor it found with artists and
intellectuals. Although so crude, and in many ways old-fashioned, the
"modernity" of its moral scheme (with its hints of Nietzsche) made it
appeal to the avant-garde of Paris, as Buchan never appealed to even the
much less advanced London equivalent. Guillaume Apollinaire founded
a Société des Amis de Fantomâs in 1912, and Robert Desnos and
Cocteau, Aragon and Colette, were enthusiastic admirers, as were Picasso's gang of friends, such as Max Jacob and Picasso himself, and other
painters like Juan Gris and René Magritte.

The fashion survives, to some degree. Introducing a 1987 edition of
Fantomâs, John Ashbery says that poets as well as proletarians loved the
story, "cubists, nascent Dadaists, soon-to-be-Surrealists," just because it
was *not* respectable adventure.[8] Ashbery asks why it was preferred to
similar and more talented work by Gustave le Roux and answers that
the latter was himself a "Surrealist sans le savoir," and the intelligentsia
preferred *Fantomâs* because it was not aimed at the literary reader and
so was more inert material for them to play with. Moreover, it gained
some of its meaning from the contemporary exploits of "la bande à
Bonnot," a gang of anarchist criminals romantically admired by the
proletariat. Buchan's heroes, by contrast, were ultimately on the side of
the police and the ruling class, and his novels were aimed at pleasing the
bourgeois reader.

Modernity

In the nineteenth-century mysteries, about London, Paris, or St. Petersburg, by Sue, Dostoevsky, Dickens, a focal point is the boardinghouse,
with so many lives, or slices of life, stacked side by side in the same

---

8. In Marcel Allain and Pierre Souvestre, *Fantomâs,* 1.

building, and outside a warren of lanes, cul-de-sacs, canals, and boule-
vards, especially bewildering and sinister at dusk or in a fog. (Both
Balzac and Sue, as we know, compared their treatments of the city to
Cooper's treatment of the forest; they knew they were bringing their
readers' lives within the scope of adventure.) The city is a place of
deceptions and of dangerous differences—between wealth and poverty,
power and weakness, fame and obscurity, order and violence—differences that generate envy, rage, and madness under every kind of cover.

Such an image of the big city finds ample confirmation in individual
experience and in crime statistics, but it can also be called a paranoid
image in that the disposition of mind it induces is unstable and tilts
easily toward irrational actions and extremes of feeling. The huge
metropolis, and by extension the modern state that creates those metro-
poles, generates paranoias in that sense. The Hunted Man adventure
expresses both that feeling and the countervailing myth of an ordinary
hero who can defeat what threatens the reader.

In the twentieth century, however, the boardinghouse is no longer the
center of this adventure; instead we have, at least in American thrillers,
the apartments, mansions, and estates of the rich. Poor and sordid scenes
are certainly described, but the really sinister suggestions emanate from
luxury. This is true of California writers especially—Raymond Chandler,
Ross Macdonald, Sue Grafton. Curiously enough, the English writers,
like Dorothy Sayers, though so interested in the criteria of class and
privilege, have not given so much attention to houses and furnishings.
The characteristic locale for them is a village or a country house—
socially speaking a nonlocale that has no relation to contemporary
forces, social or political.

For a long time the experience of alienation did not enter the world of
English adventure. Even in Buchan and Christie the idea is played with
but not realized. The highbrow-middlebrow division remained strong in
England until after 1945, and alienation belonged to the feebler high-
brow. Thus the American writers added an extra dimension to the story,
and that is why it was they, and not the British, who influenced French
and German writers after 1945. From the point of view of the Europeans, the serious American writers and the adventure writers were both
writing the same story.

Of the serious Americans, it is Hemingway who most deserves to be
named in this discussion. In a book like *To Have and Have Not* we find
the alienated hero of Chandler and Macdonald, the unwilling involve-

ment, the simplified modern prose, the situation of hunting and being hunted. The threat of the giant conspiracy derives from international politics, with representatives on a much lower level than in Buchan. Hemingway and Faulkner (the latter has also some claims to be discussed here) might challenge Buchan's right to represent the subgenre, except that they aimed at the prizes of literature and circumscribed and subdued the elements of adventure in their work. Buchan foregrounded those elements.

Buchan was in many ways an exemplary adventure writer. He attempted primarily to entertain, not to win literary prizes, yet he was a self-respecting intellectual. He tried hard with his biographies—notably those of Montrose, Scott, Augustus, and Cromwell—and he was deeply involved in maintaining the morale of England and the Empire. Thus, while his right hand was designing a story of easy excitements and diversions, his left hand brought in the colors of a conscientious post-1918 imperialism.

He called his adventures "shockers," from the phrase "shilling shockers," and claimed that his literary master was the lowbrow E. Phillips Oppenheim ("the greatest Jewish writer since Isaiah," Buchan said). Oppenheim wrote more than one hundred books, some set in diplomatic circles, some about master-criminals, some about Ruritanian royalty. Buchan's work shows a certain similarity to Oppenheim's, which is strongest when Buchan is weakest, as in *The Courts of the Morning*. But as a literary term, "adventure" belongs to Buchan more than to any other writer in English in the twentieth century. He used the word over and over in the titles of chapters, of books, and of collections of books. His fiction was periodically reissued in sets of three novels at a time with such titles as *Adventurers All* (1942).

The out-of-city action in this genre is usually minor, and in American books is confined to highways or shore cabins. In Buchan's books there is more rural action, but it is the countryside seen the way Oxford undergraduates saw it while planning a prank, which is to say a playful treatment of England as enemy territory, with the civic authorities as "the enemy" to be eluded or outwitted. The countryside (and for that matter the city too) is not taken seriously in social or political terms. In the American case, the city *is* taken seriously, within the conventions of adventure.

No doubt one can find much earlier and more fragmentary antecedents for the Hunted Man story—for instance, the images of city life in the London episodes of *Clarissa Harlow* or *Tom Jones*, or parts of *Moll Flanders* or *Colonel Jack*, or in such Elizabethan pamphlets as Robert Greene's "Cony-Catching." But the shape of the story comes first into view at the end of the eighteenth century, in William Godwin's *Caleb Williams* (1794), where a powerful paranoia about society as a whole is expressed through images of flight and suspicion and double identities. The American thrillers have made more of this than the English have.

The figure of the detective, the reader's guide through the labyrinth of conspiracy, was developed during the nineteenth century in Dickens, Dostoevsky, Hugo, and Balzac. But only in the twentieth century does that figure grow into a full-scale hero, detached from the official law-keeping agencies and able to represent the reader not only in his class interests but in his atomized privateness as well.

There are of course many variables. The English dandy detectives, like Sherlock Holmes and Lord Peter Wimsey, do not represent the reader in his ordinariness. Wimsey does not defeat political or antisocial forces; in the bulk of each story his mode of action is social—a division of the comedy of manners. Holmes is a somewhat equivocal case; Doyle uses the word adventure a good deal, but his city of London is not a real city. However, he does present groups of criminals, and his stories do have a social focus—the frontiers of the empire. Most of the early crimes Holmes faces have their origins on those frontiers (Utah, in *A Study in Scarlet*, counts as an imperial frontier for imaginative purposes), and their last acts are played out in London. The money is made, the crime is committed, the energy is generated, in South Africa, India, Australia. England is where the problem is solved, the crime is punished, justice is done. This effectively dramatizes the Englishman's sense of the relations between the home country and the colonies. And Agatha Christie does occasionally play with international conspiracies, though she is no more than a repeater of Buchan in that regard. On the whole, the English detective writers have not developed, as the American ones have, the socially significant aspects of adventure.

Women have written detective stories from the very birth of the genre, and some of them involved adventure. Over the last twenty years there has been excellent writing by women writers of stories with women detectives. This is what differentiates the work of Sue Grafton and Sara Paretsky (and Marcia Muller, Lia Matera, and Linda Barnes) from that of Ruth Rendell and P. D. James, who are equally excellent in other ways. That differentiation also divides the American women from the

British, and though there are some exceptions, there seems to be a broad tendency for the woman detective to flourish better in the United States. Especially interesting is the development that Grafton's and Paretsky's heroines inflict violence (using guns and martial arts) and so become adventurers. This marks them off not only from Miss Marple and Miss Silver but also from most of the more contemporary women. They are among the first women adventurers in modern literature, if we take into account that they remain assertively female figures even as they enter the world of violence.

The English movement has been toward a psychological or psychic development of the story, as we see in Ruth Rendell today. Graham Greene used the story to carry first religious and then political themes. Geoffrey Household, as we saw, often confined his hero in very narrow conditions, where his sufferings are passive and can easily be taken as metaphors for spiritual effort and spiritual punishment. It is not much of a step from Household to Golding, in such a work as *Pincher Martin*. And John Le Carré offers us a universe of infinite deceptions, like a literary manifestation of *maya*—an inversion of the bracingly real world of Buchan.

It is no accident that in *The Looking Glass War* Le Carré makes so much use of a religious and ecclesiastical vocabulary. He in some ways rejects the world. Ever since the war, he has said, "We've gone through a succession of lunatic ideological reversals."[9] That is all our political engagements amount to. The gun barrels have simply been swiveled from one direction to another.[10]

At the same time, Le Carré's world is socially a continuation of Buchan's, with the mood changed, optimism replaced by pessimism. His characters began life, as he says of himself, "brought up to believe that we were the best and brightest, that we'd inherited the mantle of post-war imperialism."[11] His character Bill Haydon, in *Tinker, Tailor, Soldier, Spy,* is a latter-day Lawrence of Arabia and dreams of restoring England to its former imperial powers.

Le Carré's central figure, George Smiley, is an inversion of Richard Hannay—an indoors, not outdoors, man, a cuckold, not a conqueror, physically inept and sartorially shabby, a would-be scholar—an ill-

9. Eric Homberger, *John Le Carré*, 16.
10. Ibid.
11. Ibid., 17.

tempered Hannay, if one uses "temper" in its fuller sense. He stands in relation to Hannay exactly as Chesterton's detective stands to Sherlock Holmes. In both cases, an assertively dowdy figure replaces a dazzler and proves itself the more authentic, subverting romantic ideas not only of a hero's charisma, but also of a whole world of adventure. Smiley, like Brown, triumphs over adventure as well as in it. That is why Smiley has won respectful attention from men of letters.

In the twentieth century the work of story-telling has been partly taken over from the novel by film. *Casablanca,* for instance, is a story that evokes the style and mood of Hemingway very strongly, and for that matter Bogart's whole career carried the same message. Moreover, though the Western has not been an interesting literary form, Western films were one of Hollywood's two or three main genres, and figures like John Wayne and Gary Cooper and many others were adventure heroes for Americans and the world. The *word* "adventure," the self-conscious concept, attached to films like *Raiders of the Lost Ark* or *Romancing the Stone,* was used in quotation marks, as a sign that what we are looking for was not to be found there. But the Western and the film noir were powerful adventure genres and contain many Hunted Man stories.

The liberal character of this adventure type is perhaps shown by how few examples deal with labor politics and, for instance, with trade unions. A radical adventure would surely be likely to show us strike-breaking, company spies, scabs, and so on; a conservative adventure might show us corruption and violence in the union. In fact, the detective adventure has avoided that situation altogether, and we get a great preponderance of stories about giant corporations and their private armies and their threat to democracy and justice.

The attorney is in some ways the perfect hero for this story, because he is not as a priori committed to the world of violence and illegality as the detective. He can represent the well-lighted world the reader is presumed to inhabit, and we can follow him step-by-step into that other world of darkness. Among recent writers of such stories, William Tapply has an attorney hero named Brady Coyne, and Marcia Muller has Sharon McCone.

Not all these stories uncover giant organizations at the source of the conspiracy. Sometimes (this gives a more old-fashioned effect) it is a single individual who is responsible, and he is not even always very wealthy or powerful. What makes some of such cases nevertheless belong to this genre is the feeling of paranoia, or being hunted, that the writer builds up, the feeling of danger in a normal neighborhood, a danger to the detective and thus to the reader. One example is the Hitchcock film *Rear Window,* where the villain is a petty criminal entirely without an organization to support him, but where the viewer is infected with anxiety about the whole process of living in New York and the risks involved in watching one's neighbors, or simply knowing anything about them.

The Hunted Man adventure type has no preferential connection with any one country's national identity, but it does have strong political and cultural implications. It expresses a distrust of elaborate institutions and a fear of their underside. In the cases I know best, those are capitalist institutions, but it requires very little imagination to adapt the distrust to a socialist regime. It is the highly organized character of life in a "developed" society that provokes the anxiety on which the Hunted Man story lives.

10

Conclusions

I have associated each of the seven adventure types with one of the countries involved in the expansion of the white empire or with one aspect of that movement. That association had the twin advantages of distinguishing the different types of adventure tales one from another and of suggesting the many correspondences between the literary form and large political-economic enterprises. But it would have a much greater *dis*-advantage if it made the reader think that those associations were mutually exclusive—that the Frontiersman adventure story was important to America and not to England and Germany, or that the Three Musketeers type was read in France and not in Russia and Spain (the opposite is true), or indeed that the popularity of any one type ended, in time or space, where that of another type began.

The most important single fact about the interrelations of these types is that they were all very widely popular at roughly the same period in the same countries and that their careers of popularity continued in parallel down to at least the Second World War. Since 1945, it seems likely, the first six are less read or less written. (Of course the old adventures continue to be reprinted, and it may well be that new forms are about to be invented, but there are signs that the white countries' crisis of confidence—failure in moral self-confidence—may have made it too hard for men of literary conscience to write adventure.) But the Robinson story, for instance, was read from 1719 to 1945 by everyone in the countries we are concerned with. (There were, of course, some people who read nothing, and women were less likely to read *Robinson Crusoe* than men. When I say "everyone" I mean, in effect, all those who read at all widely.) In that sense, everyone also read the Scott-type novels from 1814 on, and the Frontiersman novels from 1823 on, and the Avenger novels from 1844 on—turning from one type to another. Tolstoy, for instance, read both Dumas and Verne aloud to his children, and we know he read Defoe and Cooper for his own self-education, and so on.

We are of course interested in the exceptions to these general truths. One function of theory is to create the category "exception" or "anomaly" and to make everything more interesting. Thus we are interested in the lack of any Spanish translation of *Robinson Crusoe* in Spain until the middle of the nineteenth century, and in the paucity of American-written versions of that story. We note the predominance of the writers of France and England (or of the English language, to take account of American writers) in the production of adventure tales. Russia has not produced an adventure type popular with English or French writers, so far as I know, and neither has Germany. In the international literary market, the supply-and-demand of adventure flowed from England and France toward the countries of Europe's east and south—just like the flow of political and economic ideas. Indeed, the Russian Formalist critics found their country's lack of adventure tales an important fact about Russia's literary history.

England and France traded ideas and forms of all kinds as part of their competition for the leadership of Europe. Gerald Newman says that during Voltaire's lifetime (1694–1778) cosmopolitanism became a powerful force in Europe, largely through a quickened tempo of intellectual and social exchange between those two countries.[1] Another recent historian calls England and France "unruly twins," exchanging ideas, blows, customs, compliments, and complaints over the centuries.[2] The other countries were, comparatively speaking,

1. Gerald Newman, *The Rise of English Nationalism*, 1.
2. See Joseph Chiari, *Britain and France: The Unruly Twins*.

passive followers. The history of adventure, at least, seems to corroborate these theories.

But such differences between countries are details and modulations in the main massive phenomenon, the expansive thrust of Europe out over the rest of the world and the frothing flood of adventure tales that accompanied that thrust—accompanied it and interacted with it, equally producing and being produced, to all appearance. These types are so many fingers that all together make up one fist, the fictional equivalent of the force with which European or white imperialism exploded on the other continents and their government.

In this chapter, however, I want to look at the topic of this book historically, though in an impressionistic rather than a complete or systematic way. I offer some impressions of the way the word or the idea of adventure has been used by the series of adventure writers in English. I describe a case of adventure tale motifs persisting unexpectedly in contemporary life, which implies the unexpected persistence of the spirit of those tales. And I consider adventure's "historical" claims to serious study, meaning its claims to be studied now but claims that derive from adventure's relations with history.

The Idea of Adventure

The full title of *Robinson Crusoe* begins *The Life and Strange and Surprising Adventures of . . . .* Defoe used the word "adventures" in other titles, and so did other eighteenth-century writers after him—for instance, *The Voyages, Dangerous Adventures and Imminent Escapes of Captain Richard Falconer.* However, it seems likely that in these uses adventure lacks that purposeful meaning, and therefore that emotional color, which is primary for us today. This is not the adventure from which *we* make our words "adventurer" and "adventurous." Defoe means merely "the things that happened to" Crusoe, not "the things that Crusoe made happen." An early *Robinsonade,* called *Der Saechsische Robinson Crusoe,* said that the name "Robinson" was fast replacing the French word *avanturier* in Germany, but as it did so it changed the concept—and by Campe's time Robinson's adventures were morally most serious.

By now, of course, Campe's meaning has been combined with many others. In modern usage, the primary meaning of "adventure" is probably the literary form, cognate with romance, except when the context clearly points to some other meaning. In the seventeenth and eighteenth centuries that literary meaning does not seem to have been so clear, and an equally important allusion was to the world of finance, with which Defoe was equally familiar. Adventure could mean a financial share in a trading voyage and a ticket in a lottery. This is not to say that that middle-class commercial meaning was the original one; there were romantic and aristocratic uses of the word in the Middle Ages—knights rode out on adventures. (The two different meanings seem to have emerged at the same point in history; Michael Nerlich discusses the matter in detail in his *Ideology of Adventure*.) Thus Defoe's frequent use of the word points us first to the links between the adventure form and early capitalism, which are of great importance in understanding both of those ideas, and second to the unromantic and impersonal range of meanings the word then had.

When we turn to Scott, who was writing after England's triumph over Napoleon, we find that he does not use the word "adventure" frequently or prominently. The words that *are* used in the Waverley novels are "chivalry" and "romance," words that point us backward in time and in the direction of pathos or irony. We do not meet adventure or the adventurer in the full force of their purposefulness, their contemporary power and effectiveness. This is typical of Scott; the word "manliness," so prominent in Cooper's followers, is also largely missing. The concepts of manliness and adventure were certainly carried by Scott's stories and were put into a circulation that was of great ideological importance for the nineteenth century, but those ideas are never defined or even focused.

Scott put so much stress on compromise and common sense because he felt a strong yearning for the opposite qualities of irresponsible boldness, extralegality, and unconditioned commitment. Thus he limited his examples of pure adventure not only to the past but also to cases circumscribed by pathos and indeed by irony. In his preface to *The Talisman* he refers to Richard the Lion Hearted as "a pattern of chivalry, with all its extravagant virtues, and its no less absurd errors."[3] And in his preface to *The Betrothed,* where he does for once use the word "adventure," the tone is depreciatory; he speaks of a crusader's attempts to rescue his marital honor, "which, after all, had been endangered

---

3. Walter Scott, *Prefaces to the Waverley Novels,* ed. Mark A. Weinstein, 220.

chiefly by his forsaking his household gods to seek adventures in Palestine."[4]

His most significant use of the word is in application to Prince Charles Edward Stuart, who is referred to as "the royal adventurer" in *Waverley* and as "the Adventurer" in the preface to *Peveril of the Peak*. This title clearly distinguishes the Prince from his natural rivals, the Hanoverian king and his legitimate heirs; and it means "one who risks a great loss in the hope of a great gain" but also implies "one who fails." It does not suggest the degree of force that "adventurer" would have if applied to, say, Napoleon. The stress is on pathos rather than purpose, again, and the word "romance" is conjoined with it to the same effect; the Prince is said to look like a hero of romance. Thus Scott certainly promoted or propagated the idea of adventure, but in a mistily romantic form and of course countered by contrary ideas.

Mark Twain used the word "adventure" in several titles: *The Adventures of Tom Sawyer, The Adventures of Huckleberry Finn,* and *The Adventures of a Connecticut Yankee in the Court of King Arthur.* In his use, the word means a late nineteenth-century variant on the romantic-aristocratic idea developed by Scott. Twain's usage was ironic and sometimes sardonic; he seriously blamed Scott for the romantic-aristocratic ideas of the Southern planters, which contributed to the Civil War; and less seriously, he condemned the adventure ideas of Tom Sawyer. Indeed, by Twain's time almost any application of adventure to oneself or to ordinary people was almost bound to be ironic. And yet the whole idea of the West, on which Twain's identity as a writer was based, was profoundly adventurous. In Twain's case, this contradiction was "resolved" by Twain's presenting himself as a humorist. Humor thrives on such contradictions. But American high culture of the time was severely strained by its contrary feelings about adventure.

The same was true for England, if in a more narrowly literary sense. We see that in the work of two of Twain's successors as entertainers of the English-speaking peoples: Kipling and Wells. Their works are full of characters who think they are, or who want to be, adventurers but who ludicrously fail to measure up to that idea and yet are adventurers finally by grace of that idea, by grace of the writer's favor. One such figure is the Cockney clerk who reads about adventure—for instance, Wells's Mr. Polly. "Mr. Polly had been drinking at the poisoned fountains of English

4. Ibid., 216.

literature, fountains so unsuited to the needs of a decent clerk or shopman."[5] Literature is now the province of the Goliardic perpetual student, and adventure is the province of the aristo-military caste—two romantic groups. The other classes—the central modern social groups, the middle class, and the proletariat—like Mr. Polly, gaze at literature and adventure from a distance.

This use of adventure we may associate with the Edwardian era, which ended with the outbreak of the Great War. But, as we know, some writers, in (if not of) the postwar world tried to take the curse of irony off the word. In *Huntingtower* (1922) John Buchan makes an adventurer out of Dickson McCunn, a middle-aged, middle-class Glasgow grocer, a close relative to Mr. Polly. McCunn gets involved in romantic adventures with a beautiful exiled Russian princess, but he acts always as a grocer, and his main allies are some slum boys, who also act always as slum boys and yet like knights. Thus adventure, while remaining an aristo-military idea, makes room for the social classes it seems to exclude.

It is of some interest that *Huntingtower* was published in the same year as James Joyce's *Ulysses* and that Buchan calls McCunn Ulysses more than once. "The plump citizen was the eternal pilgrim; he was Jason, Ulysses, Eric the Red, Albuquerque, Cortez—starting out to discover new worlds."[6] Both he and Joyce may surely be said to owe their idea of the unheroic adventurer to Wells. Rather like Joyce's Leopold Bloom, Dickson McCunn is first seen using a safety razor and calculating that not using it before has cost him, from when he began shaving at eighteen until now, at age fifty-five, 3,370 hours, which makes 140 days, or between four and five months. This is modern, rational, suburban man. Buchan's and Joyce's two characters are conceived and presented quite similarly before they begin their "adventures." But Buchan's hero goes on to real though not realistic deeds of daring, while Joyce's work has no sympathy with adventure. Of course there can be no comparison between the two in literary terms; Joyce was a great artist, and Buchan was not. But because of literature's recurrent attempt to make out of Joyce's work a gnostic myth for men of letters, one must protest that of the two it is Buchan who deals in real myth—and in other books better than in *Huntingtower*.

5. H. G. Wells, *The History of Mr. Polly*, 80.
6. John Buchan, *Adventurers All!* 26.

Contemporaneity

One way to resolve our well-justified anxieties about adventure is to think (or, more likely, to assume without thinking) that it belongs to the past, to another life phase or another class or another gender, to the adolescence of the individual or the culture. Of men and women of letters, that may be true. Most of us pass beyond the life of action and into maturity early and permanently. We go through nothing like a *rite de passage*. But we are exceptional in this matter and so, judging the general case by our own reactions, are likely to make mistakes. At moments of adventurous foreign policy, we are likely to be simply disapproving and to attribute popular approval to manipulation. But several motifs of the adventure story, even the most outmoded, can often be recognized in such popular approval.

For instance, the Three Musketeers story, more than most of the types, faded before the end of the nineteenth century and ceased to be a living form for ambitious or even self-respecting writers. For that reason we easily assume that it no longer corresponds to any active cultural force, that contemporary practical imaginations no longer move in this pattern. But in fact today's ethos of masculinism corresponds to it in several ways.

Before broaching my contemporary example, I should recall that this is the masculinism of men in society, as distinct from the solitary heroism of the Robinson type. It shows men having relations with women, but also, and more important, having relations with other men: in the case of men their own age, relations of comradeship, admiration, mutual teasing, mutual loyalty; in the case of older men, relations of instruction and advice from elders, and a naive, self-denying respect, temporarily interrupted by resistance and resentment, from the younger. In Dumas's story, d'Artagnan goes through such relations with a series of older men, such as Monsieur de Tréville, Athos, and the Cardinal. The three are quite dissimilar; each represents a different aspect of maturity, and each is at certain moments separated from that image. But they are nevertheless coordinated to be a collective father to the hero, to teach him maturity.

Masculinism of ethos is so pervasive that it is difficult to discuss in any institutional terms, and we must settle for the anecdotal in trying to demonstrate its activity today. In this case we can point to Lieutenant

Colonel Oliver North as a d'Artagnan figure, and the enthusiasm with which he was made a national hero as a sign, however brief, of America's loyalty to this kind of adventure hero.

North reminds us of d'Artagnan first of all because of his strong attachment to his regiment, manifested in his insistence on wearing his uniform and his medals to the Congressional hearings. The feminist Barbara Ehrenstein says, "The real message of his silent testimony was the uniform. . . . [He] had chosen to confront the public in a costume that proclaimed his license to kill . . . he had chosen to come as a warrior."[7] Dumas's story begins and ends with, always revolves around, d'Artagnan's attempts to join the Musketeers. Of course the regiment stands for personal relations with comrades (dramatized by Dumas as Athos, Porthos, and Aramis). To be a Marine or a Musketeer gives such men an identity that is more important to them than comparable images are to other people. It is of course an identity with a clear relationship to the nations they belong to. They are the sons of their countries, who risk their lives to defend France or the United States. Their country is more, or differently, important to them than it is to other people.

Ehrenstein says that the most useful way to think about Oliver North is as a member of the warrior caste, "the oldest male elite there is." Such men obey their military commanders implicitly. At the same time, they are often in trouble with "the authorities," especially civil authorities because their devotion to their nation expresses itself in a disrespect for their society. (Contrast the words associated with society [social, socialist, sociology] with the words associated with nation [national, nationalist, patriotic] and the difference will be striking.) Men like North and d'Artagnan expect to disobey and (not quite seriously) defy society, and the response to the hearings shows that other people expect and condone that defiance. Congress is perhaps the greatest social institution in America, but a young man like North expects to defy it in his actions and remain its loyal child at heart, and so to be forgiven.

What we saw at the hearings was a confrontation between a young adventure hero (such men are always young, whatever their age) and a parental conclave—congressmen and their lawyers—which one might call in some sense maternal insofar as mothers are expected to recite the formulas of piety and prudence within the family. It was, one might say,

7. Barbara Ehrenstein, "Lieutenant Oliver North and the Warrior Caste," *Rights,* July–September 1984, 12.

the League of Women Voters whom North most insulted, and feminists across the country were the group who responded with most outrage. It is possible that some of his support came from people who wanted a revenge on feminism. It is almost certain that they saw the conflict according to the domestic archetype, in which the young man *always* breaks the rules and upsets his parents (especially his mother) but is their principal defender in times of real trouble.

Barbara Ehrenstein's article on North was published first in *Ms.* magazine, for which she was a contributing editor. She says, "I will admit that this is alien territory to me, the psychology of the warrior. . . . As feminists we ["I, and probably you, the reader"] may honor myths and tales of women warriors, but, overwhelmingly and throughout history, women have inhabited a world that warriors happily leave behind, or arrive at—only to destroy. . . . In our generation of feminist scholars, the history of wars and warriors has taken second place to 'social history'—. . . the 'hidden history' of everyday life. [Ehrenstein is of course proud to promote that change.] . . . But I do not think we will ever understand either history or women's place in it without a *feminist* understanding of the Warrior Caste."[8] That is, of course, precisely the argument of this book—that one cannot understand history without understanding the warrior caste in some sense sympathetically.

Finally, Oliver North and d'Artagnan are alike in their personal devotion to national figures—at the apex, the President, the Cardinal—for whom they front and by whom they must expect to be sacrificed. These older, colder, cautious figures sit at the center of webs of policy and intrigue, of which they will deny all knowledge if a crisis comes. The young men are naive, ardent, and energetic, and ruthless with enemies, tough with subordinates, but defenseless in dealing with these fathers of the state, who for their part do love best of all these wayward sons.

The Musketeers story is often set on the stage of national politics, not at the debates of a parliament but in the actions of a C.I.A. or a Pentagon, dramatizing not the legislature but the executive. One of the concepts to which the North hearings most directed our attention was "covert operations," the whole idea of which is, as North said, that they must be lied about to Congress and the public. Thus one of the cultural forms to which the Musketeers story is allied is our interest in and excitement about national politics in this sense.

8. Ibid., 13.

This interest is not limited to right-wingers in politics. It seems to have been strong in Washington among New Dealers under Franklin Roosevelt and among 1960s liberals under Kennedy. The game of calling the Kennedy White House "Camelot" should remind us of Scott's medievalism, which is part of this type of adventure. Wherever there is a court—perhaps wherever there is a capital city to which young men come from all over the country with a hope of taking political power and ultimately of making a historical name—an excitement that can express itself in adventure tales of this type is bred.

Another reason capital cities are a focus for this type of tale is that they are the sites of embassies and diplomats and international relations. "International" here means those aspects of power and policy which escape the supervision of society, in which sense "international" is another derivative from "nation." Diplomacy, with its immunities, is something of a private world, in the hands of a separate caste, such as the army, and the Musketeers story is allied to our interest in those institutions. The split between the public face of diplomacy, the ceremonial or ambassadorial dinners and receptions, and the back-stairs intrigues of espionage and secret payments and criminal contacts is very congenial to this kind of imagination.

By contrast, the liberal political conscience and even the liberal imagination as found in academic critics, guardians of values, find all these activities and interests uncongenial and either know them as personal enemies, to be eliminated or suppressed as much as possible, or know them not at all. A rare example of a man of letters who was fascinated by these things and made his way toward them was John Buchan, who ended his days as governor-general of Canada. The world of letters rejected him, professing to find him fascistic, but his real treachery to letters was his interest in the army, diplomacy, covert operations, and so on. It is not surprising that he wrote adventures. He would have loved Oliver North.

The Study of Adventure

Adventure ought to be studied as literature—by that I mean, of course, respectable adventure—and studied as art, though not fine art. One reason I say that is that when adventure tales are excluded, certain great names traditionally associated with literature become hard of access from literature as at present defined, except at the cost of intellectual honor. I am speaking of literature as I see it confronting me. No doubt other people see it differently, but I cannot suppose I am unique. Trying to be objective, I would describe my idea as being shaped by my experience as a teacher and a critic, part of the literary establishment, but also by my sense of the living myths of our time, literary and political. Like everyone else, I try to correct the imbalances and cut out what is dead in those myths and in "literature."

The great names alienated are Homer, Virgil, Shakespeare, and Milton—writers who offer partly narrative pronouncements on the history and destiny of their societies, made partly in the name of, the voice of, the participants in that destiny. There are elements of adventure in all four, or at least elements of epic, national or religious. Epic narratives, which give a nation its identity, need passages of danger, escape, excitement, triumph; the Bible is packed with passages of adventure.

If Goethe called the *Iliad* a glimpse into hell, Simone Weil wrote about it as a "Poem of Force," and that is what a great deal of literature has been and continues to be: a series of legends to inspire action. Such a poem therefore serves and celebrates mainly the aristo-military caste. But the interpretation of literature is the work of the Brahmin caste, and the Brahmins have masked that function of literature by rejecting most of such books as merely adventure and dignifying the few they accept by disguising them. One sees this clearly in the great Hindu epics, the *Mahabharata* and the *Ramayana*.

For the period after Milton, the equivalent texts were written by Defoe, Scott, and Kipling, but they are neglected by college and university English departments, at least in their undergraduate teaching. Even when these authors are taught, they do not reach at least the undergraduates as ideas that might have an authority like that liberal writers have. These were, of course, the adventure writers, though they did not write adventures only. As much as anything else, it is their *mixture* of adventure with other interests that makes them important writers. But "literature" has come to mean the rejection of such mixtures; it rejects, in classical authors like Jane Austen, the elements of social assent and reinforcement. Literature has become "the literature of dissent," as taught even when not as written.

I am happy, on the whole, to have English departments remain hives of discontent. But I think it is important for them to admit to themselves what they are doing, and the difference between the books they have made into living authors and, for instance, Homer and Virgil.

"Literature," as administered by teachers, critics, and scholars, has become a selection of texts biased against the adventure. There are obviously strong moral and historical reasons for that bias, and reasons of literary quality also. But within the mass of adventure books there are those I have called the respectable adventures, which are the work of considerable talent and seriousness and can repay literary study of the right kind. Far more directly and vividly than "literature," they solicit our attention to history. They invite us to think about the past, and the present and the future, as a process of force—not as a process of economic growth, and much less as one of political reason or morality, but as a barely rationalized imagination of expansion and dominance.

Literature, the canon, is a compilation of sacred texts, like the Bible. It is not sacred in the fullest or technical sense, but those texts are widely separated from ordinary texts and given extraordinary treatment. The result of that treatment is to extract from them profound meanings, which direct lives—sometimes on the surface level (the reader imitates the hero of the story), sometimes indirectly (the reader's soul reposes in the presence of those meanings).

Here I must remind myself of my own provinciality and prejudice. I grew up one of a generation who revered D. H. Lawrence above all novelists, and F. R. Leavis above all critics. About us what I have just said is so easily demonstrable that it may need no demonstration. But what about more purely scholarly critics, whose attention is dedicated to texts in all their contingency and variability, who do not appropriate meanings? And what about critical movements today, such as deconstruction, which are hostile to meaning?

For both these groups, the texts they know (including the critical texts) constitute a charter of freedom—freedom ostensibly from the idols of the marketplace, but then charters usually begin like that and usually end with a list of credal propositions and duties. Literary study becomes a cult, separating itself from other kinds of knowledge, free to pursue its own ends. In other words, both scholarship and deconstruction are, at least for many involved, forms of gnosticism, based on canons of sacred texts and dealing with only sacred meanings. So what we need, to appreciate adventure, is a new secularity.

I too am asking that a number of texts receive careful attention, with the promise that important truths will then come to light. But this will be a secular reading, nevertheless, because of the texture of those books. The reader will not intend, and the writing will not support, a sacred reading; the writing can never seem immutable and inevitable. These books so rarely have that verbal dazzle which it is fatally easy to mistake for sacred truth. Literature in the modern sense will remain as valuable as it has always been, but we will remember that what it offers is, at its best, criticism—an opposition to the social myths, such as adventure. And truth is to be found in those myths as much as in their oppositional counterparts.

I would like to leave my readers with a sense of history corresponding to the visual image I used at the beginning of this chapter: the ships setting out from Spain, Holland, and England, in the sixteenth and seventeenth centuries, establishing trading posts and factories in Africa and Asia, landing small armies in Central and South America; covered wagons crossing the North American prairie and the South African veldt; Russian expeditions going east across Siberia and Central Asia; British ships carrying convicts to Australia. Back in the core countries of the modern system, the nation-state went from strength to strength, with its characteristic cultural forms—the press and parliament, industry and the stock exchange, science and technology—and the peripheral countries strove, in various liberal and nationalist movements, to follow that example. And the yeasty ferment of all that excitement worked in the minds of white readers and writers to produce an enormous mass of adventure tales, most of which had ostensibly little to do with either home politics or empire.

Crusoe in his boat, d'Artagnan on his horse, Natty Bumppo loading his gun, Edmond Dantes ripping his shroud open in the sea, Kim and Huck, Siegfried and Grettir, Richard Hannay and Philip Marlowe—these are all smiling faces of the force Western culture has generated and employed. Adventure offers me imaginative experiences that are radically different from the experiences I associate with the literature I was trained to know and teach. It is to be read with the creak of the saddle or the mast in one's ears, the smell of the sea or of the leather worn by soldiers and sailors, which is the smell also of gunpowder and of blood. Such smells do not give me a very exhilarating sense of identification; in fact, the exhilaration I feel is momentary and rootless, contradicted by all I believe about the world and all I know about myself. I have as little sense of comradeship with those men as anybody in the world can have.

Nothing could be more disturbing to me than to feel that, as a man, I am brother to those people, one of that band. But I am, have always been, must always be; and the resolution of that disturbance brings a sobriety I would not be without.

Selected Bibliography

Allain, Marcel, and Pierre Souvestre. *Fantomâs*. London: Picador, 1987.

Allen, R. B. *Old Icelandic Sources in the English Novel*. Philadelphia: University of Pennsylvania Press, 1933.

Alocco, Luciana Bianca. *I memoirs de M. d'Artagnan*. Rome: Edizione dell'Ateneo, 1977.

Anderson, Benedict. *Imagined Communities*. London: Verso, 1983.

Andersson, T. M. *The Icelandic Family Saga*. Cambridge: Harvard University Press, 1967.

Bhabha, Homi, ed. *Nation and Narration*. London: Routledge, 1990.

Bloch, Ernst. *Erbschaft dieser Zeit*. Frankfurt: Suhrkamp, 1962.

———. *A Philosophy of the Future*. New York: Herder & Herder, 1970.

———. *Das Prinzip Hoffnung*. Berlin: Suhrkamp, 1959.

Bonington, Chris. *Quest for Adventure*. New York: Potter, 1982.

Borrow, George. *Lavengro*. London: Dent, 1906.

Bory, Jean-Louis. *Eugène Sue: Le roi du roman populaire*. Paris: Hachette, 1962.

Bowman, Anne. *The Boy Voyagers*. London: Routledge, 1859.

Buchan, John. *Adventurers All!* Boston: Houghton Mifflin, 1925.

———. *Homilies and Recreations*. London: Nelson, 1926.

———. *Montrose*. London: Nelson, 1935.

———. *Sir Walter Scott*. New York: Coward McCann, 1932.

———. *Thirty-Nine Steps*. London: Nelson, 1922.

Burke, Peter. *Popular Culture in Early Modern Europe*. New York: Harper, 1978.

Byock, J. *Feud in the Icelandic Sagas*. Berkeley and Los Angeles: University of California Press, 1982.

Cammaerts, Emile. *Discoveries in England*. London: Routledge, 1930.

Campbell, James L. *Edward Bulwer-Lytton*. Boston: Twayne, 1986.

Campe, Joachim Heinrich. *The New Robinson*. London, 1788.

Chaillu, Paul du. *The Viking Age*. London: John Murray, 1889.

Chandler, Raymond. *The Raymond Chandler Omnibus*. London: Hamilton, 1953.

———. *The Second Raymond Chandler Omnibus*. London: Hamilton, 1962.

Chiari, Joseph. *Britain and France: The Unruly Twins*. London: Vision, 1971.

Cohen, Walter. *Drama of a Nation*. Ithaca, N.Y.: Cornell University Press, 1985.

Collins, Philip. *Dickens and Crime*. London: Macmillan, 1962.

Defoe, Daniel. *The Life, Adventures, and Pyracies of Captain Singleton*. London: Oxford University Press, 1927.

Dekker, George. *Fenimore Cooper: The Critical Heritage*. London: Routledge, 1973.

Diver, Maud. *Far to Seek*. London: Blackwoods, 1921.

Dollimore, Jonathan. *Radical Tragedy*. Chicago: University of Chicago Press, 1984.

Dottin, Paul. *Daniel Defoe et ses romans*. Paris: Presses Universitaires, 1924.

Dumas, Alexandre. *La Suisse: Impressions de voyage II*. Paris, 1833–37.

———. *My Memoirs*. London: Peter Owen, 1961.

Duncan, Sara Jeannette. *The Pool in the Desert*. Harmondsworth, Middlesex: Penguin, 1984.

Eagleton, Terence. *The Ideology of the Aesthetic*. Oxford: Blackwells, 1990.

Eddison, E. R. *Styrbiorn the Strong*. New York: A. & C. Boni, 1926.

Ehrenstein, Barbara. "Lieutenant Oliver North and the Warrior Caste." *Rights*, July–September, 1984.

Eliot, George. In *Westminster Review*, July 1856.

Fiedler, Leslie. *Love and Death in the American Novel*. Torrance, Calif.: Criterion Press, 1960.

Fisher, Margery. *The Bright Face of Danger*. London: Hodder & Stoughton, 1986.

French, Allen. *The Story of Rolf and the Viking's Bow*. Boston: Little, Brown, 1924.

Fuelop-Miller, René. *Tolstoy: New Light on His Life and Genius*. New York: Dial, 1931.

Gallop, Jane. *Reading Lacan*. Ithaca, N.Y.: Cornell University Press, 1985.

Gray, Stephen. "Alan Scholefield and the African Adventure Novel." *Contrast* 14 (December 1982): 38–47.

Grettir's Saga, trans. Denton Fox and Hermann Palsson. Toronto: Toronto University Press, 1974.

Grettir the Strong, trans. G. A. Haight. London: Dent, 1914.

Haggard, H. Rider. *Allan Quatermaine*. London: Macdonald, 1949.

Healey, G. H. *The Letters of Daniel Defoe*. London: Oxford University Press, 1955.

Hemmings, F.W.J. *The King of Romance*. London: Hamilton, 1979.

Hobsbaum, Philip. *Readers' Guide to Charles Dickens*. London: Thames & Hudson, 1972.

Hoelder, Anneliese. *Das Abenteuerbuch im Spiegel der Maennlichen Reifezeit*. Ratingen: Henn, 1967.

Homberger, Eric. *John Le Carré*. London: Methuen, 1986.

Household, Geoffrey. *Rogue Male*. London: Chatto and Windus, 1939.

Huerlimann, Bettina. *Three Centuries of Children's Books in Europe*. Cleveland, Ohio: World, 1967.

Jackson, Henry E. *Robinson Crusoe: Social Engineer*. New York: Dutton, 1924.

Jameson, Fredric. *Ideologies of Theory*. Minneapolis: University of Minnesota Press, 1988.

———. *The Political Unconscious*. Ithaca, N.Y.: Cornell University Press, 1981.

Joyce, James. *Daniel Defoe*. Buffalo, N.Y.: SUNY Press, 1964.

———. *Portrait of the Artist as a Young Man*. New York: Viking, 1964.

Kamenetsky, Christa. *Children's Literature in Nazi Germany*. Athens: Ohio State University Press, 1984.

Kazantzakis, Nikos. *Report to Greco*. New York: Simon & Schuster, 1961.

Kipling, Rudyard. *Kim*. New York: Dell, 1959.

Klaus, Gustav. *The Literature of Labour*. New York: St. Martin's, 1958.

Klotz, Volker. *Abenteuer-Romane*. Munich: Hansen, 1979.

Lang, Andrew. *Essays in Little*. London: Henry, 1891.

Lawrence, George A. *Guy Livingstone*. New York: F. A. Stokes, 1928.

Leonard, Irving Albert. *Books of the Brave*. Staten Island, N.Y.: Gordian Press, 1964.

Lewis, C. S. *Rehabilitations*. London: Oxford University Press, 1939.

London, Jack. *The Call of the Wild*. 1903. New York: Random House, 1989.

———. *The Sea Wolf*. New York: Macmillan, 1964.

Mangan, J. A. "Social Darwinism and Upper Class Education in England." In J. A. Mangan and J. Walvin, eds., *Manliness and Morality*. Manchester: Manchester University Press, 1987.

Marryat, Frederick. *Frank Mildmay*. London: Macmillan, 1887.

———. *The Privateersman*. London: Routledge, 1888.

Martini, Fritz. *Probleme der Erzaehlens in der Weltliteratur*. Stuttgart: Klett, 1971.

Maurois, André. *The Titans*. New York: Harpers, 1957.

Milsand, J. *La Revue Indépendante*, March 1847, pp. 161–91.

Morris, William. *Collected Works*. New York: Russell & Russell, 1966.

———. *Selected Writings and Designs*. Baltimore: Penguin, 1962.

Nash, Roderick. *The Call of the Wild*. New York: Braziller, 1970.

Nerlich, Michael. *Kunst, Politik, und Schelmerei*. Frankfurt: Athenaeum, 1969.

Newman, Gerald. *The Rise of English Nationalism*. London: Weidenfeld, 1987.

O'Neill, Kevin. *André Gide and the roman d'aventures*. Sydney: Sydney University Press, 1969.

Ouida. *Under Two Flags*. Philadelphia: Lippincott, 1896.

Parigot, Hippolyte. *Alexandre Dumas Père*. Paris: Hachette, 1902.

Peske, Antoinette, and Pierre Marty. *Les terribles*. Paris: Chambrian, 1951.

Phillips, Walter C. *Dickens, Reade, and Collins*. New York: Columbia University Press, 1919.

Raddall, T. H. *The Pied Piper of Dipper Creek*. Toronto: McClelland & Stewart, 1943.

Rivière, Jacques. *Nouvelles études*. Paris: Gallimard, 1947.

Roelvaag, O. E. *Giants in the Earth*. New York: Harper's, 1927.

Roskill, Mark. *The Interpretation of Cubism.* Philadelphia: Art Alliance Press, 1985.

Sayers, Dorothy L. *Have His Carcase.* New York: Harper's, 1932.

Schopp, Claude. *Alexandre Dumas.* Paris: Mazarine, 1985.

Scott, Walter. *Prefaces to the Waverley Novels,* ed. Mark A. Weinstein. Lincoln: University of Nebraska Press, 1978.

Sealsfield, Charles. *America: Glorious and Chaotic Land.* Englewood Cliffs, N.J.: Prentice-Hall, 1969.

———. *The Cabin Book.* New York: St. John & Coffin, 1871.

Secord, A. V. *Defoe's Review.* New York: Columbia University Press, 1938.

Sedgwick, Eve Kosofsky. *Between Men.* New York: Columbia University Press, 1985.

Steel, Flora Annie. *Breath upon the Waters.* New York, 1897.

Stevenson, Robert Louis. *Memories and Portraits.* London: Pentland, 1907.

Tadié, Jean-Yves. *Le roman d'aventures.* Paris: P.U.F., 1982.

Thibaudet, Albert. *Réflexions sur la littérature.* Paris: Gallimard, 1938.

Tolstoy, Leo. *Sebastopol.* Ann Arbor: University of Michigan, 1961.

Tournier, Michel. *Vendredi, ou les limbes du Pacifique.* Paris: Gallimard, 1967.

Twain, Mark. *Huckleberry Finn.* London: Harcourt, 1961.

Ueding, Gert. *Glanzvolles Elend.* Frankfurt: Suhrkamp, 1973.

Vaucaire, Michel. *Paul du Chaillu, Gorilla Hunter.* New York: Harper's, 1930.

Verne, Jules. *Five Weeks in a Balloon.* New York: Parke & Co., 1911.

———. *Vingt mille lieues sous les mers.* Paris: Livre de Poche, n.d.

Vibart, Eric. *Alain Gerbault.* Paris: Editions France-Empire, 1977.

Wells, H. G. *The History of Mr. Polly.* London: Nelson, 1910.

Williams, Raymond. *Marxism and Literature.* London: Oxford University Press, 1977.

Winstone, H.V.F. *The Illicit Adventure.* London: Cape, 1982.

Index